What's
Wrong
with My
Dog?

What's
Wrong
with My
Dog?

A Pet Owner's Guide to 150 Symptoms
and What to Do about Them

Jake Tedaldi, D.V.M.

CRESTLINE

This edition published in 2011 by CRESTLINE
a division of BOOK SALES, INC.
276 Fifth Avenue Suite 206
New York, New York 10001
USA

This edition published by arrangement with Fair Winds Press, a member of the
Quayside Publishing Group

First published in the USA in 2007 by
Fair Winds Press, a member of
Quayside Publishing Group
100 Cummings Center
Suite 406-L
Beverly, MA 01915-6101
www.fairwindspress.com

10 9 8 7 6 5 4 3 2 1

ISBN-13: 978-0-7858-2769-6

Library of Congress Cataloging-in-Publication Data
Tedaldi, Jake.
  Whats wrong with my dog? : a pet owner's guide to 150 symptoms and what to do about
them / Jake Tedaldi.
     p. cm.
  Includes index.
  ISBN 978-0-7858-2769-6
  1. Dogs—Wounds and injuries—Treatment—Handbooks, manuals, etc. 2. Dogs—
Diseases—Treatment—Handbooks, manuals, etc. 3. First aid for animals—Handbooks,
manuals, etc. 4. Veterinary emergencies—Handbooks, manuals, etc. I. Title.
  SF991T43 2007
  636.7'089—dc22
                                                            2007010824

Cover design by Laura Hermann Design
Book design by Yee Design
Illustrations by Colleen Hanlon
Cover photo by Jack Deutsche
Cover model: Sparky
Author photo by Maureen Fletcher
Dog photography by Sally Andersen-Bruce, www.sabphoto.com
Special thanks to the shelter that provided most of the dogs
in the photos: www.animalwelfaresociety.homestead.com
and also to these rescue groups: www.aussierescue.org
and www.labrescuect.petfinder.org

Printed and bound in China

*To all the dogs, past and present, that have
had an impact on my life. They are the "guys,"
to use a good friend's terminology, that have left
an impression, made a difference, or simply given
me a particular memory to cherish. These are
the ones that come immediately to mind:*

Napoleon, Kip, Taurus, Baron, Jocko, Pandora,
Woofer, Lacey, Spike, Nico, Whitey, Tucker,
Nicco, Rudy, Sam, Ginger, Diesel, Charlotte, Vincent,
Grommit, Shooter, Axl, Slash, Cozmo, Murphy, Jake,
Ali, Blackjack, Ace, Pepper, Pearl, Rose, Cosmo,
Tess, Bogey, Mattie, Radio—and Tilly.

Contents

Foreword	11
Introduction	13

PART 1: THE BASICS

My Dog's First-Aid Kit	15
My Dog's Treatment Strategies	17

PART 2: MY DOG IS BLEEDING

My Dog Is Bleeding from Her Eye	28
My Dog Is Bleeding from His Ear	30
My Dog Is Bleeding from Her Nose	32
My Dog Is Bleeding from His Mouth	34
My Dog Is Bleeding from Her Neck	37
My Dog Is Bleeding from His Paw	38
My Dog Is Bleeding from Her Skin	41
My Dog Is Bleeding from His Anus	43

PART 3: MY DOG IS HAVING SKIN, FUR, OR NAIL PROBLEMS

My Dog Has Irritated Skin on Her Face	45
My Dog Has Irritated Skin on His Ears	47
My Dog Has Irritated Skin on Her Nose	48
My Dog Has Irritated Skin on His Neck	49
My Dog Has Irritated Skin on Her Chest	52
My Dog Has Irritated Skin on His Back	53
My Dog Has Irritated Skin on Her Rump	55
My Dog's Skin Is Leathery	56
My Dog Has Dark Areas on Her Nose, Lips, Gums, or Tongue	57
My Dog Has Dark Areas on His Skin	59
My Dog Has Calluses on Her Elbows	61
My Dog Has Cracked Footpads	63
My Dog Has Blisters on Her Skin	64
My Dog Has Blisters in His Mouth	66
My Dog Has Blisters on Her Genitals	68
My Dog Has a Bald Spot	70
My Dog Has a Hot Spot	72
My Dog's Coat Is Dull and Dry	74
My Dog's Fur Is Matted	77
My Dog Is Shedding Lots of Fur	78
My Dog Has a Broken Toenail	79
My Dog's Toenails Are Growing in Strangely	81

PART 4: MY DOG IS HAVING EATING AND DRINKING PROBLEMS

My Dog Is Always Thirsty	83
My Dog Is Never Thirsty	85
My Dog Is Always Hungry	87
My Dog Is Never Hungry	89
My Dog Is Drooling Excessively	90
My Dog Is Gagging	93
My Dog Is Gulping or Swallowing Strangely	95
My Dog Is Regurgitating His Food	97
My Dog Is Vomiting	99
My Dog Keeps Smacking His Lips	101
My Dog Just Ate Some Chocolate	103
My Dog Just Ate Some Plants	104
My Dog Just Ate Another Dog's Feces	106

My Dog Just Ate a Tampon	106
My Dog Has Been Gaining Weight	108
My Dog Has Been Losing Weight	109

PART 5: MY DOG HAS A DISCHARGE

My Dog Has a Discharge from Her Eye	111
My Dog Has a Discharge from His Ear	113
My Dog Has a Discharge from Her Nose	116
My Dog Has a Discharge from His Skin	117
My Dog Has a Discharge from Her Anus	119

PART 6: MY DOG HAS A GROWTH

My Dog Has a Growth on His Face	121
My Dog Has a Growth on Her Eyelid	123
My Dog Has a Growth on His Third Eyelid	124
My Dog Has a Growth on Her Ear	125
My Dog Has a Growth on His Nose	127
My Dog Has a Growth Near Her Mouth	128
My Dog Has a Growth on His Skin	130
My Dog Has a Growth in Her Armpit	131
My Dog Has a Growth in His Groin	133
My Dog Has a Growth on Her Leg	134

PART 7: MY DOG HAS SWELLING

My Dog Has a Swollen Face	136
My Dog Has a Swollen Ear	138
My Dog Has a Swollen Nose	139
My Dog Has a Swollen Neck	140
My Dog Has a Swollen Belly	142
My Dog Has a Swollen Back	144
My Dog Has a Swollen Leg	146

PART 8: MY DOG IS ITCHY

My Dog Is Scratching or Rubbing His Eyes	148
My Dog Is Scratching or Rubbing Her Ears	149
My Dog Is Scratching, Rubbing, or Licking His Nose	152
My Dog Is Scratching or Rubbing Her Mouth	154
My Dog Is Scratching or Rubbing His Neck	155
My Dog Is Scratching, Rubbing, or Licking Her Back	157
My Dog Is Scratching, Rubbing, or Licking His Armpits or Groin	158
My Dog Is Rubbing or Licking Her Anus	159

PART 9: MY DOG HAS SOMETHING STUCK

My Dog Has Something Stuck in His Ear	161
My Dog Has Something Stuck in Her Throat	162
My Dog Has Something Stuck in His Paw	164
My Dog Has Something Stuck in Her Rectum	165

PART 10: MY DOG HAS AN EYE PROBLEM

My Dog's Eyes Are Red	167
My Dog's Eyes Are Bloodshot	169
My Dog's Eyes Are Bulging	171
My Dog's Eyes Are Squinting	173

My Dog's Pupils Are Large   174

My Dog's Pupils Are Small   176

My Dog's Pupils Are of Different Sizes   177

My Dog Has Dark Pigment in Her Eye   179

My Dog Has a Problem with His Third Eyelid   181

My Dog Has a "Stye"   183

PART 11: MY DOG IS HAVING WALKING PROBLEMS

My Dog Is Limping   185

My Dog Keeps Falling Down   188

My Dog Keeps Losing His Balance   190

My Dog Keeps Fainting   192

My Dog Can't Use His Front Legs   193

My Dog Can't Use Her Hind Legs   195

My Dog Can't Walk Up or Down Stairs   196

My Dog Is Walking in Circles   198

My Dog Keeps Walking into Things   199

My Dog Is Stiff   200

My Dog Is Dragging the Tops of His Paws   202

My Dog's Head Is Tilted   203

PART 12: MY DOG IS HAVING GENITAL PROBLEMS

My Dog's Testicles Are Enlarged   205

My Dog's Nipples Are Enlarged   207

My Dog Has a Constant Erection   209

My Dog's Vulva Is Enlarged   211

PART 13: MY DOG IS CRYING OUT

My Dog Cries Out When He Tries to Chew   213

My Dog Cries Out When She Tries to Open Her Mouth   215

My Dog Cries Out When He Tries to Turn His Head   217

My Dog Cries Out When She Tries to Stretch   219

My Dog Cries Out When He Breathes Deeply   221

My Dog Cries Out When She Tries to Move Her Leg   222

My Dog Cries Out When He Tries to Urinate   224

My Dog Cries Out When She Tries to Defecate   226

My Dog Keeps Yelping   228

PART 14: MY DOG IS HAVING BEHAVIOR PROBLEMS

My Dog Is Acting Funny   229

My Dog Is Pressing His Head into Corners   231

My Dog Keeps Tucking Her Tail between Her Legs   233

My Dog Is Barking at Night   234

My Dog Is Barking Hoarsely   236

My Dog Is Constantly Chasing Things   237

My Dog Is Attacking People or Animals   239

My Dog Is Afraid of Strangers   241

My Dog Is Afraid of Other Animals   243

My Dog Is Afraid of Children   244

My Dog Is Afraid of Shiny Floors   245

My Dog Is Afraid of Certain Objects   247

PART 15: MY DOG IS HAVING BATHROOM ISSUES

My Dog Is Peeing Everywhere 249

My Dog Is Urinating Where He Shouldn't 251

My Dog Urinates When Strangers Approach 253

My Dog Is Pooping Everywhere 254

My Dog Is Dragging Her Bottom 256

My Dog Is Straining to Urinate 258

My Dog Is Straining to Defecate 259

PART 16: MY DOG SMELLS FUNNY

My Dog Has a Funny Smell Coming from His Ears 261

My Dog Has a Funny Smell Coming from Her Mouth 263

My Dog Has a Funny Smell Coming from His Skin 264

My Dog Has a Funny Smell Coming from Her Anus 265

PART 17: MY DOG HAD AN ACCIDENT

My Dog Fell from a Height 266

My Dog Was Hit by a Car or Heavy Object 268

My Dog Was Rescued from a Car Accident 270

My Dog Was Rescued from a Burning Building 272

My Dog Was Rescued from a Frozen Lake 274

My Dog Was Sprayed by a Skunk 275

My Dog Was Quilled by a Porcupine 276

PART 18: MY DOG SEEMS SICK

My Dog Is Coughing 278

My Dog Is Sneezing 280

My Dog Is Always Seeking Heat 281

My Dog Is Always Seeking Cold 282

My Dog Just Had a Seizure 284

My Dog Is Shaking His Head 286

My Dog Is Shaking All Over 288

My Dog Is Shivering or Trembling 290

My Dog Is Weak and Lethargic 291

My Dog's Nose Is Wet/Dry When It's Usually Dry/Wet 292

My Dog Is Wheezing 293

My Dog's Tongue Hangs Out in a Strange Way 295

My Dog Is Panting Heavily 296

Index 298

About the Author 303

Acknowledgments 304

Foreword

Jake Tedaldi takes care of our two dogs. He knows a great deal about dogs (and other animals, but I'm a dog guy). Much of what he knows is of course the result of his training and involves veterinary medicine. But that alone is not what makes him a great vet. What makes him great is other stuff. He knows how important dogs are to the people who own them. He doesn't sentimentalize this fact, he simply knows it. He doesn't sentimentalize the dogs either. He knows they are dogs. He knows their limitations and respects them as such. But he also respects them as dogs. He also knows that they are individuals. He cares about their dignity. Like any good doctor his patients are never just patients.

A vet, especially a really good vet, has the special responsibility of treating two species. It is always about the animal and the owner, and neither is ever slighted. It is a special challenge, and, for this challenge, Jake Tedaldi has a special gift. You can trust his advice here. He knows what he's doing. But what matters most is the degree to which his professional knowledge is grounded in his humanity. He knows that the fundamental fact of his profession is the bond between the animals and their people, both of whom he treats with meticulous compassion.

—Robert B. Parker,

Best-selling author of the Spenser novels, including Paper Doll, School Days, Hundred-Dollar Baby, *and many others*

Introduction

Since you are reading this introduction, you are obviously a dog lover. The book in your hands was designed to help you be a better dog owner, especially when it comes to handling your dog's inevitable injuries and illnesses. It is written in a way that should make it easy to use as a reference or guide, and serves as an approximation of what it is like for my clients when they call me for help.

I have tried to be general when too much detail would be confusing, and specific when the details are critical and appropriate. Some of the details may come across as a bit gross or disgusting—for that I apologize. Medical care tends to include some rather unsavory aspects some of the time. This is what makes my job fun for me and occasionally revolting to others!

In writing this book, I realized that the use of gender-specific pronouns can become a bit of a burden. You will notice that my editors and I have solved the he/she, his/her problem by alternating their use chapter to chapter, except when the chapter is gender-specific.

I have tried to include a few anecdotes where appropriate, so that they might provide additional insight to a particular problem. Such boxes are titled "My Patient's Story."

You'll also find two other types of special boxes in this book. "Warning" boxes will alert you to dangers to you and your family. They will also alert you to potential hazards you may encounter in attempting to perform various procedures or examination techniques; be cautious but not overly timid. "When to Get the Vet" boxes signal situations that require an immediate call to your dog's vet or even a dash to a veterinary hospital.

While this book should be thought of as a guide, it should never be used as an alternative to establishing a trusting relationship with a veterinarian. My hope, in fact, is that through the use of this book you will become a better-educated dog owner and that as a result, you become one of your veterinarian's better-informed clients.

As a veterinarian, I also realize that being intellectually aware of your dog's problems is all well and good, but you, the dog owner, would occasionally like to avoid the costly process of seeking professional help for every last injury and ailment in your dog's life. By using this book properly, you should be able to do just that.

Remember two important facts as you do your best to help your dog through whatever issue is at hand. First and foremost, this is your dog—the companion you love and who trusts you and loves you back. Even though you may be hesitant to approach your dog's problem, your best effort may relieve some acute suffering or at least avoid some future suffering. Second, the worst you can do is fail and get no result or improvement, in which case you can always resort to consulting your veterinarian—which is what you would have done anyway.

So consult the book, roll up your sleeves (and put on some latex gloves), use your common sense, and help your dog out of whatever situation he has gotten himself into. You and your dog will be glad you did.

My Dog's
First Aid Kit

Every dog owner should have the peace of mind that comes from knowing that there is a plan in the event of an animal emergency. In order to achieve such a level of comfort, you need the following:

1. Your veterinarian's office and cell phone numbers

2. The number of a local or regional twenty-four-hour animal emergency center

3. Your own canine first-aid kit

The first two items on the list are easy to find in the phone book or on the Internet. The third is something you can put together easily, with most of the items likely to be found in your own bathroom medicine cabinet. What you don't already have in the house, you can probably pick up in one quick visit to your local pharmacy.

Canine First-Aid Kit

- **HYDROGEN PEROXIDE (A ONE-QUART BOTTLE AND A SMALLER BOTTLE).** The large bottle will come in handy as the main ingredient in the de-skunking mixture listed later. The smaller one will be used as a wound disinfectant or to promote vomiting if your dog swallows something he shouldn't.

- **STERILE SALINE SOLUTION (A LARGE SQUIRT BOTTLE).** This can be used to flush debris out of your dog's eyes as well as for general wound cleansing. In order to keep the solution sterile, be sure to prevent the tip from coming in contact with any part of your dog.

- **KARO LIGHT CORN SYRUP.** This is to be given orally or rubbed over your dog's gums if your dog appears to be weak from overexertion without enough nutrition or if your dog is a diabetic and appears to be suffering from hypoglycemia.

My Dog's First Aid Kit

- **RUBBER TUBING OR A DOUBLE-RING BUCKLE BELT.** This is to be used as a tourniquet in case of heavy bleeding from one of your dog's limbs.

  Note: If you are forced to use this technique to control excessive bleeding be sure to make a note of the time the tourniquet was applied.

- **ALL-PURPOSE ANTIBIOTIC OINTMENT,** such as Bacitracin, Bactroban, or Polysporin

- **MILD ALL-PURPOSE STEROID OINTMENT OR CREAM,** such as hydrocortisone

- **BENADRYL** tablets or liquid

- **PEDIATRIC STRENGTH (81 MILLIGRAMS), ENTERIC-COATED ASPIRIN**

- **BITTER APPLE** or an equally foul-tasting spray to use as a lick or chew deterrent

- **ROLLS OF TWO-INCH TO THREE-INCH WIDE GAUZE OR PADDED GAUZE**

- **NON-ADHERENT "TELFA" PADS**

- **ROLLS OF ADHESIVE TAPE**

- **ROLLS OF SELF-ADHERENT WRAP**

- **MANUALLY-ACTIVATED ICE PACKS**

- **RUBBER EXAM GLOVES**

- **TUBE OF K-Y JELLY**

- **Q-TIPS,** or cotton swab equivalents

- **CAUTERIZING POWDER OR STICKS**

- **COTTON GAUZE PADS AND COSMETIC COTTON BALLS**

- **AMMONIA SMELLING-SALT CAPSULES**

- **INFLATABLE AIR SPLINT**

- **LARGE BOTTLE OF ISOPROPYL RUBBING ALCOHOL**

- **SIZE-APPROPRIATE MUZZLE** (Always use this if there is even a slight chance that whatever you are trying to do for your dog may cause pain.)

- **SIZE-APPROPRIATE ELIZABETHAN COLLAR**

- **FLASHLIGHT WITH A SHARP, BRIGHT BEAM**

- **BOTTLED, NON-CARBONATED WATER**

- **WIDE-TOOTHED METAL COMB**

- **STANDARD HAIR BRUSH**

- **PAIR OF LONG BLUNT-TIPPED HAIR-CUTTING SCISSORS**

- **HEATED BLANKET** that can be plugged in to a car outlet and adapter

- **ANBESOL** (oral analgesic)

- **ANUSOL HC** (hemorrhoid cream)

My Dog's
Treatment
Strategies

If you are a devoted dog owner and you not only love your dog but also have a hard time watching him suffer or run the risk of even a few moments of discomfort, it will be helpful for you to have a few simple strategies at your disposal in case a situation like one of those listed below presents itself. Even if you have occasion to put only one of these strategies to use in the course of your dog's lifetime, it will be worth the price of this book.

How to Make Your Dog Vomit

If your dog has recently (within the last few minutes) swallowed something dangerous to his health and you are *absolutely certain* that it won't cause more damage coming up than it would traveling through his digestive system, then you can use the hydrogen peroxide in your first-aid kit to induce vomiting. Make a 50/50 mix of the hydrogen peroxide and water and pour between a teaspoon and a tablespoon, depending on the size of your dog, down his throat. If it doesn't work within five minutes, repeat the procedure, but not more than one additional time (three times total).

If you are not sure how dangerous the substance is or whether it would be worse coming up than going down, call the ASPCA National Animal Poison Control Center at 888-426-4435 for advice.

How to Check Your Dog's Temperature

The most effective and accurate way to take your dog's temperature is rectally. This is tolerated better than you might expect, as long as you are gentle, use enough lubricant (K-Y jelly is perfect), and have a friend to offer treats as a distraction during the process. You can buy a rectal thermometer at your local pharmacy (they even have mercury-free ones, so if yours breaks by accident there will be no danger). Normal temperature for most dogs is between 98°F and 102°F.

How to Assess Severity of Bleeding

Start by identifying the approximate source of the bleeding. Using a clean, moist towel, blot the area directly, absorbing and cleaning at the same time. Once the bulk of the recent and dried blood has been cleared, switch to a dry, light colored towel and press it to the area for a few moments. If the blood you take away from the site when you remove the towel is significant, get started on controlling the bleeding (as described below). If the amount of bleeding is moderate, explore the area further to identify more specifically where the source is and how dramatic the flow of blood. In general, spurting or pulsing is a severe bleed (requiring an immediate trip to a veterinary ER), flowing or dripping is very serious (requiring an immediate trip to your vet's office), and seeping or oozing is usually possible to control at home.

How to Control Bleeding

If your dog is bleeding profusely, start by applying direct pressure with a sterile gauze pad if you have it; if not, a clean towel will do.

Applying Direct Pressure

In addition, try to elevate the source of bleeding so that it is above the level of your dog's heart. (This mainly applies to limbs, but if your dog's hind end is bleeding, propping it up with pillows will help as well.)

If this isn't enough to stop the bleeding or at least slow it significantly, a tourniquet may be needed. Only apply one on the advice of a veterinarian or human physician, or if you see no other way to control the bleeding before getting the dog to an ER. Tourniquets are best used on limbs.

To apply a tourniquet, find a rubber tube, belt, or even a shoelace. Tighten the device around the limb somewhere between the wound and your dog's body. Be sure to take note of the exact time the tourniquet was applied, including a.m. or p.m., and attach a note to this effect to the tourniquet if you are turning over your dog's care to someone else.

How to Clean a Wound

It is always best to decide as soon as possible whether you are capable of dealing with a wound yourself or if you're ultimately going to need help from your veterinarian. Start by assessing how painful it is.

Next, trim the hair from around the area, allowing you to get a better look at the wound while making further treatment easier. If you are planning to apply a dressing to the wound after cleaning it, you should extend the area of trimming to a distance of two to three inches on all sides to allow bandaging and adhesive attachment.

Trimming Hair

without slipping or bunching. This can be tricky, depending on the location of the wound!

Wound Dressing

My Dog's Treatment Strategies

If there is enough crusted blood and debris present to make this difficult, try softening this material with warm water and soft toweling and use a gentle blotting technique. Then use a wide-toothed comb to help clear this softened material before attempting any trimming. Once the wound has been fully revealed, squirt the entire area aggressively and liberally with sterile saline, then blot once again with sterile gauze or a clean cloth. Finally, disinfect the wound by gently dabbing the entire area with sterile gauze or cotton that has been soaked in hydrogen peroxide.

How to Dress a Wound

Once a wound has been thoroughly cleansed and disinfected, it is usually best to apply a therapeutic, protective dressing. Start by spreading a thin coat of antibiotic ointment, such as Bactroban, Bacitracin, or Neosporin on one side of a non-adherent pad and applying it directly to the wound, ointment side down. Using a roll of cotton gauze, trap the pad against the skin and wrap the gauze around the body part in a manner that will keep the pad in place

Be careful not to wrap the gauze too tightly, cutting off circulation, or too loosely, allowing the dressing to slip. Next, cover the gauze with a protective, self-adherent wrap and finish by using one layer of adhesive tape around each edge of the dressing, half of the width covering the edge of the dressing, the other half sticking directly to your dog's recently trimmed skin/fur. Always plan to change wound dressings every one to two days to monitor progress.

Blanket Stretcher

How to Transport an Injured Dog

If your dog is injured seriously enough to warrant hospitalization, or at least veterinary attention, you'll need to transport him in a way that will protect him from further harm while ensuring that you don't get injured in the process. Start by applying a muzzle. If you don't have one, you can tie some gauze around his muzzle without compromising his ability to breathe through his mouth and nostrils.

does. If this threatens his injury in any way, or if the injury prevents him from walking normally, use a blanket, dog bed, or large bath towel as a means of lifting him into a vehicle.

For a small dog, a box may be just the thing to carry him in.

Box Carrier

Muzzle

If the injury doesn't prevent your dog from walking, help him to your car and allow him to get in the way he usually

For a dog that is only partially ambulatory, but stubborn enough to resist being carried, a large towel slung under the chest or belly and grasped from above the dog's back is often enough to help him move more effectively.

It is always wise to have at least one helper to guide the process and avoid jarring moves or collisions. Remember, go slowly and speak comfortingly to your dog to reduce his stress and the possibility of causing further injury.

How to Remove Mats from Your Dog's Fur

If the matted fur is a result of crusted blood or pus, first be sure to address the wound or infection. Next, try using your wide-toothed comb to gently pry away any larger clumps of fur and debris. If your dog is resistant, a muzzle may be needed. Once you get to the point where the comb is no longer enough to dislodge the clumped and matted fur, use your hair-clipping scissors, but never to cut the fur! With the tips closed, insert the pointed end of the scissors between the skin and the mats and gently but firmly open the scissors in a spreading motion, separating the hairs that have been anchoring the matted fur to the skin. After repeating this motion (but never cutting the hairs) enough times, you should be able to go back to using your wide-toothed comb to remove the remaining mats. Use this method on each individual matted area on your dog's body.

How to Flush and Treat Your Dog's Itchy, Irritated Eyes

Start by using a squirt bottle of sterile saline solution to liberally flush out your dog's eyes. Once you're confident that any matter that might have been irritating your dog has been flooded out of his eyes, use a cotton swab to clear out any pus,

mucus, or other tenacious material that could have remained behind. Following this process you can place a few drops of commercially available soothing eye drops, such as Visine, in the eyes to reduce any residual discomfort.

Applying Eye Drops

Repeat this process two to three times a day. Most cases of simple irritation and even viral conjunctivitis will respond at least partially to this treatment alone. Some will resolve completely within a few days. If you see little to no improvement within two days, you will need your vet's help.

How to Tell If Your Dog Is in Pain

The most obvious signs are the ones we have come to expect from humans, such as crying out or howling. More subtle signs of pain and discomfort include restless pacing, panting, lip smacking, tooth grinding, or repetitive swallowing.

How to Treat Your Dog's Fleas

Treating fleas should always involve a three-pronged approach. First, you must kill the fleas and flea eggs that are on your dog. Second, you must kill the fleas and eggs that remain in your dog's environment. Third, you must find out where your dog was exposed to the fleas in the first place and either kill the fleas and their eggs in that place or prevent your dog from having access to that spot in the future. Commercially available products are less expensive than the ones you can buy from your vet and sometimes they are enough to solve the problem. If the problem is not resolving, always seek your vet's help and advice.

Flea

How to Treat Your Dog's Mites

With the exception of those that affect your dog's ears, mite problems are rarely eradicated without the help of a veterinarian. In fact, the two most common mites that affect dogs—sarcoptic and demodex—are difficult for even a vet to cure. Trust your vet, not yourself, to solve the problem.

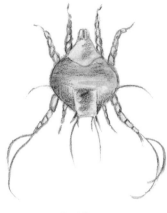

Ear Mite

How to Remove a Tick from Your Dog

Ticks are interesting to some, disgusting to others, and potentially dangerous to all. If you discover even one tick on your dog, remove it immediately. Once ticks have attached, they don't begin to feed, and potentially spread disease, for up to around twenty-four hours. By pulling them off right away you may be able to avert the spread of such tick-borne diseases as Lyme disease and Ehrlichiosis. Removing a tick can be accomplished by grasping the tick with your fingers or a pair of tweezers, as close to your dog's skin as possible, and pulling it directly out. If you are disgusted by the idea, cover the entire tick with Vaseline and wait until the lack of oxygen causes it to back out of its attachment site. Then it will be easy to remove it and dispose of it. In the future, you can avoid ticks entirely by treating your dog with a tick-preventive medication such as Frontline.

How to Treat Your Dog's Intestinal Parasites

Many of the intestinal parasites that can affect your dog are also capable of affecting humans. If you are even remotely suspicious that your dog has intestinal parasites (as indicated by rubbing his rectum on the floor, or the actual sight of worms in his stool or around his anus), consult your veterinarian right away. The proper medication should resolve the problem in short order.

How to Adjust Your Dog's Diet in Order to Manage a Case of Diarrhea

Boil a few pounds of lean ground beef or lamb, skim the fat off the surface, drain the meat and refrigerate it. Prepare a few cups of white rice and refrigerate it. At meal time, mix the boiled meat and rice—equal parts of each—and give your dog roughly half the amount of what you would offer if it was his regular food. Warm it up on the stove or in the microwave to make it smell more appetizing.

Continue with this program until his stools have returned to normal. Then, and only then, start mixing in his regular food, in ever-increasing amounts, every two

days, until you have successfully weaned him from the meat and rice back to his old dog food.

How to Empty Your Dog's Anal Sacs

If your dog has been showing signs of difficulty defecating and you notice the telltale bulges at 5 o'clock and/or 7 o'clock on your dog's anus, your dog probably needs to have an anal sac expression performed. There are two ways to accomplish this. The most effective way is with a gloved, lubricated forefinger inserted in your dog's rectum and the thumb of the same hand on the outside of the anus used as leverage. By trapping the swollen sac between these two fingers, you can use them to gently squeeze the contents toward you and out of the pore that lies right at the rim of the rectum. This is an awkward procedure for the inexperienced, on a number of levels!

The alternative technique, used by most adventurous owners and groomers, is to wear a rubber glove, grab a few sheets of paper toweling and press them directly against your dog's rectal region. Then, imagining that your dog's anus is like the end of a sausage and your goal is to squeeze its contents out toward you, press in from the sides of the anus, squeezing gently but firmly. If you are successful you may hear or feel a squirting action, but the real test will be if you see the material in the toweling once you pull it away from your dog. The material has a distinctly pungent odor, quite unlike fecal matter. Be ready to gag!

Anal Sac Expression

pound. If your dog weighs 20 pounds, you would want to give about 100 milligrams. Since the products on the market come in pediatric or cardiac dosage of 81 milligrams or adult dosage of 325 milligrams, round down or up using your best judgment. It is always safest to round down. Useful to know is that buffered products are buffered throughout, so it's okay to divide them using a pill cutter or knife. Enteric coatings should never be cut, as cutting destroys its benefits.

Since most owners balk at the mere thought of administering any medications to their dogs, a few helpful hints might make things easier. Some dogs will tolerate any pill placed in the back of their throats as long as you shut their mouths afterwards and massage their throats. Another successful technique is to hide the medication in cheese, peanut butter, or meat.

How to Treat Your Dog with Anti-Inflammatories

A multitude of anti-inflammatory agents are available and effective for use in dogs. By reducing inflammation, these medications are often successful in reducing pain—and therein lies their most valued effect.

Before resorting to the ones typically prescribed by your veterinarian, it is often safe to try a buffered or enteric-coated aspirin product. These are over-the-counter human medications, such as Ascriptin (buffered) and Ecotrin (enteric-coated). Only do so if your dog has no known clotting disorders or previous issues with gastric or intestinal bleeding. Dose your dog by giving 5 milligrams per

How to Clean and Treat Your Dog's Dirty and/or Infected Ears

You will need cotton balls, cotton swabs, ear flush, and an appropriate ear medication (antibiotic for bacterial infections, antifungal for yeast infections, and mite-killing for mite infestations). Start by attempting to clear out as much wax, pus, and other materials as possible from your dog's ear using the dry cotton swabs. Do not moisten them in any way, as leaving them dry allows the materials you are removing to adhere to them better.

Next, gently squeeze some ear flush down into the ear canal. Try to have an idea of about how much you put in because you are going to try to remove close to all of it before introducing any medication. Next, flip the ear flap back down over the canal and massage the entire ear, feeling the flush sloshing around inside the ear. Go gently, since this has to sound pretty awful from your dog's perspective! Next insert one cotton ball deep into the canal and repeat the massage technique. When you remove the cotton it should be soaked with ear flush and coated with the wax, pus, and debris from your dog's ear canal. Repeat the cotton ball technique until there is little to no moisture or residue on the cotton when you remove it. Next, apply the appropriate medication, following the directions on the package. Be sure to get the medication into the canal, then massage the entire ear thoroughly to ensure that the medication coats the entire ear canal. The medication will work best if you finish by distracting your dog for a few minutes following the medication, allowing it to be absorbed by the ear canal lining before your dog has a chance to shake it out.

How to Treat Your Dog's Allergic Symptoms

If your dog shows signs of an allergic response, your first priority should always be to ensure an open airway without any respiratory difficulties whatsoever. If there is even a hint of a struggle to breathe, get your dog to an emergency facility immediately.

If breathing is normal and your dog's allergy symptoms are topical itching or local swelling, try applying cold compresses. If this doesn't help significantly, try an over-the-counter human antihistamine, such as Benadryl, Tavist, or Claritin.

These can also be used to effectively treat allergy-related coughing and sneezing, but it is better to consult your veterinarian before going ahead with treatment, as the dosage and frequency will depend on more than just the size of your dog.

Most antihistamine medications are available as either liquid, chewable tablets, or capsules. The tablets and capsules can be given by emptying the capsule contents into a food that your dog finds delicious. The liquid form is best given through a dosing syringe, which can be teased in between your dog's teeth and carefully squirted into his mouth, but not too forcefully. An overly aggressive squirt might cause your dog to aspirate the medication, which could result in other problems.

How to Treat an Abscess

An abscess, formerly known as a boil or furuncle, is a localized, subcutaneous infection, usually caused by a puncture or other penetrating wound that has introduced bacterial organisms beneath the skin. Once there, in a warm, moist, protected environment, these organisms flourish, multiplying rapidly, and causing much swelling and discomfort. The body, in its attempt to solve the problem, sends white blood cells and other inflammatory cells to gobble up the infective ones and combat the infection. If the infection is serious enough, the body needs help in fighting it—otherwise the pet could become septic and die.

Most superficial abscesses have a noticeable point of entry. This would look like a puncture hole or cut of some sort that would permit entry of bacterial organisms through your dog's skin. Apply a warm compress to soften the surrounding skin and clean any crusts or other accumulated materials from the opening. After a few minutes, replace the warm compress with a clean absorbent cotton or paper towel soaked in hydrogen peroxide. Now firmly but gently apply pressure to the swollen area. If the warm compress was successful in clearing the opening of all obstructions, you should get a steady flow of pus, serum, and blood from the opening and into your disinfectant-soaked towel. Continue the process until you are satisfied that you have drained all there is to drain. Finish by cleaning again with hydrogen peroxide and applying an antibiotic ointment, such as Bactroban, Bacitracin, or Neosporin, to the opening. To ensure that the abscess will not return, check with your vet for follow-up antibiotic therapy.

If you are not successful in your attempts to drain the abscess, leave it in the more experienced hands of your veterinarian. It is possible that you are treating something other than an abscess or that the opening has healed enough to prevent you from reopening it. Do not under any circumstances try to open the abscess by using a sharp object. This is always best left to your veterinarian.

How to Treat a Hot Spot

You'll probably need a helper to hold your dog while you do this, especially if the wound you're treating is bothering him. Using your clippers and scissors, try to trim away as much hair as possible over the wound and extending an inch beyond the wound in every direction. If the hair over the wound is caked with discharge,

try the next step first, and then come back to the trimming. Soak a clean cloth or towel with a 50/50 mixture of hydrogen peroxide and warm—not hot—water and repeatedly blot the entire wound, rinsing the cloth off frequently. You'll soon find that the wound doesn't look nearly as awful as it did earlier. Once it seems to be clear of dirt, debris, and dried blood, put away the cloth. Now use the anti-itch spray and give the entire area a few good squirts, taking care to go all the way to the edges of the trimmed hair.

Once you have determined the size of non-adherent dressing to use, apply a thin film of antibiotic ointment, such as Bactroban, Bacitracin, or Neosporin, to one side of the dressing and press that side directly to the wound. The next step will depend on the anatomical location of the "hot spot." If it is on an extremity, simply wrap gauze around the limb 2–3 times and then use adhesive tape to encircle the ends of the gauze. If the site is on an area such as the shoulder or hip, it is sometimes possible to wrap gauze in a figure 8 around the front or rear limbs.

Now, apply the bitter apple or equivalent spray to the bandage to prevent licking or chewing. The addition of an Elizabethan collar will improve your chances of success. If you can keep the dressing on for 3–5 days, you'll be surprised at how much improvement will take place!

Finally, be sure to scrutinize the area daily to check for signs of increased swelling, heat, or sensitivity. If any of these signs are noticed, or if your dog develops a fever, he'll probably need systemic antibiotics and should see your veterinarian.

How to Manage Superficial Injuries and Irritations of Your Dog's Neck

This is quite similar to dealing with "hot spots." Start by trimming away any excess hair. Next, blot and eventually scrub the area with your 50/50 hydrogen peroxide and water mixture until you have succeeded in clearing away all crusts, discharge, and debris. Now apply a cold compress. Ideally such a compress should be flexible, so create one by taking an appropriately sized towel, soaking it in water, ringing it out, and putting it in the freezer for about 15 minutes or until it is cold but only slightly stiff. Apply the compress by wrapping it completely around your dog's neck for about 10 minutes.

After removing the compress, apply the appropriate medication (antibacterial, antifungal, steroid, etc.) and protect the neck from further scratching by using a modified turtleneck. This can be either one of your own winter neck warmers if your dog is large, a cut out turtleneck if your dog is small to medium in size, or a sweatband or gauze bandage if your dog is small. Just be sure it isn't too tight!

How to Check Your Dog's Hydration Status

Start by lifting your dog's lips to closely examine his gums. They should be wet, slippery, and reflective. If they appear to be dry, sticky, or dull, there is a strong possibility that your dog is at least somewhat dehydrated. Confirm this by grasping the area of loose skin at the back of his neck between his head and his shoulder blades, lifting it up and releasing it. If your dog is dehydrated, this handful of loose skin will slowly return to its original, flat state (see figures on page 85). A properly hydrated dog's skin would return to its normal position immediately, with no noticeable delay.

What do you do about dehydration? The simple answer is to offer your dog something to drink. Water is an obvious first choice, but ice cubes or electrolyte solutions such as Pedialyte, Gatorade, Powerade, etc. are excellent alternatives if your dog will accept them. This is not always the complete answer, however, since it fails to address the reason behind the dehydration. If it's simply a matter of your dog's overexertion without access to liquids, the fluids should solve the problem. If the fluids alone don't do the trick, trust your vet to help find the reason and arrive at a plan of action.

My Dog's
Treatment
Strategies

PART

2

MY DOG IS
BLEEDING

My Dog Is

Bleeding from Her Eye

Blood coming from a dog's eye is almost always the result of some type of trauma. The origin of the blood is usually the skin and tissues immediately surrounding the eye and much less often the eye itself. This is because the eye is not as delicate as most dog owners imagine. Trauma to the face and eyes, even with sharp objects, may cause bruising, abrasions, tears, and even punctures to the tissues around the eyes without resulting in any more damage to the eye than a corneal abrasion or tear.

Less commonly, bleeding from the eye itself may be caused by a mass in or near the eye or some disease process of the eyes or the tissues immediately surrounding them.

What to Look For

Settle your dog in a comfortable position under bright light. Speak softly to her and stroke her gently to reassure her. Slowly work your way toward her head. Carefully examine your dog's entire head for the source of bleeding. Look for signs of injury, such as swelling, scrapes, tears, or punctures.

Next look at the actual globe of your dog's eye for a penetrating foreign body, blood coming from the eye itself, or an unusually small or large pupil.

Try examining the conjunctival tissues beneath both the upper and lower lids of your dog's eye. They should be a healthy pink color.

If you think your dog's third eyelid could be the source of the bleeding, take a look at it. To examine the third eyelid closely, press gently on the upper eyelid, forcing the globe of the eye slightly deeper into its socket. This will allow the third eyelid to rise passively, partially covering the lower half of the eyeball.

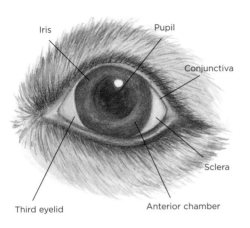

Iris

Pupil

Conjunctiva

Sclera

Third eyelid

Anterior chamber

Anatomy of the Eye

What to Do

Next, ask yourself these questions:

Is your dog fully conscious, walking with balance, and able to see with both eyes? This question is designed to determine whether your dog is suffering from the after-effects of serious head trauma.

Is there evidence of injury to the eyes or the tissues around them, such as swelling, scrapes, tears, or punctures? Provided that you can stop the bleeding and the answer to all parts of the first question is yes, then you should feel safe to treat your dog's injuries at home. (See "How to Flush and Treat Your Dog's Itchy, Irritated Eyes" on page 21.)

Does the bleeding appear to be coming from the eye itself? If so, and if the eyeball looks normal and appears to be functioning properly, are the conjunctival tissues beneath both the upper and lower lids a uniform, healthy pink color? If they are bleeding slightly, apply gentle pressure with a clean cold pack over the eye for a

few minutes. If these tissues are free of blood yet there is accumulated blood around the eye, gently use a cotton swab in a twirling motion to remove the blood.

Is your dog's third eyelid the source of the bleeding? The third eyelid is a protective membrane that, under normal circumstances, rests comfortably tucked below the medial canthus of the eye. If the third membrane is torn or noticeably damaged, it should be surgically repaired to avoid ongoing problems.

When to Get the Vet

Contact your dog's vet if:

- There is any evidence of injury to the actual globe of the eye, such as a penetrating foreign body, blood in the eyeball, or an unusually large or small pupil, get immediate veterinary help.

- Your dog is unconscious, not able to walk with balance, or not able to see with both eyes, wait thirty minutes for the situation to improve. If it does not, seek veterinary attention immediately.

Does the bleeding appear to be coming from a growth or mass in or near the eye? Bleeding can arise from a variety of masses in and near the eyes. Many of the masses that typically occur in these areas are benign and treatable, so don't assume anything! If this is the first you have noticed a bleeding mass, chances are it hasn't been there that long. The fact that it has begun to bleed, though, means something about it has changed. It may simply have been rubbed or chafed, in which case the bleeding should subside quickly enough with some gentle pressure.

If the bleeding has occurred for any other reason related to a mass, it should be examined closely by your veterinarian and possibly biopsied.

My Dog Is
Bleeding from
His Ear

My Dog Is
Bleeding from His Ear

Your dog's ears are highly vascular, meaning that they have lots of blood vessels. This allows them to function well in dissipating heat, sense temperature and pressure changes, and receive auditory information. There are five common reasons for there to be blood coming from a dog's ear. The most common is trauma, either self-induced by shaking or scratching, or from some outside source. A variety of masses—including polyps, warts, and sebaceous adenomas, most of which are benign—can arise from the pinna, or ear flap, or from inside the ear. All of them are capable of bleeding.

Parasites—such as ticks and mites and, less frequently, fleas and flies—can cause bleeding from the ear. Bacterial and fungal infections usually cause dogs to scratch aggressively at their ears, resulting in the self-induced trauma described above. In some cases, though, an infection of the inner ear can cause a perforation of the tympanic membrane, or eardrum, and bleeding may result.

What to Look For

The first step is to figure out where the blood is coming from. Gently take a look at the outside and inside of your dog's ears. If the source of the bleeding is not immediately clear, use a cotton or paper towel soaked in water to blot and wipe away the excess blood. Since ears bleed a lot and dogs with bleeding ears tend to shake their heads repeatedly, expect a bit of a mess!

Check your dog's ears for punctures and lacerations. Look outside and inside for lumps, bumps, and growths. Next, check both of your dog's ears for parasites. Look for lesions on the tips of your dogs ears and hair loss, cracking, and bleeding.

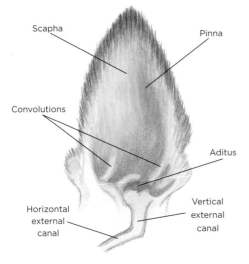

Anatomy of the Ear

What to Do

Ask yourself a few questions to determine what to do:

Precisely where is the blood coming from? It is important to establish the site of the bleeding first since this usually dictates why the bleeding is occurring and how to handle it. It is even possible that the blood is not coming from your dog, but from one of your dog's playmates.

Is there a puncture or laceration to any part of the ear? These are the toughest to deal with because of the size and location of the blood vessels in the ears. If you find punctures, clean them thoroughly first with water, then with a 50/50 mixture of hydrogen peroxide and water. If you've got the nerve, soak a cotton swab in the hydro-

gen peroxide mixture and insert the tip right into each of the puncture holes. This will disinfect the wounds and also give you an idea of how serious the bleeding is.

If you find lacerations, treat them similarly to the punctures, but only if they are superficial.

After you clean the wounds, bandage and protect your dog's ears to promote proper healing and prevent aural hematomas following trauma.

Do you see any unusual lumps, bumps, or growths in or on the ear? If the blood appears to be coming from any one of these types of lesions and it is not excessive, you may be able to stop the bleeding with a cauterizing chemical or clotting agent like Kwik Stop or an equivalent powder, gel, or topical "spot-on." Apply it directly to the source of the bleeding. These products are available at most human pharmacies and pet supply stores. This, of course, is only likely to be a temporary solution until the growth itself is taken care of.

Are there any parasites in your dog's ears? Here's how to deal with ticks, fleas, mites, and flies.

TICKS can be removed with tweezers or forced to detach by covering them with Vaseline, which blocks their ability to "breathe." As they suffocate, they'll back out of your dog's skin within a few days. You should probably consider using a tick preventive collar or topical liquid to protect your dog in the future.

FLEAS are not often found inside the ear, but fleas on your dog's outer ear or head would probably cause enough scratching to result in bloody ears. Treat the fleas with a commercially available product, and the ears will respond quickly to wound management.

MITES are microscopic in size, but the ear wax produced in response to them is distinct in appearance. It resembles the color and granularity of coffee grounds. Remove this material from your dog's ears and use mite-specific medication to kill the mites and their eggs. Ear flush and mite remedies to accomplish this are available over the counter at your pet store. (See "How to Treat Your Dog's Mites" on page 22 for directions on how to clean and medicate your dog's ears.)

FLIES can be the source of bleeding in and around a dog's ears, but only in unusual circumstances, usually when a dog is sick or compromised in some other way. If you notice flies landing in and on your dog's ears, look for pre-existing wounds or lesions. Clean the ears thoroughly and try spraying a bandana with your favorite fly repellant and tying it around your dog's neck.

Did you see lesions on the tips of your dog's ears along with hair loss, cracking, and/or bleeding? This could be caused by a nutritional deficiency. Try adding a multivitamin containing zinc to your dog's diet.

When to Get the Vet

If lacerations extend through the entire thickness of the ear, they will probably need sutures to ensure proper healing.

My Dog Is
Bleeding from Her Nose

Bloody noses are quite common in humans, and rarely anything to get very upset about. When your dog's nose is bleeding, however, it may seem more worrisome, especially since dogs are likely to begin sneezing once they get the sensation of blood in their nostrils. This usually creates quite a mess!

What to Look For

Take a few moments to get a look at your dog's nose. Wipe away the bleeding with a clean, damp, white cloth. Try to figure out exactly where the bleeding is coming from. Check for cuts and bruises on your dog's nose.

Next, check your dog's breathing by carefully placing your cheek close to her nostrils. Check if the passage of air through those nostrils is roughly equal during respirations, or if one nostril seems partially blocked.

If you think the bleeding might actually be coming from your dog's mouth instead, see "My Dog Is Bleeding from His Mouth" on page 34.

When to Get the Vet

Dramatic bruising and lacerations require immediate attention to control bleeding and prevent your dog's condition from deteriorating.

What to Do

Ask yourself these questions to determine the best solution:

Did your dog recently have some trauma, such as a collision with a door or baseball bat? The trick is to stop the bleeding, then make sure that there is no serious injury. Apply a cold pack to your dog's nose while keeping it pointed up to the sky.

Once you have successfully controlled the bleeding, check your dog carefully for signs of physical injury and neurological damage. Swelling, redness or bruising, pain or discomfort, confusion, or balance issues represent enough to warrant an immediate trip to the veterinary hospital.

Did the bleeding seem to start spontaneously without any obvious reason? It is important to first establish how severe the bleeding is and then what might be the reason. With the bleeding controlled, if you can't explain the onset of the bleed, you and your veterinarian need to investigate the possibilities of exposure to anticoagulants like rodenticide, clotting disorders like Von Willebrand's disease, and other various factors that may have caused an increase in your dog's blood pressure.

Is there any sign of traumatic injury to the nose or muzzle? Minor cuts and bruises typically associated with bleeding in this area are usually treatable at home using common sense and your dog's first aid kit. (See "How to Control Bleeding" on page 18 and "How to Dress a Wound" on page 19.)

Is there any evidence of injury to your dog's mouth? Any injury to the oral cavity, which has a direct connection to the nasal sinuses, could easily result in blood coming from the nose, especially if the dog is sneezing. (See "My Dog Is Bleeding from His Mouth" on page 34.)

Does your dog have a history of prolonged bleeding during or after having surgery? Dogs that have had prolonged bleeding episodes in the past may have problems (such as with Von Willebrand's disease) that predispose them to bleeding more easily or for longer periods of time than other dogs. Deficiencies in a dog's clotting cascade prolong bleeding time.

My Dog Is Bleeding from Her Nose

Is your dog taking any medication? Some medications, such as aspirin products, can make a dog more prone to bleeding.

Does your dog seem congested in one nostril? Sometimes the blocked nostril makes a significantly higher pitched sound as air is forced through a narrower passage. This would suggest that the nostril is swollen or has a foreign body or mass partially occluding the nasal passage. If any of these possibilities is present, further diagnostics will be in order.

My Dog Is
Bleeding from
His Mouth

My Dog Is
Bleeding from His Mouth

While bleeding from any part of your dog is serious business, there are many locations that may not mandate immediate veterinary attention. The mouth, in some instances, is one of those sites. Before you bundle your dog into the car and rush off to the hospital, take a moment to identify the source of the bleeding.

Not every dog likes to have his mouth pried open, or even his lips lifted to expose the teeth and gums. This is especially true if your dog's mouth is clenched shut in an attempt to protect something painful inside. Go slowly and speak soothingly.

Because the mouth is a sensitive, highly vascular area, injuries inside the mouth are often painful and usually bleed quite profusely, so exercise caution during your examination!

What to Look For

Get a flashlight or take your dog to a spot with very good light. If you can, get someone else to help out.

Begin by petting your dog the way you normally would. In a few minutes, begin rubbing his ears and working your way to his muzzle. Search your dog's muzzle and head for signs of external injury before opening his mouth to look inside.

Sit beside your dog and place the palm of your hand that's closest to his nose beneath his chin. Place the palm of your other hand flat against his cheek. Use the thumb of that second hand to apply gentle pressure against the outside of his upper lip, sliding it up to reveal the teeth and gums beneath. Similarly, use the thumb of your lower hand to slide your dog's lower lip down, revealing his lower teeth and gums.

Mouth Examination

Take your time. By shifting the position of your hands and patiently starting and stopping repeatedly, you should eventually be able to take a look at your dog's teeth and gums on that side of his face.

Now it's time to check out your dog's tongue and hard palate (the roof of his mouth). To do this, place your left thumb on the right side of your dog's upper lip, just behind the large canine teeth. Place your left index and middle fingers on the left side of your dog's upper lip, just behind the large canine teeth. Do the same with your right hand on his lower lip, and then open his mouth like a clam shell. Take a good look inside. Don't forget to check under the tongue.

Now repeat the side exam from the other side.

What to Do

Ask yourself the following questions to figure out how to proceed:

Is your dog between four and six months of age? Be on the lookout for loose teeth or areas where "baby" teeth have recently fallen out. There is usually blood associated with the loss of these deciduous teeth. No reason for concern.

Are your dog's gums swollen, angry red in color, and bleeding? Your dog has gingivitis. This is not a reason for an emergency appointment, but it is important enough to do something about. You should think about changing your dog's diet to one that includes more dry kibble rather than canned food, and/or beginning a dental hygiene program involving brushing his teeth regularly. Your vet might also suggest the use of fluoride-containing rinses.

Teeth Brushing

Does your dog have an abnormal growth or swelling in his mouth? Not all the masses that can grow in a dog's mouth are tumors, and not all oral tumors are cancerous. If you notice any new growth in your dog's mouth, look at it closely and think of how to describe it to someone else. The color, texture, and consistency of a growth is important in deciding what course of action to take in diagnosis and treatment.

If your dog is young and these masses are white to gray in color, pebbly or frond like in appearance, and there are a few of them, they could be warts, in which case they will probably go away on their own.

If the growth you see is very hard and located near a tooth or even between two teeth, it could be an epulis. These are often highly aggressive yet benign tumors and should probably be removed as soon as possible. Such a growth could also be cancerous, which is even more reason to have it professionally treated.

If the growth is a soft mass, know that they occur in the mouth frequently. Many of them are cysts or benign tumors, but they could also be cancers such as melanomas or sarcomas. If the bleeding is not a significant amount and you can get it to stop, try waiting a few days and see if it recurs or if the mass gets any larger.

Is there evidence of a traumatic injury to your dog's mouth? Tears and punctures to the inside of a dog's mouth, including

When to Get the Vet

If the mass recurs or gets larger or if the bleeding persists over the next few days, go see your vet.

the tongue, are often the result of some external force causing the dog's own teeth to lacerate or puncture the soft tissues of the oral cavity. Another common source of injury to the inside of a dog's mouth is the act of chasing, catching, and chewing foreign objects. Sticks and bones are frequently the culprits. They can be found stuck in between a dog's teeth, lodged across his hard palate (the roof of the mouth), penetrating the tissues of the cheek, or under the tongue. Sometimes the object is gone and only the results are apparent. In all such cases, extreme caution is advised to avoid causing your dog more pain or getting bitten yourself. Flushing the dog's mouth out with water from a hose can be helpful in dislodging a foreign body and in evaluating whether the bleeding is serious enough to warrant a trip to your vet.

My Dog Is Bleeding from His Mouth

My Dog Is

Bleeding from Her Neck

Your dog's neck is not only a handy place for you to attach a controlling collar, but it also happens to be the most popular target for attack by other animals. As this area contains some of your dog's most important blood vessels and nerves, it's important to take it very seriously if you ever notice blood coming from anywhere near your dog's neck.

What to Look For

Your first order of business is to establish if the blood is actually coming from your dog. Assuming that it is, and without getting bitten in the process, identify the source of the bleeding and whether it is oozing, flowing, or spurting. If it is a superficial injury and the blood is oozing slowly, you can probably treat it at home.

What to Do

Ask yourself the following questions:

Where has your dog been immediately prior to your discovery of the blood on her neck? If your dog has been in the house all day, your expectations will be different than if your dog has just returned from a romp in the woods with her favorite dog walker. If the former is true, you should be looking for self-induced trauma like hot spots or injuries from

household items like appliances, utensils, and furniture. (See "My Dog Has a Hot Spot" on page 72.) If your dog has been outdoors, the list of possibilities increases dramatically. Your dog could have a small amount of blood coming from the site of a tick attachment just as easily as she could have a sharp stick penetrating her throat! This is why it is so important to be cautious, yet efficient in your exam.

Is this the first time you've seen blood coming from your dog's neck? If this has happened before and you know for certain that your dog does not have some sort of clotting disorder, chances are you are dealing with a chronic problem, such as one of the many skin diseases that can result in mild bleeding, some type of skin mass or masses that bleed when they are traumatized, superficial parasites, or some allergy that prompts your dog to scratch at a specific area enough to cause bleeding. Be sure to look first for the same problem your dog has had before. Since you are familiar with how to deal with it, you can probably follow the same course of action. If this is the first time you have noticed blood coming from your dog's neck, you'll need to quickly assess the source and severity of the bleeding.

Using a clean, moist cotton or paper towel, blot the bloody area to clear off any excess blood and try to identify the source of the bleeding. If there is a scab or crust, clean only the area immediately surrounding it without dislodging the crust. If there is no such scab, try to establish whether the bleeding is coming from a puncture, laceration, or scrape and exactly how dramatic the flow of blood is. If the blood flow

is very slow and more like an ooze, follow the cleaning and bandaging directions in "How to Control Bleeding" on page 18 and "How to Dress a Wound" on page 19. Remember, this is your dog's neck, so any bandaging or applied pressure must be done with caution in order to avoid compromising your dog's ability to breathe!

My Dog Is
Bleeding from His Paw

A bloody paw is a fairly common occurrence in dogs. Identifying the source of the blood is critical in determining whether the injury is minor, serious, or grave. If you know how the injury occurred, you may already have a good idea what to expect when you examine your dog's paw more closely. If you don't, prepare yourself for anything. If the injury possibly includes a fracture, make plans to see your vet.

(sidebar)

My Dog Is Bleeding from His Paw

What to Look For

Start by following the directions on how to assess severity of bleeding as outlined in "How to Assess Severity of Bleeding" on page 17. In the process, you will undoubtedly discover the source of the blood and determine whether or not you feel comfortable proceeding at home or doing your best to temporarily control the bleeding until your vet can have a look.

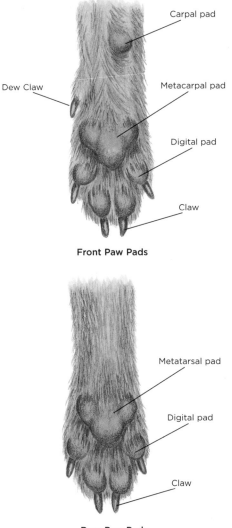

Front Paw Pads

Rear Paw Pads

What to Do

Now, ask yourself the following questions:

Is the bleeding severe, moderate, or mild? Moderate to severe bleeding should always be handled by your veterinarian. Follow the directions for controlling bleeding as outlined in "How to Control Bleeding" on page 18, but get your vet to see the injury as soon as possible.

Is the bleeding from a cut or laceration? If you can see the full extent of the slice, and the bleeding is minimal, clean the entire area with your 50/50 water and hydrogen peroxide mixture. If your dog resists strenuously, it may be safer to allow your vet to handle this. Alternatively, if you think you can handle your dog, apply a muzzle and resume your efforts, possibly with the help of a friend. You may find it easier to dip the whole paw into a bowl of the hydrogen peroxide mixture to thoroughly disinfect the wound and the areas around it.

Once you're finished, apply a non-adherent dressing and bandage to the paw, being certain not to wrap it too tightly. If possible, always leave the toes exposed so that you can easily check for signs of swelling. This would result if the bandage were too tight and would require re-bandaging the wound more loosely. White athletic socks make excellent over-bandage protection since you probably have some

My Patient's Story

My Dog Is Bleeding from His Paw

I once had an elderly client call to ask that I see her ten-year old standard poodle, Tabitha, as she had done something to her paw and it was bleeding. I asked my client how much blood there was, to which she replied "Oh, I don't know, enough to notice, but not so much. I think she may have caught her toenail on the threshold." I told her I could get there after my next appointment and she seemed satisfied. As I hung up the phone something didn't feel quite right, so I decided to postpone the next appointment and go directly to her. It was lucky that I did!

When I arrived, my client's entire kitchen floor was covered in semi-congealed blood and she and her dog were slipping on newspapers placed like islands in an attempt to sop up the blood while providing some traction. Tabitha had pulled out her entire dewclaw. The immediate application of a pressure wrap and a trip to the hospital for supportive care solved the problem, but another fifteen minutes might have been the end of her.

The lesson here is to never be cavalier about continuous or non-responsive bleeding. If you can't stop it right away, get your veterinarian's help immediately.

already, you can cut them as needed, and blood shows up well when it seeps through them, providing you with a signal that you may need your vet's help after all.

Many of the lacerations to the paw area involve the interdigital webbing and require suturing to ensure proper healing. If the laceration is to the pads of your dog's paw, sutures are only worthwhile if the slice is deep enough to reach the flesh beneath the pad. This is probably best left to your vet to decide.

Is there a foreign body stuck in the wound? Always be cautious when a foreign object is lodged in your dog's skin. Unless you know exactly what it is *and* that it won't cause any more harm if you remove it, you're better off leaving it for your vet to handle. If you feel confident

that there is no danger in removing it, do so carefully, and be ready to control any bleeding that may result from its removal.

Is the bleeding coming from a damaged toenail? A cracked or broken toenail can be a painful and bloody mess. If the bleeding is minimal, proper disinfecting, cleansing and dressing may allow healing and recovery without veterinary intervention. If the bleeding persist after you have done your best to control it and/or bandage the paw, your veterinarian may need to cauterize the blood vessels in order to stop the bleeding. (See "My Dog Has a Broken Toenail" on page 79.)

My Dog Is
Bleeding from Her Skin

Your dog has the advantage of a thick coat of hair that provides protection for most of her skin. This serves as a barrier to many of the day-to-day annoyances that affect human skin, such as sunburn, minor scrapes and scratches, and even contact allergies such as poison ivy.

Unfortunately, this wonderful protection can serve as a major nuisance when you notice that your dog is bleeding. In such cases, the fur gets caked with blood and prevents you from getting a good look at the actual source of the bleeding.

Don't be dissuaded! It's important to look at the source of bleeding because it will tell you how severe the problem is and whether or not it is something you are capable of handling yourself, even if it is only temporarily.

- **IDENTIFY** the exact location on your dog's body. Knowing where on your dog's body the bleeding is coming from is critical in determining treatment and prognosis.

- **DETERMINE** if the site has been contaminated with dirt or debris.

What to Look For

Use the moist towel technique outlined in "How to Assess Severity of Bleeding" on page 17 to get an accurate assessment of the origin of the bleeding. Once, you've found the source of the bleeding, look for the following four things. They're easy to remember; just think of the word IDEA.

- **ESTABLISH** the size and severity of the source. In other words, how big is the wound and how bad is it?

- **ASSESS** the potential blood loss. This is just a fancy way of saying "figure out if you are capable of stopping the blood flow yourself or if you're going to need help!"

What to Do

The following questions reiterate the IDEA concept and should help you determine if you can proceed on your own or if a vet's attention is required:

Where is your dog bleeding? This is important because it will determine whether or not you can treat your dog at home. For instance, a laceration on your dog's paw might be handled safely at home by cleaning and bandaging, while a similar laceration near your dog's eye might require an immediate visit to your veterinarian, sutures, protective ophthalmic ointment, and an Elizabethan collar to prevent your dog from scratching at the injury during recovery.

Elizabethan Collar

Is the wound clean or dirty? Wounds that are fresh and clean can be repaired more easily and safely than those that have been exposed to dirt and other contaminants. A contaminated or dirty wound, despite appearing to be perfect for stitches, may need to be left open, to heal on its own because of the risk of infection and subsequent abscess formation. These decisions are best left to your veterinarian.

How big and severe is the wound? This question is critical for similar reasons. A bloody mass that is one centimeter in diameter is significantly less worrisome than a four centimeter bleeding mass. Likewise, an excoriation that invades one or two layers of skin is much less serious than a laceration that extends through the skin and into the muscle tissue beneath it.

Can you stop the bleeding? It is always helpful to try to control and isolate the bleeding. See "How to Control Bleeding" on page 18 for helpful advice.

When to Get the Vet

If you're unable to stop the bleeding, or if the wound looks large and deep, take your dog to the vet.

My Dog Is
Bleeding from His Anus

Blood coming from anywhere is disturbing, but blood coming from your dog's anus can be especially alarming. As you might imagine, your dog's rectum is a sensitive and vascular part of his anatomy, which means it has a lot of blood vessels. So it can bleed—a lot. Damage to this sensitive area can be very painful for your dog.

What to Look For

The best way to examine your dog's hind-quarters is to put on a pair of rubber gloves and, while he remains standing, lift his tail up and have a good look. Here's what to do:

Once your dog's tail is elevated and his anus is easy to see, look all around the area for injuries, growths, or swelling. Try to use one gloved finger to feel the edges of his anus for bulges and to check for irritation and blood.

Use the towel technique outlined in "How to Assess Severity of Bleeding" on page 17 to identify the source of the bleeding and to evaluate the severity of the flow. It's possible that the blood is actually coming from your dog's tail. It may appear to be arising from your dog's rectal area because of the way he tucks his tail against his anus when something is bothering or frightening him.

The best way to refer to anything unusual that you might see is to identify its location in relation to your dog's anus as though you were talking about a clock. So, if your dog has a dark spot at the top of his anus, closest to his tail, you would say that it was located at twelve o'clock.

Also take a look at your dog's stools, checking for blood. This blood could appear as a bright red or as a brick red to black color, depending on where in your dog's intestinal tract it arose from.

What to Do

Here's what to do, depending on what you found:

INJURIES: In the midst of a dog fight, some dogs trying to escape their attackers get bitten in the hindquarters. Puncture wounds to the region will bleed; how much depends on the location and depth of the bite. Clean the wound carefully with water and hydrogen peroxide and call your dog's vet if you can't stop the bleeding.

But what looks like a bite might not actually be one. Some dog breeds, especially German Shepherds, can develop draining tracts. These are often associated with some immune-mediated problem and are part of a disease called furunculosis. The treatment is long term and requires a dedicated and patient pet owner for success.

An injury that looks like a bite could actually be an anal sac problem. All dogs have anal sacs, which can rupture and form draining sores. Anal sacs are actually scent glands similar to the ones we find so objectionable in skunks, but less developed in size and smelliness. The glands are embedded in the muscles that surround your dog's rectum and are located at approximately four o'clock and six o'clock. They each have a pore that exits at the rim of the anus at around five o'clock and seven o'clock, respectively. The sacs usually empty their contents when your dog defecates. But occasionally, for a variety of reasons, these sacs become inflamed or infected and unable to empty their contents. This can form an abscess, which can then rupture through the skin, resulting in a draining, open wound. Except for their characteristic location, these can easily be mistaken for nasty, infected bite wounds.

You can clean and disinfect anal sac abscesses with hydrogen peroxide and water, but call your dog's vet for wound management and antibiotic therapy. Despite the proximity to the rectum, a bacteria-rich spot to be sure, these wounds heal remarkably quickly with the proper treatment.

My Dog Is Bleeding from His Anus

Impacted Anal Sac

GROWTHS OR SWELLING: The area surrounding a dog's anus can be affected by various types of tumors, which can bleed readily if rubbed or scratched enough. If your dog is an intact male, he may be suffering from any one of a number of testosterone-responsive tumors. Consult your vet about neutering him if this appears to be the case.

When to Get the Vet

Contact your dog's vet if:

- You are unable to stop the bleeding.

- You suspect an anal sac abscess.

- You see blood in your dog's stools.

If the bleeding seems to be coming from such a swelling or growth, apply gentle pressure with a moist towel. This will accomplish two things. First, it will tell you how hard or soft the mass is. If it happens to be a blood-filled cyst, it may also allow you to drain the rest of the blood and maybe even solve the problem. If this happens, be sure to go back and look closely at the structure that used to contain blood.

Check for legs! Engorged ticks often look and behave like blood-filled cysts. Once you squeeze the tick and drain the blood from it, remove it from your dog's skin like you would remove any other foreign body, such as a splinter.

Regular Tick vs. Engorged Tick

BLOOD IN YOUR DOG'S STOOLS: If you see blood in your dog's stools, it's best to take your dog and the stools to the vet. Besides the blood coming from the rectum, it could be coming from your dog's gastrointestinal tract or from his anal sacs.

PART 3: MY DOG IS HAVING SKIN, FUR, OR NAIL PROBLEMS

My Dog Has

Irritated Skin on Her Face

When the skin on your dog's face is red and irritated, she can easily worsen the problem with persistent rubbing and scratching. If you can get an idea of why the problem began, your chances of finding a solution are much better.

What to Look For

First put on a pair of rubber gloves to protect your skin in case your dog has anything contagious that you could contract. Now get a good look at the irritated area, checking for evidence of trauma, such as scratches, punctures, or lacerations. Next, check for any pustules or rashes in the immediate and surrounding areas. Finally, search for any discharge associated with the irritated area.

Warning

Always wear rubber gloves when examining your dog's skin. This is to protect yourself against infections that are transmittable to humans, such as ringworm.

What to Do

Now, ask yourself a few questions:

Is there evidence of a wound in the irritated region? If you see a wound in the area, treat it appropriately by disinfecting it with a 50/50 mixture of hydrogen peroxide and water, medicating it with an antibiotic ointment, such as Bactroban or Neosporin, and protecting it by covering it with a bandage. But don't be surprised if you can't identify the original trauma. They are often unidentifiable once the dog begins to scratch or rub the area. See "My Dog Has a Hot Spot" on page 72 for additional advice.

Is there any noticeable discharge from the area? If the discharge is yellowish to green in color, the area is infected and will probably need antibiotic therapy. You can try treating the area topically by following the directions in "My Dog Has a Hot Spot" on page 72.

Is the area circular to oval in shape and clearly defined? Irritated areas of skin that are sharply outlined and circular to oval in shape may be fungal in origin. These are commonly referred to as *ringworm* and are highly contagious among animals and to humans. (Good thing you put on those gloves!) The treatments mentioned above may help such a lesion, but are unlikely to resolve it. You can try using a topical antifungal, but ringworm infections are best handled by your vet since a correct diagnosis and proper medication are essential to ensure the recovery of your dog and the protection of your family.

Is the area still covered with hair? If so, you are fortunate to have noticed it before your dog started pestering it herself. If the area is just red and irritated, or even if there are bumps or blisters, try using cool compresses followed by a thin film of an antibiotic/steroid ointment, such as Corticin. If your dog begins to scratch or rub the area at any time, use an Elizabethan collar to prevent her from doing any damage. This will guarantee the speediest resolution to the problem.

If this treatment has no effect within a few days, your vet should be able to prescribe the proper therapy.

My Dog Has
Irritated Skin on His Ears

Your dog's ears are sensitive in many ways. Sure, they provide an abundance of auditory information, but they also allow your dog to pick up changes in air currents and temperature. This sensitivity can be a burden when some element in your dog's environment results in an irritating stimulus to his ears. His natural instinct is to scratch and/or rub the area, or shake his whole head until it feels better. These actions, individually or together, can result in much more serious problems. It is always best to be aggressive in managing ear problems before they develop into much more than a simple irritation or infection.

What to Look For

Put on a pair of rubber gloves. Choose a well-lit room in which to take a close and thorough look at all aspects of both your dog's ears. Your exam should include both the outside, hairy part of the ear flap, or *pinna*, and the inside portion or ear canal. (See the illustration on page 31.) It may help to use a flashlight and even a few cotton swabs to clear away debris and get an accurate idea of what you're dealing with.

What to Do

Next, ask yourself a few questions:

Is the area of irritation well-defined or is it more generalized? Well-defined areas of irritation, especially with hair loss in an oval or round area, suggest the fungal infection ringworm. Pat yourself on the back for wearing your exam gloves (as people can catch ringworm too), but get to your vet for treatment of your dog's lesions.

Well-defined but simply red and raw areas, with or without discharge, may be the result of a bite, wound, or infection. For these, check for evidence of a penetrating foreign object (remove it only if you can do so without further injury to your dog or yourself!), clean the area with hydrogen peroxide, and apply a thin coat of Bacitracin or other antibacterial ointment. Continue this treatment only as long as you feel that there is ongoing improvement.

Generalized areas of irritation on the ears suggest more dramatic diagnostic challenges. You can try cold compresses and topical anti-itch products, combined with an Elizabethan collar to prevent your dog from inflicting more trauma to the area. If there is no immediate improvement, see your veterinarian.

Is there obvious evidence of infection?
Any sign of yellow to green pus or distinctly malodorous discharge from the ear means infection. Infections of the outer ear can often be treated at home with the use of antibacterial agents, cool compresses, and topical ointments such as Bacitracin. An Elizabethan collar is usually necessary to prevent your dog from doing himself any harm during the course of therapy. Keep in mind, however, that if things are not getting better, systemic antibiotics may be needed and your vet can help.

Infections inside the ear are more difficult to treat. If you have an idea what type of infection you are dealing with, you may try treating your dog at home. Do so cautiously by following the directions for treating your dog's infected ears as outlined in "My Dog Has a Discharge Coming From His Ear" on page 113.

My Dog Has
Irritated Skin on Her Nose

Your dog's nose is a delicate part of her anatomy. She uses it to gather information constantly throughout the day and even while she is sleeping. Any irritation to the sensitive tissues of her nose will be poorly tolerated and will likely be dealt with by attempts to lick, rub, scratch, or sneeze until the irritation ceases. Most of the time these attempts only seem to make matters worse. Your best course of action in such instances is to first get a precise idea of what is causing the irritation. Next, try to determine how likely it is to be something you can help her with. Finally, you should either begin some course of action yourself or get your dog to her vet as soon as possible.

What to Look For

Put on a pair of rubber gloves before you begin and get a flashlight. This will protect both you and your dog by preventing your exposure to any unsavory or hazardous components of the nasal discharge, while also protecting your dog's delicate nose from your fingernails. Bright lighting is important as you begin your exam. First look closely at your dog's nose for changes in color, texture, topography, moisture, and overall symmetry. Next use your gloved fingers to gently feel for any areas of swelling or tenderness. Finally, use your flashlight to get a look inside your dog's nostrils.

What to Do

Ask yourself a few questions to figure out what to do next:

Is there any sign of injury? Injuries to the nose of your dog are usually obvious, and it is often immediately apparent whether they are simple enough to handle at home or serious enough to warrant veterinary intervention. If it is at all unclear, consult your vet. Remember that your dog's nose is an entry port to both her respiratory and digestive systems. Keeping it healthy is therefore of paramount importance.

Is the irritation confined to the main tissues of the nose or does it seem to mostly involve the edges of the nose where they meet her muzzle? Irritations to the main tissue of the nose are often the result of direct trauma (including insect bites and stings) or exposure and may be resolved using the standard techniques outlined in "How to Clean a Wound" on page 18 and by using an Elizabethan collar to prevent self trauma. When the irritation is at the transitional border between the nose and the mouth, it may be more difficult to assess. Irritations in this area may well be part of a wide assortment of nutritional, immune-mediated, infectious, or even parasitic problems. Because of the wide variety of possibilities, don't spend too much time treating these irritations at home unless the techniques already mentioned are indeed working.

My Dog Has

Irritated Skin on His Neck

Your dog's neck is probably the easiest place for him to scratch and as a result tends to be the area that he will scratch more often than any other. Sometimes, even if the part of your dog that is truly bothering him is his ear, he'll end up scratching his neck because it's easier to reach! Because of this factor, if your dog's neck seems red and irritated, first think in terms of what might be prompting your dog to scratch.

While you're doing this, take the time to trim his toenails and if he's not completely stressed, try filing or buffing them to dull the tips. Only after you've determined that your dog isn't causing the problem should you move on to other reasons for the irritation.

What to Look For

Before focusing on the worrisome portion of your dog's neck, start from a much broader perspective. Try to evaluate his overall health status by asking yourself if he has been eating and drinking well, urinating and moving his bowels appropriately, and behaving in a normal fashion. Ask yourself if his coat has been in good condition and if he has been bathed or groomed recently. Go over his entire body, searching for clues of other problems that might cause him to focus on scratching his neck. Eventually you will work your way to the neck itself and then you will determine exactly how much of the neck is affected, how severe the irritation is, and what needs to be done about it.

What to Do

Ask yourself the following questions:

Does your dog have fleas? If so, treat the fleas before you even try to resolve the neck irritation. See "How to Treat Your Dog's Fleas" on page 22.

Does your dog have an ear infection? Follow the directions for cleaning and treating your dog's ears as outlined in "How to Treat Your Dog's Mites" on page 22 before you attack the neck problem.

Does your dog have any chronic or recently diagnosed disease? It is important to try and resolve other disease and illness before focusing on this, more superficial one.

Does your dog have a new collar of any kind, including bark collars or electronic fence collars that may only be worn part-time? If so, remove all collars and only use a harness for walking your dog until the neck irritation has resolved. This is generally a good practice for all neck problems and for dogs prone to neck and spinal injuries.

Does your dog eat and/or drink from rubber or plastic bowls? Some dogs are allergic to petroleum products. To be safe, switch his bowls to stainless steel.

Is your dog licking, rubbing, or scratching other parts of his body? Allergies are often a reason for a dog to scratch at his neck. If your dog is paying attention to these other areas as well as his neck, allergies are quite likely. Ask your dog's vet to suggest the appropriate course of action.

Is the irritation confined to a small focal area of the neck or a much broader, poorly defined region? The small areas are often easier to identify and certainly easier to correct. Bites, punctures, and sites of tick attachment are all good examples. Larger areas of irritation are often more challenging. Since an Elizabethan collar is of little value when treating irritations of the neck region, a much better approach is to use a cold compress and modified turtleneck as described in "How to Manage Superficial Injuries and Irritations of Your Dog's Neck" on page 27. Take off the protection once or twice daily to check for signs of improvement. If none is noted within a few days, see your vet.

My Patient's Story

A number of years ago one of my more affable patients, Sam, a 5-year-old Golden retriever, was found to be in a bit of a predicament when his owner returned from a trip to the market. When she called me she described Sam as having a possible ear infection with some moisture below his ear that she thought was sticky and possibly coming from the ear. She hoped that I could stop by that day, but tomorrow would be okay if I couldn't. She went on to say that she had to go out shortly but her husband had a short day and would be home in two hours. It just happened that a cancellation in my schedule allowed me to head over to their home within the hour and it was a good thing I did.

When I arrived I found Sam lying in a huge puddle of what I had to assume was a mixture of vomit, urine, and diarrhea and panting heavily. He was dehydrated with a fever of 104°F and purulent discharges from both infected ears. There was an area the size of my fist under each ear that looked like raw, bloody meat soaked in pus.

True to his nature, Sam's tail was making a weak attempt at a wag while I started in on my efforts to treat him. I called Sam's owner at work and explained to him that Sam was in dire straits. He said that he was just finishing up and that he would be home in about forty-five minutes. I urged him to make it as quick as possible, as Sam was going to need critical care at the nearest major veterinary hospital with full emergency facilities and 24-hour care. With that taken care of, I started in on cleaning up the mess that involved both of Sam's ears and the fur and skin below them. I trimmed, shaved, and cleaned the entire area, treated Sam with injectable antibiotics and steroids, administered fluids to combat his dehydration, and put a protective Elizabethan collar on him. At this point I still didn't feel great about Sam's condition, but I left a note for his owner reiterating the importance of rushing him in to the hospital and asking him to call me as soon as he had done so. With that I headed off for my next appointment.

Sam's owner called me two hours after I left his house. When I asked him how things had gone at the hospital and how Sam was doing he said, "Fine. When I walked in the door he greeted me in the front hallway with his tail wagging. I figured you must have solved the problem so I'll just give him the antibiotics you prescribed and spray his neck twice a day like you said in your note, OK?"

Taken somewhat aback by this response, I quickly considered whether I needed to intervene or simply trust my client. The client, a surgeon at a major local hospital, was certainly someone capable of evaluating whether or not his dog was in grave danger, so I chalked this one was up to the incredible ability of some dogs to bounce back from the worst of situations. Sam is now 13 years old and still plugging along!

My Dog Has
Irritated Skin
on His Neck

My Dog Has
Irritated Skin on Her Chest

Your dog's chest is a prime spot for a vast array of skin irritations. Most frequently occurring are those that arise in long-haired or thick-coated dogs that like to dig troughs in the dirt in order to cool off during hot weather. Certainly, seasonal inhalant allergies, contact allergies such as poison ivy, and food allergies are common sources as well. Sometimes, as is the case with most hot spots, the initial cause of irritation is unidentifiable due to the ability of your dog to reach the area with her rear paws and scratch away the evidence. It is often a good idea to minimize further damage by trimming and dulling your dog's rear nails before thinking about addressing the irritation itself.

What to Look For

Take a broad-perspective look at your dog's general condition before beginning your specific examination of her chest irritation. Try to get a grasp of her overall health by evaluating her enthusiasm, bowel and bladder habits, appetite, and thirst. Is her coat glossy and is her skin soft and supple? Once you're confident that you've fairly evaluated her, move on to a more critical assessment of the irritation on her chest.

What to Do

Now take a few moments to answer the following questions:

Does your dog suffer from any form of allergies? Many skin irritations can be traced to some form of allergy. If the source can be eliminated, the irritation will be easier to solve. Investigate food, environmental (including regional plants, household materials, and chemicals), and parasitic allergies. If you suspect allergies and wish to test your theory more quickly, try administering a weight-appropriate dose of Benadryl while removing all the potential allergens you can. (See "How to Treat Your Dog's Allergic Symptoms" on page 25.) The dose may need to be repeated every twelve hours if tolerated well, and if the irritation resumes each time the medication wears off.

Are you using any new cleaning products in the house, especially where your dog spends time? If so, go back to the original ones just to be safe.

Have you recently changed the brand or formula of your dog's food? If so, switch back in order to ensure that the food is not responsible.

Does your dog have an injury or infection in the irritated area? The pain, tenderness, or even mild discomfort of an injury or infection is enough to prompt a dog to focus on that area and begin to lick, scratch, rub, or chew at it. If this is the case, try treating it the way you would a hot spot as detailed in "My Dog Has a Hot Spot" on page 72.

Does your dog have any swelling associated with the irritation? Occasionally a swelling or mass will cause irritation to an area of skin either by its presence alone or due to chafing. If you find a mass in the area of irritation, seek advice from your veterinarian right away.

My Dog Has
Irritated Skin on His Back

Irritation of the skin on your dog's back is usually a straightforward problem, rarely complicated by the effects of licking, chewing, rubbing, or scratching, simply because the location makes it a difficult part of your dog's body to reach. (However, since some dogs will go to rather heroic lengths to satisfy an itch, don't assume this is an *impossible* place to reach.) To begin the evaluation process, start by assessing your dog's overall health and then focus in on the problem on his back.

What to Look For

Only after getting a good look at your dog's entire body, look at the part of his back that seems to be bothering him.

Brush the hair of his entire back first with the direction of growth, then against it, to get a clear view of the skin beneath. Look for evidence of parasites, bleeding, wounds, excoriations, rashes, crusts, discharge, or other signs of infection. Also be on the lookout for growths, swellings, or suspicious changes in pigmentation.

What to Do

Asking yourself the following questions should help you figure out what to do next:

Does your dog have dry skin? Dry skin is often a source of irritation, and the back is a common site for it to occur. A typical time of year for this is when the heat is turned on, removing even more moisture from your dog's skin. Giving your dog food or supplements fortified with omega-3 fatty acids may help this. Also, make sure that your dog is always well hydrated by offering plenty of clean, fresh water.

Does your dog suffer from allergies? Usually food and environmental allergies will affect more than just your dog's back. If it is only your dog's back that is irritated, however, contact allergies and flea allergies are still distinct possibilities.

Does your dog have fleas? Fleas alone can cause quite an awful mess simply by making your dog uncomfortable enough to rub his back against objects or even the floor. Their constant biting can also induce a hypersensitivity reaction known as flea allergy dermatitis.

Treat the fleas and it may be enough to solve the problem, but the allergic response may take a while to resolve. (See "How to Treat Your Dog's Fleas" on page 22 and "How to Treat Your Dog's Allergic Symptoms" on page 25.)

Does your dog have any new clothing, bedding, or bath products? Sensitivities to any of these items could be causing an irritant reaction, so put them aside for the time being, until you can get the irritation under control.

Did your exam reveal any wounds or infection? Treat minor wounds and infections by following the directions outlined in "How to Clean a Wound" on page 18. More dramatic wounds, ulcers, and infections that cover substantial areas of your dog's back should always be handled by your veterinarian.

Did you notice any lumps or bumps associated with the irritation? Rashes, infections, tumors, and other types of swellings can often appear as irritations to the skin of a dog's back. If initial attempts at topical treatment don't seem to be working, consult your veterinarian.

My Dog Has
Irritated Skin on Her Rump

When the hindquarters of a dog become uncomfortable or irritated, her first reaction is to lick or chew at the area. If a dog can't reach the actual site that is bothering her, the closest spot she can reach will do. The simple act of repetitive licking or chewing will promote the release of endorphins, the body's own form of narcotic, and provide a sense of comfort. Unfortunately, the euphoric results can become somewhat addictive, driving the dog to continue the process and cause more damage.

What to Look For

Before checking the severity of the actual irritation, closely examine your dog's rectal region. Look for any abnormal sign or evidence of discomfort such as redness, swelling, irritation, open wounds, discharge, or foreign body, including dried fecal residue. Any of these could prompt the type of response described above.

What to Do

Now, ask yourself a few questions:

Did your exam reveal any evidence of an anal problem? If so, and if it appears to simply be that your dog's anal sacs are full, you may wish to follow the directions from "How to Empty Your Dog's Anal Sacs" on page 23. If you are unsuccessful or uncomfortable with the thought of trying this, or if the problem seems more serious, it is important to have it evaluated by your veterinarian.

Did you see any other abnormality anywhere between your dog's anus and the site of irritation? Treating that problem first, while attempting to control your dog's efforts to lick and chew, should solve the problem. An Elizabethan collar may be needed. If the irritation itself is the only problem, treat it like you would any other wound, rash, or injury. (See "My Dog is Rubbing or Licking Her Anus" on page 159 and especially "My Dog Has a Hot Spot" on page 72.)

My Dog's
Skin Is Leathery

Some dogs have thicker skin than others, and not in the proverbial way. While thicker skin may, in some cases, provide added protection and insulation, it is usually a sign of some problem. Most of the time the problems that cause thickening of the skin are treatable; sometimes they are even curable. A close look at your dog as a whole, and his skin in particular, may yield some clues as to the cause of his thick skin.

What to Look For

Look closely at your dog's entire body, noticing all his skin, not just the area in question. Check for variations in color, texture, thickness, temperature, and elasticity. You can check elasticity by stretching the skin and releasing it, noting how quickly it returns to its original position and shape. Also check for evidence of trauma, such as excoriations, or scratch marks, and bleeding. Look for signs of infection, such as moisture and discharge. Finally, check for parasites. You might see external parasites, such as fleas and lice, or their droppings on your dog's skin. You might see overall dullness of coat, or gastrointestinal symptoms like vomiting or diarrhea if your dog has internal parasites.

Warning

Always wear rubber gloves when examining your dog's skin. This is to protect yourself against parasites or other infections that are transmittable to humans, such as ringworm.

What to Do

Now ask yourself the following questions:

Is your dog itchy? Itchy dogs may have allergies, parasites, or even autoimmune disorders like lupus or pemphigus. First try shampooing your dog with a soothing, emollient-type shampoo. There are many oatmeal-based products that fit the bill—I like Malaseb, a DVM Pharmaceuticals product available through your veterinarian—to calm the itch. If this doesn't work, keep questioning.

Have you recently changed your dog's brand of food? The skin problems could be caused by a food allergy. Try switching back to the old food or trying another new one and see if he tolerates it better. Give it two to three weeks to notice improvement.

Is your dog also losing hair? Dogs with thick skin and hair loss are often diagnosed with either an endocrine disorder or an immune system disorder. Take your dog to his vet for the appropriate blood tests.

Does your dog have parasites? External parasites such as fleas, ticks, and lice can drive a dog crazy with itchiness. The scratching then causes injuries to the dog's skin, and the skin responds by becoming thick, dark, and leathery. The dog then loses his hair. Treat the parasites effectively and the skin will improve. (See "How to Treat Your Dog's Fleas" on page 22.)

The same holds true for internal parasites. If they are suspected, your veterinarian can conduct the appropriate tests and recommend the correct treatment. Treat them and the quality and texture (and smell) of your dog's skin will improve.

My Dog Has
Dark Areas
on Her Nose,
Lips, Gums,
or Tongue

My Dog Has

Dark Areas on Her Nose, Lips, Gums, or Tongue

As is the case for many parts of your dog's anatomy, the mucus membranes of the nose, lips, and gums and even the inside of the mouth are commonly pigmented. This pigmentation can be overall, lending a deep blue to black color to some or all of these tissues with little to none of the reassuringly healthy pink color we expect to see. In some breeds, such as the Chow Chow for example, the entire tongue is darkly pigmented, taking on a deep bluish color. The pigmentation can also be patchy or spotted, and to make matters even more challenging, some of this pigmentation does not appear until the dog has reached adulthood.

What to Look For

For all of these reasons, it is wise to have a very good look inside your dog's mouth when you first acquire her. This will serve as a baseline for future comparison. Then in the process of your dog's development, if new pigment is noticed, it can be followed accurately. If, however, you did not take a look in the past, have a good look inside your dog's mouth now to check for any abnormalities.

Get a flashlight or take your dog to a spot with very good light. If you can, get someone else to help out. Begin by petting your dog the way you normally would. In a few minutes, begin rubbing her ears and working your way to her muzzle. Sit beside your dog and place the palm of your hand that's closest to her nose beneath her chin. Place the palm of your other hand flat against her cheek. Use the thumb of that second hand to apply gentle pressure against the outside of her upper lip, sliding it up to reveal the teeth and gums beneath. Similarly, use the thumb of your lower hand to slide your dog's lower lip down, revealing her lower teeth and gums. (See the illustration on page 35.)

Take your time. By shifting the position of your hands and patiently starting and stopping repeatedly, you should eventually be able to take a look at your dog's teeth and gums on that side of her face.

Now it's time to check out your dog's tongue and hard palate (the roof of her mouth). To do this, place your left thumb on the right side of your dog's upper lip, just behind the large canine teeth. Place your left index and middle fingers on the left side of your dog's upper lip, just behind the large canine teeth. Do the same with your right hand on her lower lip, and then open her mouth like a clam shell. Take a good look inside. Don't forget to check under the tongue.

Now repeat the side exam from the other side.

What to Do

When a new area of pigment is identified, the two most important factors in deciding whether it is something to be concerned about are your dog's age at the time of occurrence and the specific appearance of the area of pigment.

Most forms of pigment in or around your dog's mouth are normal, especially if your dog is less than five years old.

If your dog is less than two years old, it is likely that any new pigmentation associated with her nose, lips, or mouth is simply the normal appearance of genetically predetermined coloring. Watch it closely for any changes in texture, shape, and color. If such changes, especially in texture, occur rapidly, they are worth having examined by your vet. Normal pigment development will occur slowly, and changes in shape and color will come on gradually and eventually stop.

If your dog is between two and five years old, it is possible that any pigmentation you notice may have been present all along but had escaped your notice until now. Examine it carefully, paying particular attention to the exact color of the pigment. Normal pigment is most often dark blue to black and occasionally medium to dark brown. Red "pigment" is not normal. Check the edges for irregularities in shape and color. If those edges are rough or jagged looking and/or there is redness associated with them, a biopsy may be advised.

My Dog Has
Dark Areas on His Skin

Every dog has variations in skin color. These variations can range from subtle differences in shading to spots as dramatic as those on a Dalmatian. In most cases, dark areas of skin, even when they exist against a background of much lighter skin, are quite normal. Because most dogs have skin that is covered with a thick coat of fur, we are often not acutely aware of these variations. With this in mind, always approach skin-related issues in your dog with an open mind and an eye toward what might be considered normal.

What to Look For

I would venture to say that most dog owners would find it difficult to describe the color of their dog's skin. So now is a good time to take a few minutes and get a good look.

First, put on a pair of rubber gloves. Now take your time and using a wide-toothed comb, part your dog's fur to get a look at his skin (if your dog will let you). Note any differences in color and keep an eye out for hair loss as well.

What to Do

Here's what to do, depending on what you saw. Ask yourself the following questions:

Does the texture of the pigmented skin appear similar to the skin around it? Normally pigmented skin will have the texture and appearance of the skin immediately surrounding it, with no observable differences in the transition from the dark area to the lighter surrounding area. If the texture of the pigmented region is rough, raised, leathery, or scaly, this is not normal.

Do you see areas of hair loss? If the skin is scaly, it's especially worrisome if combined with hair loss in the area, as this combination may suggest a fungal infection called ringworm that is often transferable to humans and is very itchy! (Bet you're glad you put on those gloves!)

Does your dog seem to be aware of this patch of skin? If the area is itchy or bothersome in any way, it may represent an injury, infection, or a reaction to something

When to Get the Vet

If you notice redness around the edges of the dark area—particularly if the perimeter of the dark region is poorly defined with jagged edges—take your dog to the vet immediately, as this could mean that your dog has a type of cancer called melanoma. A skin biopsy will be necessary to find out.

If your dog is losing hair over an area where the skin is heavily pigmented, it can mean that he has been so bothered by some irritation that his constant licking, chewing, or scratching has resulted in the pigmentation that you are now noticing. Alternatively, it could mean that both the hair loss and the pigmentation are side effects of some systemic disease process. In either case, veterinary care is called for.

your dog was exposed to. If a dog "worries" any patch of skin long enough, the trauma alone will cause an increase in the pigment to the area. If you can figure out what the underlying problem is, correct it and, in turn, eliminate the licking, chewing, or scratching, the pigment should gradually diminish.

Have you ever noticed this specific area of skin without the dark coloring you are noticing now? If so, check to see if the dark color is present in a similar location on your dog's other side. Bilaterally symmetrical lesions of the skin and hair are often linked to endocrine disorders such as hypothyroidism.

Is there any other color associated with the dark area in question? Redness within the dark patch could be the result of trauma from injury or self-induced by your dog due to irritation. See "My Dog Has a Hot Spot" on page 72.

See "My Dog Has a Hot Spot" on page 72.

My Dog Has
Calluses on Her Elbows

Callused elbows—patches of tough, leathery skin—are a common occurrence, mostly among large breed dogs, particularly those stubborn enough to refuse the cushioned bedding provided by their owners! While the calluses are not dangerous or even abnormal, they can become a nuisance to the dog. They also have the potential to develop into something worse.

What to Look For

With your dog lying down or standing, take a good look at her elbows. Note which elbows have calluses and what they look like. Check for bleeding, discharge, and swelling. If the area is swollen, note if the area is hot and painful and whether the swelling is hard or soft.

What to Do

Ask yourself the following questions:

How long have the calluses been present? True calluses are the result of repeated trauma to the skin. Over time, repeated pressure or friction to the skin anywhere on a dog's body will result in a protective formation of a tough, leathery area of skin. If the area on your dog's elbow has cropped up seemingly overnight, you may be dealing with something other than a callus.

Is there any bleeding or discharge near the calluses? Because calluses are formed from hardened, keratinized skin, they often crack and bleed and will sometimes get infected. In most cases, if the cracking, bleeding, or discharge is not substantial, home care is easy and effective. Clean the entire area with your 50/50 hydrogen peroxide/water solution then spread a thin film of an antibiotic ointment, such as Bacitracin or Polysporin, over the infected site.

If you see only cracking and minor bleeding but no pus discharge, you can use a soothing, moisturizing salve such as Bag Balm or A&D Ointment instead of the antibiotic ointment. If your dog spends much time outside, this ointment or salve is going to act like a dirt magnet, so it is important to protect the area. Use adhesive tape to anchor a non-adherent wound dressing over the area, then take a clean white cotton athletic sock and cut out the toe area. Pull the sock over the elbow, trapping the recently placed dressing in position under the "heel" of the sock. Place additional tape around the top and bottom of the sock, immediately above and below the elbow, respectively.

Sock Bandage

Is there noticeable swelling of the area?

Calluses by themselves are rarely a very serious problem, but swelling of the area beneath and surrounding a callus can represent something more grave. Examine the area gently but thoroughly to determine if the swollen area is painful or non-painful, soft or hard, hot or normal body temperature, and baggy or fluid-filled.

If the swelling is painful, there may be an injury in addition to the callus. Rest and anti-inflammatory medication may help. (See "Treating Your Dog with Anti-Inflammatories" on page 24.) If you don't see improvement within a day or two, call your dog's vet.

If the swelling is hot, there may be an infection present so look more closely for evidence of a puncture or scratch to the area. If your dog is acting normally, try an antibiotic dressing like the one mentioned above. If no improvement is noted within twenty-four hours, check with your dog's vet.

If the swelling seems to be filled with fluid but is normal in temperature, your dog may have a hygroma. This is a fluid-filled swelling, usually of both elbows, that may respond to rest and protective care. Since most of the dogs that develop these are large or giant breed, human elbow pads can often serve as effective protection. Over time, the fluid should be resorbed and the swelling should subside.

If the swelling is hard, there may be a mass present, in which case further diagnosis by your vet is recommended.

My Dog Has
Cracked Footpads

The soles of your dog's feet are quite well-protected by the thick fatty tissue of the digital pads that are themselves covered by the toughest skin on your dog's body. The surface of this skin is rough due to the heavily keratinized conical papillae that make it up. If you take a close look at your dog's footpads, you'll see that these papillae look like tightly packed rows of corn. They can be identified easily with the naked eye, except in those dogs that are walked on rough surfaces, which smooth the papillae down.

What to Look For

Observe your dog moving around for a few minutes. Cracked and bleeding pads are often enough to cause your dog to limp in discomfort. Now have your dog sit or lie down comfortably. Speaking soothingly, gently examine each footpad in turn. Check to see how deep the cracks are and if they are bleeding. Then carefully wipe away any excess blood or dirt with a clean white cloth to get a sense of how much the pads are bleeding.

What to Do

Ask yourself the following questions to get your dog feeling better:

How deep are the cracks? It is important to distinguish between pads that are bleeding superficially due to dryness and cracking and pads that have deeper fissures due to trauma and injury. It is unusual for injuries to footpads to require surgical intervention except in severe circumstances. This is mostly due to the composition of these pads. The conical papillae, since they are long and separate, present a challenge to the surgeon who cannot gain any purchase for his sutures except in the deeper layers of the dermis.

Does the crack extend in one or more directions? Cracks that extend in more than one direction are often not cracks at all, but just the normal separation of the conical papillae that can be demonstrated if the pads are manipulated just so. (This activity is probably best left to your vet to perform.) In such cases where cracks are visible, there is rarely any bleeding present. However, if a crack is solitary and deep, chances are that it is the result of drying or injury. If the crack is bleeding, but not dramatically, a simple pressure wrap may be enough to control the bleeding and solve the problem. (See "How to Control Bleeding" on page 18.)

Does the crack extend below the superficial layers of the pad and is the bleeding steady? If both criteria are met, this may be one of those instances where sutures are called for. Try to clean the wound enough with a 50/50 mixture of hydrogen peroxide and water and a clean towel to get an idea of how deep the wound is and how serious the bleeding is.

When to Get the Vet

If the crack is deep and the flow of blood is steady, see your vet.

My Dog Has
Blisters on Her Skin

Most of us are familiar with how uncomfortable it can be to have blisters on our hands as a result of excess activity, such as chopping wood. Similarly, the itchiness of poison ivy blisters is probably something many of us have experienced. Dogs can get blisters just like we can, and they can be just as uncomfortable.

Also just like humans, blisters on dogs can arise from a variety of sources. These include infections (bacterial and viral), parasite infestations, burns (including sunburn), allergic reactions, and trauma. While the blisters themselves are rarely a cause for alarm, it's important to identify the reason for their appearance as it may have an impact on your dog's recovery. In addition, your own health might be affected by whatever it is that is causing your dog's blisters. Rather than worry yourself about the various sources of danger to you, make sure that you wear protective rubber gloves each and every time you examine your dog's skin.

What to Look For

With your rubber gloves on, settle your dog in a comfortable position under bright light. Slowly and carefully check her skin for blisters. Take note of how many you find, where they are, and what they look like.

What to Do

Blisters, which are also known as bullae, result when some agent causes a separation of the epidermis from the dermis. Ask yourself the following questions to figure out what to do next for your dog:

How many blisters did you find? The number of blisters is important because solitary blisters are likely to be the result of some sort of trauma or direct, isolated contact with something noxious. Multiple blisters, however, are more suggestive of some sort of systemic reaction to an infection, allergen, or parasite infestation.

When to Get the Vet

Blisters' presence, if related to exposures like those listed above, does not necessitate a visit to your vet. In these cases, remove the suspected contact or medical element from your dog's environment and apply cool compresses to soothe your dog's skin. However, if you don't see improvement within a week, contact your vet for a professional opinion.

Where are the blisters on your dog's body? Location is an important clue to figuring out the reason behind the presence of blisters on your dog's skin. For example, a single clear blister, which is also called a vesicle, on your male dog's foreskin paints an entirely different picture than a galaxy of pustules, or pus-filled blisters, between your dog's toes.

Are the blisters itchy? This is a trick question to some extent. When blisters are itchy, like the ones resulting from demodex mites, you don't often get a chance to see them because as soon as the dog feels the itch, she'll lick, scratch, or chew the area until all that's left is a raw, bloody area, or hot spot. (See "My Dog Has a Hot Spot" on page 72.)

What, if any, color are the blisters? Pink to red blisters can be present in cases of autoimmune disease (such as pemphigus), mite infestations, burns, and drug eruptions. The presentation of such blisters should always prompt a visit with your veterinarian.

Clear blisters, or vesicles, can also be present in all of the above cases. White blisters, or pustules, are white because they are filled with inflammatory cells, or pus. They are usually present in cases of infection and infestation. If topical treatment by cleansing, disinfecting, and topical antibiotics is unsuccessful, your vet should be consulted.

Has your dog been on any medications over the past few months? Many dogs will develop blisters as part of an adverse reaction to medications. By simply taking your dog off the drug, the blisters will usually go away within a few weeks. Talk with your vet before taking your dog off of any prescribed medication, however.

My Dog Has Blisters on Her Skin

Have you recently changed your dog's diet or begun offering some new treat? Food allergies are a common cause of skin blisters. Stop offering the new food or treat, and the symptoms should abate.

Have you been using any new detergents or cleaning products? Direct contact between the hairless portions of your dog's skin and any allergenic substance or chemical can produce a blistering contact dermatitis. In these cases, use a milder detergent or even just water to clean the surfaces your dog comes in direct contact with to alleviate your dog's symptoms.

Did you recently buy new plastic or rubber dog bowls? If the blisters are clustered around your dog's mouth and chin and you are using plastic or rubber bowls for food and water, it is quite possible that your dog has an allergy to petroleum products. Switch to stainless steel or ceramic bowls and avoid other petroleum products as well.

My Dog Has
Blisters in His Mouth

Blisters in a dog's mouth can result from many of the same causes as those occurring on a dog's skin. (See "My Dog Has Blisters on Her Skin" on page 64.) In the majority of cases, they are the result of some viral illness, but other common causes are allergic responses to foods, medications, and chemicals; and burns from spices, heat, or electricity.

What to Look For

Get a flashlight or take your dog to a spot with very good light. If you can, get someone else to help out.

Begin by petting your dog the way you normally would. In a few minutes, begin rubbing his ears and working your way to his muzzle. Sit beside your dog and place the palm of your hand that's closest to his nose beneath his chin. Place the palm of your other hand flat against his cheek. Use the thumb of that second hand to apply gentle pressure against the outside of his upper lip, sliding it up to reveal the teeth and gums beneath. Similarly, use the thumb of your lower hand to slide your dog's lower lip down, revealing his lower teeth and gums.

Take your time. By shifting the position of your hands and patiently starting and stopping repeatedly, you should eventually be able to take a look at your dog's teeth and gums on that side of his face.

Now it's time to check out your dog's tongue and hard palate (the roof of his mouth). To do this, place your left thumb on the right side of your dog's upper lip, just behind the large canine teeth. Place your left index and middle fingers on the left side of your dog's upper lip, just behind the large canine teeth. Do the same with your right hand on his lower lip, and then open his mouth like a clam shell. Take a good look inside. Don't forget to check under the tongue.

Now repeat the side exam from the other side.

What to Do

The following are questions that you need to answer in order to ascertain the cause of the blisters are quite straightforward:

Does your dog appear to be otherwise healthy? Illnesses that result in blistering of the mouth may also be responsible for fever and lethargy. Use a rectal thermometer to check your dog's temperature, especially if he seems lethargic. If he has a fever (any temperature greater than 102.5°F), he could be fighting some systemic illness. If your dog remains unhealthy for more than a few hours, the blisters are unlikely to resolve without first treating the underlying illness, so place that call to the vet.

If your dog does appear to be in otherwise good health and the blisters do not appear to be itchy or infectious in origin, they should resolve on their own within a week to ten days. If they persist, call your vet.

Has your dog recently ingested a spicy food or had exposure to any unusual plants or chemicals? Even brief exposure to some plants or chemicals can result in blistering on the sensitive mucus membranes of the mouth. If this is the case, flush your dog's mouth immediately with cold water or rub ice cubes over the affected tissues. If you know the type of plant or the exact chemical or brand name, call the ASPCA National Animal Poison Control Center at 888-426-4435 for immediate advice.

My Dog Has
Blisters on Her Genitals

Genital blisters sound like something you'd like to avoid speaking about in public! Most of the time, however, they are the result of an easily treatable bacterial infection or a not-so-awful viral infection that will probably resolve on its own within a few days. Occasionally, other sources of genital blisters occur, and most of them are treatable as well.

What to Look For

Settle your dog in a comfortable position in bright light. It would be helpful to have someone help you out with this. Take a close look at the blisters by gently parting your dog's hair and examining her skin. If your dog is male, examine both his penis and the surrounding tissues, including his scrotum.

What to Do

Here's what to do, depending on what you saw:

What exactly do they look like? The "blisters" you see on your dog's genitals may not be blisters at all, so look at them closely. If they look like clear, fluid-filled bubbles arising from the surface of your dog's skin, you are correct in describing them as blisters. If the material they contain appears milky white to slightly yellow in color, they are probably pustules—pus-filled blisters. If they are blood red to brick red in color, they are probably hemorrhagic in origin. Pustules will require antibiotic therapy prescribed by your veterinarian, while hemorrhagic blisters are more worrisome and definitely require a veterinary evaluation.

Is your dog bothered by the blisters?
Itchy blisters and pustules can be brought on by mite infestations, bacterial infections, and allergic reactions. If they are really itchy, you probably won't get a good look at them because your dog will destroy them before you have a chance. In such cases what you will see are known as epidermal collarettes, which are the result of former pustules or blisters that have been scratched off by your dog's licking, rubbing, or scratching.

Epidermal Collarettes

When to Get the Vet

If your dog seems unaffected by the blisters, it's probably fine to leave them be while monitoring them closely. But if she is even moderately annoyed by them, seek treatment quickly before the situation progresses to something much worse.

If your dog is bothered by the blisters, apply a cold compress. This will be soothing and will reduce the sensitivity of the nerve endings in the area. Don't use warm compresses on the blisters to "bring them to a head," however. Warm compresses will probably not make a difference, and they may actually make the area more uncomfortable than when you started.

My Dog Has Blisters on Her Genitals

My Dog Has
a Bald Spot

Hair loss is a constant event in the life of a dog. With the exception of some breeds that tend not to shed much, most dogs shed enough to make weekly sweeping or vacuuming a necessity. But when your dog loses so much hair that areas of bare skin are exposed, something is definitely wrong.

What to Look For

Wearing rubber gloves, slowly and carefully look over your dog's coat for other bald spots. It's helpful to speak softly to your dog and gently rub him with one hand while checking his fur for bald spots with the other hand.

Warning

It is important to wear disposable rubber gloves when examining bald spots! Sometimes they can be caused by ringworm, which is highly contagious, even to people.

What to Do

Reasons for hair loss are numerous, but by answering a few simple questions you should be able to figure out the source of the problem.

Is the hair loss generalized, patchy, or confined to one small area? Generalized hair loss usually indicates a more systemic problem. Endocrine disorders such as hypothyroidism are commonly associated with hair loss that involves significant areas of the body, often in a bilaterally symmetric pattern. (This means, for example, your dog has one bald spot on his left shoulder and a similar one on his right shoulder.) If you observe such a pattern, you'll need to take your dog to his vet for blood testing.

Patchy areas of hair loss may be due to a variety of sources, including infection or parasite infestation. These will also require a visit to the vet.

A single, isolated bald spot could be due to a simple injury (see below) or the first noticeable lesion of a more dramatic problem. Monitor the spot and consult your vet if it looks suspicious or if more spots appear.

Does your dog have an injury? A common reason for the loss of hair in a particular area or isolated spot is an injury. The injury itself can cause hair loss, and the compulsive licking of the site of the injury performed by most dogs will remove hair as well. In such instances it may be necessary to treat the injury *and* protect it from further attention by your dog. Cover the injury with a bandage and place an Elizabethan collar on your dog to keep him from licking the wound. You can buy this type of collar at most pet supply stores. (See "How to Dress a Wound" on page 19.)

Methods for treating the injury can vary tremendously depending on the severity of the wound. You can probably treat superficial scratches and abrasions at home. If they don't respond well, your vet's help should be sought. Take any puncture or laceration seriously because it may represent a more dramatic injury than you think and have a way of getting worse in a hurry.

Does your dog have a rash? A rash or other irritation can directly affect the health of hair follicles, resulting in hair loss. The discomfort the dog feels from the area will usually prompt him to lick or scratch, making things worse. Again, treat the problem, but be sure to protect the area from further trauma by the patient!

Is the bald area clearly defined with a distinct round to oval shape? Such bald areas are often the result of ringworm, a highly contagious fungal infection. The exposed skin is usually slightly scaly and a bit shiny. See your vet for the appropriate testing (and be happy you were wearing your gloves!). If members of your family develop dry, itchy spots on their skin as well, they should be seen by a doctor immediately.

Is there any moisture or discharge in the area? Licking alone could cause a bald area to be moist, but look more closely for signs of discharge. Blood is a sign of injury, and pus is a sign of infection. You can clean mild abrasions and excoriations with an antiseptic such as hydrogen peroxide, but anything more serious should be seen by a professional. Your dog may need antibiotics.

My Dog Has
a Hot Spot

My Dog Has
A Hot Spot

Any area of skin that is angry pink to red, warm to hot, moist to wet, irritated to bloody, and possibly seeping pus can be called a "hot spot." It is important to realize, however, that the term "hot spot" is a general description and not a specific diagnosis. Simply put, a hot spot is a patch of your dog's skin that is bothering her so much that she can't leave it alone. Because of this overwhelming discomfort, she has rubbed, scratched, and licked it into the condition you see before you.

What to Look For

Gently separate your dog's hair around the hot spot to get a good look at it. Look for open skin and raw, bloody patches of flesh. Then slowly and carefully look over your dog's skin for other hot spots. It's helpful to speak softly to your dog and gently rub her with one hand while checking her skin for hot spots with the other hand.

What to Do

No doubt, you feel badly for your dog and want to figure out what caused this mess. Although it is wonderful to be able to get to the bottom of such a condition and to diagnose the inciting cause, it is not always possible, nor is it all that critical compared to treating the lesion.

The treatment usually involves three separate parts. First, you'll shave the hot spot and the surrounding area to get a better look at the full extent of the problem and to make ongoing treatment easier. Second, you'll clean and medicate the entire area. And third, you'll come up with a therapy plan to control infection, reduce itchiness, and protect the area from further trauma.

Don't gag; don't sweat; as long as the wound is not an open one, revealing the muscle or fat beneath, you should be able to treat it yourself. Grab the following supplies and get to work:

- Electric hair clippers, if you have them

- Scissors that you are comfortable using

- Soft, clean cotton cloths or towels, or a generous supply of paper toweling

- 50/50 mixture of hydrogen peroxide and warm (not hot) water

- A commercially available soothing, anti-itch spray, preferably alcohol-free

- Bacitracin, Polysporin, or another broad spectrum antibiotic ointment

- Size-appropriate non-adherent wound dressing

- Cotton gauze on a roll

- Adhesive tape

- Bitter apple or other awful-tasting spray

- Plastic Elizabethan collar

You'll probably need a helper to hold your dog while you do this, especially if the wound you're treating is bothering her.

1 Using the clippers and scissors, try to trim away as much hair as possible from the wound, extending an inch beyond the wound in every direction. (If the hair over the wound is caked with discharge, try the next step first, and then come back to the trimming.)

2 Soak your cloth or towel with the hydrogen peroxide and water mixture and repeatedly blot the entire wound, rinsing the cloth off frequently. You'll soon find that the wound doesn't look nearly as awful as it did earlier. Once the area seems to be clear of dirt, debris, and dried blood, put away the cloth.

3 Now give the entire area a few good squirts of anti-itch spray, taking care to go all the way to the edges of the trimmed hair.

4 Apply a thin film of antibiotic ointment to one side of the non-adherent dressing and press it directly to the wound.

5 If the hot spot is on an extremity, simply wrap the gauze around the limb 2–3 times and then use adhesive tape to encircle the ends of the gauze. If the site is on an area such as the shoulder or hip, it is sometimes possible to wrap gauze in a figure 8 around the front or rear limbs. If the spot is on your dog's belly, back, or chest, you may need to get enough gauze and tape to wrap entirely around her abdomen or thorax.

6 Almost done; now apply the bitter apple or equivalent spray to the bandage to prevent licking or chewing. (The addition of an Elizabethan collar will improve your chances of success.) If you can keep the dressing on for 3–5 days, you'll be surprised at how much improvement will take place!

When to Get the Vet

Scrutinize the area daily for signs of increased swelling, heat, or sensitivity. If you notice any of these signs or if your dog develops a fever, she'll probably need systemic antibiotics and should see your veterinarian.

You should also call your vet without delay if your dog's hot spot has progressed far beyond hair loss and red irritated skin and now appears as fur sticky with accumulated discharge, covering raw to bloody, excoriated patches of flesh.

**My Dog's
Coat is Dull
and Dry**

My Dog's
Coat Is Dull and Dry

A healthy dog is usually covered in a thick, shiny coat of fur. Even if your dog is a mischief-loving rogue that loves nothing better than to escape and go wading through the nearby swamp or rolling in something absolutely horrid, if he is healthy, a good brushing should bring the luster back to his topcoat.

In some instances, your dog's breed may be the driving force behind the texture and appearance of his coat and you are probably aware of this. If, however, you have a dog that lacks the glowing coat you expect, there is probably a reason behind it.

What to Look For

You should have a good quality brush and comb for the care and maintenance of your dog's coat. Not every breed of dog is suited to the same type or brand of grooming device, so get some guidance from your veterinarian, groomer, or friends with dogs.

To evaluate the health of your dog's coat, start by brushing his fur against the grain, beginning just forward of his tail and moving toward his head. Repeat this a few times, then conduct similar exams on each of his four limbs, starting at the paw and working upward toward the body. Examine your dog's head, face, armpits, groin, and belly with a soft brush or just your hands (wearing rubber gloves, of course), since these areas on your dog tend to be more sensitive. This motion will give you a good look at the full length of your dog's individual hair shafts while also providing you with an opportunity to check for parasites and irregularities of the skin and fur.

If you notice anything suspicious in the course of these long, slow brush strokes, go back over the areas in question with a wide-toothed comb. This will allow you to identify a specific spot with a minimum of trauma to the area. Once that spot is located, you can scrutinize it with additional finer tools like a magnifying glass and a finer-toothed comb.

Take a look at your dog's stools and around his anus, checking for signs of internal parasites, such as bleeding.

What to Do

Now ask yourself the following questions:

Do you feed your dog a nutritionally complete diet with all the necessary vitamins and minerals? Most commercially available kibbles fit this description, but the ingredient list may not necessarily agree with your dog's metabolism. Sometimes the simple addition of some missing or poorly absorbed vitamins, minerals, or fatty acids is enough to dramatically improve the luster of your dog's coat.

Be particularly aware of the omega-3 fatty acids. You can buy these supplements in most natural food stores and even in some grocery stores. Liquids are ideal since dosing can be precise. Alternatively, you can give your dog capsules directly or hide them in food. Or you can puncture the capsules and drizzle the contents over food. Zinc, the various B vitamins, and vitamins A, C, D, and E are the others to consider adding. When in doubt, a call to your vet may help.

Did you notice any wounds, bites, rashes, or irregularities on your dog's skin? Any one of these could significantly contribute to the loss of a shiny coat, either directly or indirectly (through the resulting licking and scratching). Unless the problem is solved, your dog could start losing his hair. Treat the wounds and bites in a manner consistent with their severity. Treat mild ones with persistent application of disinfectant and topical antimicrobials such as Bacitracin or Neosporin. Treat rashes by substituting mild topical steroid ointment or lotion like Cortaid or Corticin. "Irregular-

ities" can describe just about anything that seems abnormal, such as a lump, bump, crust, or unusual pigmentation. In general, if they don't bother your dog, just keep an eye on them for further developments. If they prompt attention from your dog, check with your vet for advice.

Is there evidence of external parasites? If you see fleas or their telltale droppings, you should begin treatment immediately before your dog and his entire environment become infested. Besides treating your dog, treat all other pets in the household, as well as the house and any other places the dog frequents, such as the car, the dog carrier, all dog beds. Also be sure to treat the furniture, as fabric is a common place for fleas to reside while waiting

Warning

- Your fingers may be the most valuable and effective tools for this purpose, but be sure to wear rubber gloves to protect yourself against possible fungal infection or parasites like fleas or mites.

- Never assume that the absence of fleas on your dog means that there is no flea problem. The presence of the tiny, comma-shaped feces of fleas is strong enough evidence to merit aggressive treatment of both your dog and your home. For more information, see "How to Treat Your Dog's Fleas" on page 22.

- Take internal parasites very seriously. Many of these parasites can be transmitted to humans. Get your dog treated right away.

My Dog's Coat is Dull and Dry

for a new host. Commercially available parasitic-fighting products are a good place to start, but if they are less than completely effective, seek your vet's assistance.

The other type of superficial parasite common to dogs is the mite. Mange is caused by a type of mite that burrows beneath the skin, causing intense itching, mostly on your dog's underside. The demodex mite is another type that can cause skin lesions. In many cases a dull, lackluster coat may be the first indication that something is wrong. Suspicion of either type of mite is usually enough to prompt immediate aggressive treatment by your veterinarian.

Is there evidence of internal parasites? Diarrhea or blood in your dog's feces could be due to intestinal parasites. An easy and inexpensive way to check this is to simply drop off a stool sample at your veterinarian's office for analysis. You'll have an answer in short order. In some instances, you may see actual worms or larvae in the stool or around your dog's anus.

Does your dog seem completely healthy in every other way? Dogs with an underlying illness will often have subtle changes such as a dull coat. Pay attention to other signs of illness that might be present at the same time, such as changes in appetite, bowel and urinary habits, or energy level. Continue to be on the watch for these things while you attempt to get to the bottom of why your dog's coat has changed. If enough minor signs are present simultaneously, it may be time for a visit to your vet.

Is the heat in your house turned up? If so, and if your dog tends to like the warmth from the heater or stove, his dull coat may be a result of the drying effects of the heat. Try combining essential fatty acids, such as the omega-3s, with the use of a shampoo with emollients (moisturizers).

My Dog's Coat is Dull and Dry

My Dog's
Fur Is Matted

If your dog's normally sleek, shiny coat suddenly develops one or more areas of clumped, matted fur, it is not a reason to fret. It is, however, worth looking at more closely before you attack her with scissors or rush her off to a professional groomer.

What to Look For

Start by looking your dog over carefully, examining her entire body with a keen eye to any signs of coat dullness, dishevelment, or textures you are not accustomed to seeing. Providing your dog is compliant, lift the hairs involved in any of those abnormal areas in an attempt at getting a closer look at the skin beneath. If your dog is still tolerating all this without complaint, use a wide-toothed comb to try to comb through the clumped, matted, crusted, or entangled fur, removing as much of it as possible or until your dog won't tolerate it any longer.

What to Do

Next, ask yourself the following questions:

Is there moisture or discharge mixed in with the matted fur? Any time that there is moisture or discharge involved with matting fur, you should be suspicious of infection. Follow the directions in "My Dog Has a Discharge from His Skin" on page 117.

Do you notice dry, flaking skin beneath the matted fur? When the matted fur occurs above a patch of dry, flaking skin, it usually means that your dog's skin has been dry enough to cause her discomfort. Her rubbing or scratching has probably caused the fur above the area to snarl, resulting in the clump you have noticed. Start by removing the clumped fur either with a wide-toothed comb, broad-bristled brush, or even your fingers. (Always wear gloves for this in order to avoid possible exposure to infection or parasites.) Next, clean any excoriations or dry patches with a 50/50 hydrogen peroxide/water mix. If there are no excoriations, rub some mild bath oil, such as Avon Skin So Soft, into the dry area and consider supplementing your dog's diet with omega-3 fatty acids, which you can buy at pet supply stores.

Is there fresh or dried blood in the area? Be cautious in approaching these mats, since there is often an open wound hidden underneath. Follow the directions listed in "My Dog Is Bleeding from Her Neck" on page 37 and "How to Remove Mats from Your Dog's Fur" on page 21.

Do you notice any parasites in the region? Fleas, mites, and lice usually cause extreme itchiness, which, in turn, causes scratching and licking that results in snarled and matted fur. Remove the mats (see "How to Remove Mats from Your Dog's Fur" on page 21), treat the parasites (see "How to Treat Your Dog's Fleas" on page 22), and you and your dog will both be happy!

My Dog Is
Shedding
Lots of Fur

My Dog Is
Shedding Lots of Fur

Dogs shed. This is an inconvenient fact of life unless you own a non-shedding breed, such as a poodle, wheaten terrier, or bichon frise. That said, if your dog starts losing fur in clumps, or so steadily that his skin is in full view, there is something wrong. In your efforts to get to the bottom of the problem, focus on your dog's nutritional status, immune system, and endocrine system.

What to Look For

Start your thorough scrutiny of your dog's entire body surface by putting on a pair of rubber exam gloves. Slowly look over your dog's skin, paying strict attention to any unusual pigment, texture, temperature, sensitivity, and/or smell. Then review your dog's recent medical history, bowel and urine habits, appetite, thirst, and activity.

What to Do

Now take a moment to answer these questions:

Has your dog been eating a balanced diet over the past month? The health of every dog's coat of fur is directly dependent on his nutritional status. That status is, in turn, directly dependent on the food the dog is fed and the dog's ability to digest and process the nutrients contained in that food. If there is a breakdown or deficiency anywhere in the sequence of food choice, ingestion, breakdown, and eventual absorption and distribution of nutrition, any of the organ systems that benefit from that nutrition may suffer. Your dog's skin and coat of fur are part of one of those systems. If your dog's diet has been deficient over the past week to month, that could be the cause of fur loss.

Has your dog recently been suffering from some generalized illness? Any illness dramatic enough to occupy a dog's immune system or negatively affect his nutritional status could be the reason for significant hair loss. If you successfully treat the illness, you may resolve the symptoms of hair loss.

Does your dog have a history of skin disease? Eczema is a chronic skin condition that typically presents as dry, rashy, irritated skin. Seborrhea is a chronic condition that can present as either a dry or oily irritation with a smelly surface. Both are skin diseases that often result in dramatic hair loss. When hair loss is combined with red, itchy, or scaly skin that also happens to smell rather unsavory, chances are that the hair loss is related to one of those skin diseases. If you treat the primary skin disorder, you may solve the entire problem.

Is there a pattern to the hair loss? When there is a pattern to a dog's hair loss, especially when that pattern is bilaterally symmetrical, it's very possible that an endocrine disorder is the reason for the hair loss. In dogs, the most common endocrine source of hair loss is hypothyroidism. This is when your dog's thyroid gland produces less than the necessary amount of thyroid hormone needed for maintaining a normal rate of metabolism. A simple blood test can diagnose hypothyroidism, and oral medication, once to twice daily, will manage it and allow for regrowth of your dog's coat of fur.

My Dog Has
a Broken Toenail

A broken toenail may seem like no big deal to most people, but to a dog it can mean something quite serious. A dog's toenails, like our finger- and toenails, protect the very sensitive tissue that lies beneath them. This tissue is loaded with blood vessels, so in addition to being very painful, any injury to a dog's toenail can result in quite a bit of bleeding and may invite a bacterial or fungal infection.

Only pull the damaged nail off if you are certain that the attachment is only nail and does not involve any blood vessels or the quick, which is located within the center of each toenail and provides the blood and nerve supply for the nail.

If you feel the injury is minor enough to handle at home, dip the entire paw in a 50/50 mixture of water and hydrogen peroxide. This will start the disinfecting process and give you an idea how much bleeding, if any, is present.

Dry the paw gently with a clean, white towel or paper towels to check if the site is still bleeding and whether there remains any discharge.

If the injury is mild to moderate with no discharge and minimal to no bleeding, place a light bandage on the cracked nail to stabilize it and protect the area from bacteria, dirt, and further trauma. (See "How to Control Bleeding" on page 18 and "How to Dress a Wound" on page 19.)

What to Look For

Watch your dog walk around for a few minutes to see if she is favoring that paw or limping. Then get her to lie down in a comfortable position. Gently examine the paw with the broken nail. Look for bleeding or pus and check if the crack in the nail is open or closed.

What to Do

What you'll do next will depend upon what you observed during your exam. Ask yourself the following questions:

Is your dog limping? Limping and nonweight bearing lameness are sure signs that a broken toenail is causing your dog a significant amount of discomfort. Look closely to get an idea whether the injury is confined to the toenail alone or if there is damage to the toe and paw as well.

Is there any bleeding? If there is bleeding along with the cracked toenail, the quick of the nail has been traumatized and will continue to cause discomfort until something is done to correct the injury.

When to Get the Vet

See your dog's vet right away if:

- Your dog is putting no weight on the affected paw for more than an hour.

- There is so much bleeding that you can't get it to stop.

- A smelly discharge recurs even after you have cleaned and disinfected the entire paw.

- Your dog is in so much pain that she snarls or tries to bite you each time you try to examine the paw.

- The cracked nail is dislodged from the rest of the nail, but is still attached by a substantial portion of nail and you can see that the quick is exposed.

Quick

Nail Quick

Is there any discharge? Other than blood, any discharge from the area is cause for concern since the nail beds are popular sites of entry for bacterial and fungal elements. If you see pus, an infection is already present and immediate action is necessary.

Is the crack closed or open? If there is space between the two edges of the crack, it is described as "open." In such a situation it is possible that there is movement of those edges that could cause painful trauma to the underlying tissue, as well as prolonged bleeding.

Is any part of the nail loose and hanging? If part of the nail is dangling, the situation is surely uncomfortable for your dog. In most such cases, if the site of attachment is just a small bit of nail, a swift pull will remove the damaged nail.

My Dog's Toenails Are Growing in Strangely

My Dog's Toenails
Are Growing in Strangely

Your dog's toenails, like your own, grow throughout life. This makes it necessary to keep them trimmed in order to prevent problems for your dog or injury to others. Dogs that are always walked on abrasive surfaces such as paved roadways or concrete sidewalks, however, may never need their nails trimmed.

If you happen to notice that your dog's nails are growing in a strange way, a number of possible explanations exist. A closer look may help you deduce which applies to your dog and if any action is necessary.

What to Look For

Many dogs are shy about having their nails examined. I know a few German Shepherds, in fact, that would prefer to jump out a window before submitting to having me so much as hold one of their paws! In such instances, patience and outright bribery go a long way toward building confidence and trust.

In your careful examination of each of your dog's toenails, be sure to start at the base of each toe, where it joins the paw, and work your way slowly out to the tip of each nail. Do your best to check all four aspects of each nail (top and bottom surfaces and both sides) to ensure that no inconsistency goes unnoticed.

What to Do

Now ask yourself a few questions:

Are all your dog's nails growing strangely, just a few, or only one? If they are all growing strangely, it may be because they haven't been trimmed in quite a while, which causes them to grow so long that they begin to curl. If this is the case, trim them carefully and admire the results. If it seems to be more a case of a new and strange appearance that you're sure is different than what you are accustomed to seeing, you should probably consult your veterinarian.

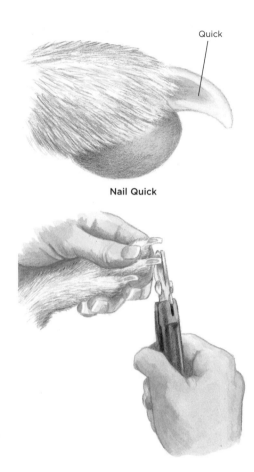

Nail Quick

Trimming the Nail

Has your dog recently suffered a paw or toe injury to the limb in question? Following an injury to any digit, the first time the associated nail grows back in, it may grow in abnormally due to trauma to the germinative cells of the nail bed. Sometimes the nail will eventually grow back normally, but not always.

Has your dog recently been suffering from an infection of the affected toes? Fungal, and occasionally bacterial, infections of the nail bed will result in abnormal nail growth for as long as the infection persists. Treat the infection successfully and you may solve the entire nail problem. For the proper therapy, however, you will need your veterinarian's advice and a prescription.

For the future, the best way to prevent your dog's nails from becoming a problem is to trim them regularly (approximately every two weeks) in order to avoid even the possibility that they will ever get long enough to affect their pattern of growth or your dog's comfort level.

My Dog Is
Always Thirsty

PART

4

MY DOG IS
HAVING
EATING AND
DRINKING
PROBLEMS

Maintaining hydration is an important aspect of your dog's instinct to survive and stay healthy. Since water accounts for more than 60 percent of a dog's body weight, and because breathing, salivating, defecating, and urinating are all responsible for significant losses of water from a dog's body, it stands to reason that dogs need to take in a good amount of fluid each day from what they eat and drink. This is accomplished by a number of intricate feedback mechanisms that directly control a dog's urinary output and thirst center. Most average-sized dogs (around twenty-five pounds) will consume at least sixteen ounces of fluid in a day, either directly or as part of their food. Warmer weather and increased exercise, however, will put greater demands on them and require greater fluid intake.

A little extra drinking and peeing is usually not much to be concerned about. If you are noticing steep increases in these two important functions, however, it is probably worth paying closer attention.

What to Look For

Start by measuring the amount of water your dog is actually drinking in a twenty-four hour period. An average healthy dog drinks about ½ to 1 ounce of water per pound of body weight per day.

The amount of water your dog is drinking is an important piece of information to share with your veterinarian and can help avoid unnecessary testing. Keep in mind that dogs are very sloppy, inefficient drinkers. They lap their water instead of drinking the way we do, so take this fact and the amount of water that ends up on the floor near your dog's bowl into account.

What to Do

Ask yourself the following questions to determine what to do next:

Have you recently changed anything in your dog's diet? Foods and treats that are rich in certain ingredients (such as sodium) will tend to increase your dog's thirst.

Is your dog taking any medication? Some medications can increase a dog's thirst, particularly steroids and those directed at cardiac disease and seizure control.

Does your dog have a fever? Like people, dogs become thirsty when they have elevated body temperatures. While the use of a rectal thermometer is the most accurate way to measure, you can get a pretty good idea of whether or not your dog has a fever simply by feeling her ears and groin. Dogs with high fevers tend to radiate heat from these areas.

Does your dog have an infection? Bacterial and viral infections are often the cause of fever in dogs, resulting in an increased thirst. Other feedback mechanisms related to infection may stimulate a dog's thirst as well, explaining why infected dogs often have an insatiable desire to drink.

Is your dog dehydrated? Dehydration is probably the most obvious reason why a dog would be drinking excessively, but noticeable dehydration suggests that some outside influence, such as illness or restricted access to water, has prevented the dog from keeping up with her needs. To check for noticeable dehydration, grasp a handful of skin at the scruff of your dog's neck. Lift it up as far as it will stretch, then release it. A well-hydrated dog's skin will snap briskly back into place, while that of a dehydrated dog will return slowly to its original position, forming a "tent" in the process.

If this test seems inconclusive, try lifting your dog's lip to inspect her gums. (See "My Dog Is Drooling Excessively" on page 90 for instructions on how to do this.) Wet, slippery, reflective gums are healthy. Dull, sticky gums confirm dehydration.

Is your dog acting sick? Dogs that drink excessive quantities of water without an obvious explanation should always be examined for underlying illness. Usually those dogs happen to be urinating large quantities too, since the urinary tract and the thirst center are closely associated. Don't be fooled into thinking that this is a

When to Get the Vet

If your dog is dehydrated despite drinking excessively, she should be seen immediately by her veterinarian to determine why she is not meeting her body's hydration needs.

Grasp skin at neck to check for dehydration.

If "tent" forms, dehydration is present.

simple explanation. Without testing, it will remain unclear whether the drinking is causing the peeing or vice versa! Blood tests can identify diseases, including diabetes and Cushing's disease, which might be responsible for increases in thirst.

My Dog
Is Never Thirsty

The consumption of water is essential to the health of every dog. Thus, when a dog stops drinking for more than twenty-four hours, it is always a concern. Keep in mind that it is rare that a dog stops drinking yet continues to eat normally. The two usually go hand in hand, so observe your dog closely for other signs of illness—such as decreased appetite, vomiting, diarrhea, or lethargy—before deciding whether your dog needs to be evaluated by your vet.

What to Look For

When your dog stops drinking, your primary concern should be to figure out the reason why, and then check for the possibility of dehydration. You can start to assess both by using the technique for examining your dog's mouth in "My Dog Is Drooling Excessively" on page 90. In the process, you may discover a reason for his reduction in water intake.

While conducting your examination, pay particular attention to your dog's gums, making note of their slipperiness and reflective quality. Continue your exam by grabbing the scruff of your dog's neck and lifting a handful of skin, then releasing it. If it snaps back into place immediately, there is only a slight chance that your dog is dehydrated. If the skin "tents," remaining in its raised position, then returning slowly to its original, flat position, dehydration is very likely. (See the illustration on page 85.)

Finally, with your dog in a standing position, gently place one hand, palm up, against your dog's belly, just behind the hind edge of his rib cage. With a slow but firm pressure, press upward toward his spine, checking for signs of discomfort. If your dog resists or flinches at any point, discontinue the exam.

What to Do

To determine what to do next, ask yourself the following questions:

Is your dog dehydrated? If you notice the "tenting" of your dog's skin described above, and/or his gums are dull and tacky, you are likely dealing with dehydration. This symptom can be corrected simply by administering fluids either orally, subcutaneously, or intravenously. The first method, oral administration, is one you can accomplish at home, but with some difficulty since your dog is not interested in drinking. Try using a spoon, syringe, or even a turkey baster as a means of getting fluids into your dog.

The second method, subcutaneous administration, can also be accomplished at home, but you'll need to get the necessary equipment from a nurse, doctor, or veterinarian. The third method, intravenous hydration, should only be performed professionally, in a hospital setting.

When to Get the Vet

- Has your dog recently suffered some form of head trauma? Head trauma can cause a number of behavioral changes, including decreases in appetite and thirst. If your dog loses his interest in food and water following an episode of head trauma, have him evaluated by a veterinarian as soon as possible.

- Has your dog recently gotten into any unusual chemicals or medications? Since many toxins have a direct effect on the nervous system, it is common for exposure to a variety of substances to result in abnormal behaviors or neurological symptoms. Some may even cause temporary blindness. If you know what chemicals or medications your dog has possibly ingested or inhaled, call the ASPCA National Animal Poison Control Center at 888-426-4435 for immediate advice. Plan to make a trip to the nearest animal emergency facility as well.

My Dog
Is Never
Thirsty

Is your dog showing other signs of illness? Loss of appetite, vomiting, diarrhea, and lethargy are signs that often coexist with decreased fluid intake. In some cases, dehydration can cause the others, and in some cases the other symptoms result in the onset of dehydration. It is often difficult to identify the order of occurrence. By starting with the symptom you are most likely to correct at home (dehydration), you stand a better chance of sequentially correcting the others. If you fail to improve your dog's symptoms, you can always seek veterinary help.

Has your dog recently eaten something he shouldn't? Dogs that scavenge for garbage, eat rich or spicy food, or chew on inedible objects are most likely to suffer from gastrointestinal problems. Try to figure out if your dog swallowed something unusual and, if so, take the appropriate measures to solve the problem.

Had your dog been drinking excessively prior to the recent loss of thirst? In some rare instances, dogs that have been drinking excessively, for whatever reason, will experience a medical condition known as hyperhydrosis. The result will often be an extended period with little to no interest in drinking. In cases when a dog that is well hydrated loses all interest in fluids, try to be patient for a day or two. Providing the dog remains free of other signs of illness for that period of time, waiting out your dog's loss of thirst may be the proper solution, but you should try to assess why he was drinking excessively to begin with.

My Dog Is
Always Hungry

Dogs are survivors. In the wild, they live in packs and hunt as teams, surviving from kill to kill on whatever prey is available, occasionally scavenging the kill of other predatory animals. In order to tolerate this existence, dogs are capable of gorging themselves to the point of regurgitation. They are also happy to eat their own vomit as a way to conserve calories!

In a domestic setting, with few of the survival pressures they are confronted by in the wild, dogs are capable of establishing an eating routine based on the convenience of their owners and their good health. This routine, though, can be disturbed by illness, schedule changes, and outside pressures. In such cases, a dog may seem to be willing to eat more or different foods than usual and may even resort to pilfering foods from storage locations.

What to Do

In order to figure out what's up with your dog's appetite, ask yourself the following questions:

Is your dog taking any medications? Some drugs, particularly steroids and seizure-control medications, cause an increase in appetite. If your dog is taking medication, check with his veterinarian to see whether it is one that might increase appetite.

Is this the only dog in the house? If not, and particularly if a new dog has recently joined the household, competition for food may be the driving force behind the increase in your dog's appetite. Try feeding the dogs separately.

Have there been recent scheduling changes in the household? Sometimes dogs that have always been fed on a strict schedule and have recently been forced to wait longer than usual for their meals will become aggressive around food. In such cases, a return to a strict schedule may solve the problem. In order to accomplish this, owners are occasionally forced to hire someone to feed and walk their dogs while they are at work.

Another circumstance that can result in food-related behavioral changes is the introduction of a new pet or child to the household. This will either bring on depression, which is typically coupled with a decrease in appetite, or protective behavior, which is typically coupled with a dramatic increase in appetite.

Is your dog's voracious appetite a recent development? If not, evaluate your dog's diet to determine whether it is nutritionally sound. Check the ingredients and call your vet for some advice. Diets lacking some important nutrients may not be capable of satisfying a dog's hunger. If the diet is sound and the dog is underweight, you may just need to increase the amount of food offered per meal. If the diet is sound and the dog is overweight or if the appetite has recently increased, take your dog to the vet for blood testing to check for endocrine disorders such as Cushing's syndrome.

If you have examined all the possible explanations for your dog's hunger and it seems that you have an otherwise healthy dog that just happens to love food, you have a choice to make. If she is a reasonable weight, feed her frequently throughout the day, but give her healthy food in small amounts. If she is overweight, try weaning her gradually from a standard maintenance diet to a "light" diet, lower in calories. Alternatively, or in addition, try replacing one third of each of her meals with canned pumpkin. It is high in fiber and very filling, and is often the supplement capable of and successful in reducing a dog's appetite.

My Dog Is
Never Hungry

Not every dog is capable of regulating his dietary intake perfectly. In fact, because the natural social structure of dogs is that of the pack, they will often be willing to eat whenever food is offered to them. Because most dog owners expect this food-driven behavior and are actually pleased when their dogs wolf down their food with gusto, there is an abundance of overweight dogs in our society! It is no surprise then that most dog owners are more than a little concerned when their dogs refuse a meal.

While one or two missed meals never hurt a dog, when your dog refuses food for more than a day, it is definitely cause for alarm.

What to Look For

Your first objective is to figure out whether your dog isn't eating due to lack of interest in the food offered, overall illness, or simple nausea. It's usually easy to rule out the lack of interest in the food offered by simply presenting your dog with a variety of different, interesting foods. Don't be too creative, though, because what started out as a spell of hunger loss could change to diarrhea if the new food is too rich in ingredients your dog can't tolerate well. It is usually best to start with something bland, such as boiled beef and rice.

What to Do

Ask yourself the following questions to figure out what to do next:

Is this a sudden, abrupt change or has your dog's appetite been diminishing gradually? The answer to this question generally helps distinguish between acute, obstructive reasons for loss of appetite and those that result from chronic illness.

When to Get the Vet

If your dog shows no interest in food for more than twenty-four hours, take him to his vet. X-rays or an ultrasound exam are often required.

My Dog Is
Drooling
Excessively

Is your dog a thief? Dogs that steal food, items of clothing, etc., are more likely to develop a gastrointestinal obstruction from swallowing one of those items. While some dogs are able to regurgitate those items before any damage is done, surgery is often the only alternative for dogs that are not.

Has your dog been gagging or vomiting? Nausea and vomiting often go hand in hand. While it's certainly helpful to know that nausea or vomiting is the reason for your dog's lack of hunger, it is still impor-tant to figure out what the source of that nausea is. This will usually require a thorough physical exam, blood work, and X-rays/ultrasound.

Has your dog recently eaten something unusual in amount or ingredients? When dogs eat a particularly large meal or they are given a new type of food, it may take them longer to process what they've eaten. This could result in a longer period of digestion, so they won't be ready for their next scheduled meal. Be patient!

My Dog Is
Drooling Excessively

It's a fact of life: Dog's drool. Glands in your dog's mouth produce saliva, which is an enzyme-rich liquid that helps lubricate your dog's food and begins the digestive process while she is chewing.

But you can have too much of a good thing. Excessive salivation is not normal. In fact, in extreme cases it can lead to dehydration. In order to figure out why your dog is producing so much saliva, you need to get a good look inside her mouth.

What to Look For

Get a flashlight or take your dog to a spot with very good light. If you can, get someone else to help out. Here's what to do:

Begin by petting your dog the way you normally would. After a few minutes, start rubbing her ears and working your way to her muzzle. Sit beside your dog and place the palm of your hand that's closest to her nose beneath her chin. Place the palm of your other hand flat against her cheek. Use the thumb of that second hand to apply gentle pressure against the outside of her upper lip, sliding it up to reveal the teeth and gums beneath. Similarly, use the thumb of your lower hand to slide your dog's lower lip down, revealing her lower teeth and gums. (See the illustration on page 35.)

Take your time. By shifting the position of your hands and patiently starting and stopping repeatedly, you should eventually be able to take a look at your dog's teeth and gums on that side of her face.

Now it's time to check out your dog's tongue and hard palate (the roof of her mouth). To do this, place your left thumb on the right side of your dog's upper lip, just behind the large canine teeth. Place your left index and middle fingers on the left side of your dog's upper lip, just behind the large canine teeth. Do the same with your right hand on her lower lip, and then open her mouth like a clam shell. Take a good look inside. Don't forget to check under the tongue.

Now repeat the side exam from the other side.

What to Do

Here's what to do, depending on what you found:

FOREIGN OBJECTS: Look for anything that obviously doesn't belong in your dog's mouth, such as wood splinters, fish hooks, bone fragments, or bits of plant matter or fabric. These could be embedded in your dog's gums or tongue or wedged between her teeth or across the roof of her mouth.

If you find a foreign object in your dog's mouth, use common sense to decide whether it is something you feel comfortable attempting to remove. First, consider the immediate results, both those hoped for and those dreaded. For instance, if there is a large wood splinter stuck in your dog's throat, does it look like it can simply be dislodged, or is it embedded in tissue and cause more pain, damage, or bleeding if you try to extract it? When in doubt, check with your dog's vet.

INJURIES: Look closely for bleeding or wounds. Other signs of injuries and irritations are indicated by changes in color. The normal healthy pink or pigmented color of your dog's gums will be an angry red or even purple when those tissues are injured or infected.

If you find one injury, don't stop there. Complete your exam in case there are others, making note of each one as you go. Scrutinize the teeth as well. Sometimes a hairline crack right at the border of the gums can extend into the root, causing pain and salivation. You might see a lot of blood. Since the area inside a dog's mouth is loaded with blood vessels, injuries there bleed a lot. For the same reason, small cuts, scratches, and even ulcerations in the mouth often heal quickly without you doing a thing.

As long as the bleeding is not excessive, place some hydrogen peroxide on a cotton swab or gauze pad and place it on your dog's wound. The hydrogen peroxide is a disinfectant and it can also clean the area so you can get a better look at it.

INFECTION: The presence of pus— usually a slightly yellow to green sticky, pasty material—indicates a bacterial infection. Infection is usually accompanied by a distinctly foul odor that's different from typical "dog breath."

If you spot signs of infection, take them seriously. You can probably take care of a small amount of pus, irritation, or even mild gingivitis by simply dedicating yourself to a strict tooth-brushing schedule. But most of the time oral infections need veterinary treatment since they can lead to more serious infections such as bacterial endocarditis—an infection of the heart.

DENTAL PROBLEMS: Areas of red, sensitive gum tissue, often with tartar accumulation and parts of the tooth roots exposed, with or without pus indicates gingivitis, which is a common symptom of dental disease.

When to Get the Vet

Contact your dog's vet if:

- You spot a foreign object that you can't safely remove yourself.

- You are unable to stop the bleeding in your dog's mouth.

- There's more than a small amount of pus, foul odor, or discoloration in your dog's mouth.

- Your dog has a fractured tooth.

- You see any growth in your dog's mouth other than a wart.

- You believe your dog may be drooling because of pain, nausea, or a neurological problem.

If you discover any fractured teeth, your dog is probably going to need some veterinary attention. Only the simplest cracks and breaks, right near the tip of the tooth and not exposing any of the pulp cavity, can safely be left untreated.

GROWTHS: Any lumps, bumps, or abnormal-looking tissue in the mouth can be referred to as a mass or growth. These can be as benign as warts (see the illustration on page 129) or as devastating

as squamous cell carcinoma, a highly invasive and usually fatal form of cancer.

Warts are the only oral masses you can ignore. They typically go away on their own. Any other swellings, enlargements, or abnormal growths in the mouth should be seen by a veterinarian.

PAIN: If at any time when you're examining his mouth, your dog whimpers, snarls, squirms, or attempts to bite you, it is likely that you are causing pain. Stop your exam immediately.

Now, you're probably wondering, "What do I do if I didn't see anything at all unusual in my dog's mouth?" The truth is that drooling can be caused by things outside your dog's mouth, such as pain, nausea, or a neurological difficulty. These issues are best left to your dog's veterinarian to diagnose.

Excessive salivation is rarely cause for a high-speed dash to an emergency room, but it is important enough to address and resolve.

My Dog
Is Gagging

What exactly is a gag? Is it a choke, cough, gasp, or your dog's attempt to clear his throat? All of these actions, at one time or another, have been described by my clients as gagging. The truth is, any respiratory event that mimics the act of vomiting, without actually producing any vomit, can legitimately be termed gagging.

So what do you do for your dog when he is doing it? In many instances, if the gagging continues, unless your dog has also not been eating for some period of time, he will eventually produce some vomit. If you are fortunate enough to swiftly identify the gagging, you may be able to get him outside before things get messy.

What to Look For

Conduct a thorough oral exam like the one outlined in "My Dog Is Drooling Excessively" on page 90. Be acutely aware of the possibility of a foreign object either penetrating the tissue of your dog's cheek, gums, or palate, or being lodged between his teeth, under his tongue, or across the roof of his mouth.

What to Do

Next, ask yourself these few questions:

Did your exam reveal any foreign objects? If so, and if you are absolutely certain that removing it will cause no further harm to your dog, you may wish to cautiously attempt to remove it. If this doesn't seem like a reasonable approach, get your vet's help right away.

Has your dog recently eaten anything new or unusual? New foods, spices, and other products that he has never had before might bring on either a temporary gag reflex or repetitive retching due to an allergic response.

When to Get the Vet

If your exam revealed any swelling or inflammation, get your vet's help right away. Sometimes a bacterial or viral infection or even an allergic response will cause enough swelling and inflammation to cause a dog to retch repeatedly to try to rid himself of that space-occupying thickening of the tissues in his mouth and/or throat. If this appears to be the case, see your vet immediately before the swelling has a chance to get worse.

Also, if your dog has recently gotten into any unusual chemicals or medications, be prepared to seek immediate help. Since many toxins have a direct effect on the nervous system, it is common for exposure to a variety of substances to result in abnormal behaviors or neurological symptoms. Gagging could be one of these. If you know what chemicals or medications your dog has possibly ingested or inhaled, call the ASPCA National Animal Poison Control Center at 888-426-4435 for immediate advice. Plan to make a trip to the nearest animal emergency facility as well.

Similarly, if your dog was recently stung by a bee or bitten by an insect, spider, or snake, immediately rush him to an emergency facility. Any of these events could bring on an acute and violent reaction, including gagging.

In general, if the gagging continues for more than a few minutes, take it seriously. If your dog ever appears to be having difficulty breathing, rush him to an emergency facility!

My Dog Is Gagging

My Dog Is
Gulping or Swallowing Strangely

A gulp is like a bigger version of a swallow, and a swallow is what we do when we are eating or drinking. We are also compelled to do these things when there is no food or drink involved, and so are our dogs. If the activity becomes a persistent one, however, it usually means that something is awry.

What to Look For

Follow the same directions for examining your dog's mouth as outlined in "My Dog Is Drooling Excessively" on page 90. In addition, carefully open her mouth as wide as possible and, using your flashlight, get a good look down her throat. Be on the lookout for any foreign bodies or unusual redness. Also be prepared for a vomiting episode! Dogs that gulp, smack their lips, or make mock swallowing efforts often do so in preparation for a vomiting episode.

What to Do

Ask yourself the following questions:

Is your dog a Bernese mountain dog? "Berners" commonly present with a mysterious, transient swallowing problem some-

time within their first few years. If your Berner doesn't improve over a seventy-two-hour period, get her in to see a veterinary neurologist for further evaluation.

Is your dog coughing as well as gulping? If there is coughing involved, see "My Dog Is Coughing" on page 278.

Is your dog vomiting or regurgitating as well as gulping? If so, check "My Dog Is Vomiting" on page 99 and "My Dog Is Regurgitating His Food" on page 97.

Does your dog have a fever? If so, she is probably fighting a viral or bacterial infection and either has a sore throat as part of her symptoms or she is getting dehydrated and her gulping is an attempt to lubricate her throat. Try giving her some water to cool off, make her throat feel better, and hydrate her.

Has your dog been eating something dangerous? When dogs eat things they're not supposed to, they often do so in a hurry, taking little time to chew properly. If those things happen to contain bones or other sharp pieces, their passage down your dog's throat could be quite abrasive. If you suspect that your dog's throat has been traumatized by something harsh, try giving her a dab of petroleum jelly at the back of her throat and force her to swallow it as a means of lubricating her throat and esophagus. This will also help her swallow anything stuck in her throat.

Has your dog been eating something unusual? This could be anything that she doesn't often eat—such as grass or even popcorn—that might adhere to the sides or back of her throat or esophagus. Try the same method of using petroleum jelly (as described above).

Has your dog recently gotten into any unusual chemicals or medications? Since many toxins have a direct effect on the nervous system, it is common for exposure to a variety of substances to result in abnormal behaviors or neurological symptoms. Some may even cause temporary blindness. See box at right for how to proceed.

Does your dog have cardiac disease or a heart murmur? Dogs with even mild congestive heart disease or a murmur will often have a slight cough or some sporadic gulping or swallowing behavior. You probably already know how to proceed to help your dog feel better.

Has your dog been dropping her food or acting off balance or uncoordinated lately? A serious, progressive disease known as myasthenia gravis often starts out as gulping and excessive swallowing, followed by gradual loss of motor function starting with the head and neck and moving backward. This is a very rare disorder, so before you assume anything awful, have your vet do the blood test for myasthenia gravis and then make the appropriate plan.

When to Get the Vet

If you know what chemicals or medications your dog has possibly ingested or inhaled, call the ASPCA National Animal Poison Control Center at 888-426-4435 for immediate advice. Plan to make a trip to the nearest animal emergency facility as well.

My Dog Is Gulping or Swallowing Strangely

My Dog Is
Regurgitating His Food

In every dog's life, there are bound to be some episodes of regurgitation. In fact, regurgitation serves as both a protective response and a strategy employed by canine mothers to feed their young during the period immediately following weaning them from breast milk and before they are capable of consuming freshly killed prey.

Regurgitation is simply a way of emptying the stomach of its contents before the initial stages of digestion have been completed. The reasons for this evacuation vary, but the one possibility that every dog owner and veterinarian should be most concerned about is an obstruction somewhere along the dog's digestive tract. In such instances, food and water cannot pass beyond the obstruction and have nowhere to go. The dog's system senses this and attempts to evacuate these materials in the opposite direction. Because the system is designed to try to correct the problem, increased muscular contractions of the gastrointestinal tract begin in an effort to move the obstruction along. Your dog may feel a cramping sensation and act restless and uncomfortable. Eventually, if these contractions are unsuccessful at moving the obstruction, the intestines can be perforated. Once intestinal contents are spilled into the abdomen, rapid infection and inflammation follow and the consequence is frequently fatal.

What to Look For

In cases of regurgitation, it is best to proceed in a straightforward manner. Begin by examining the contents of what your dog has just regurgitated. Continue by conducting a thorough oral exam as outlined in "My Dog Is Drooling Excessively" on page 90. Moving on, feel your dog's neck and throat for swelling or lumps.

Next, with your dog standing, kneel beside him. Place one hand, palm facing up, on your dog's abdomen, just behind his rib cage. Forming a "U" shape with your thumb as one side and your remaining four fingers as the other, gently lift, squeeze, and slide your hand back and forth along your dog's underbelly in order to check for areas of discomfort or tenderness.

Finally, lift your dog's tail up check his anus for signs of swelling, irritation, blood, diarrhea, or parasites.

What to Do

Now ask yourself these questions:

What did you see in the regurgitate? Because regurgitation is an effective way for a dog's body to reject what his appetite won't, you may find the reason for the episode right in front of you. Look for the usual culprits—inedible objects, plant or animal matter, and any evidence of spicy or unusual foods.

Has your dog recently eaten anything that he shouldn't have? As stated above, new or unusual foods, especially spicy ones, and anything that might have been tainted with bacteria or chemicals, should be rejected by your dog's system shortly after it is ingested. If so, wait for an hour, then give your dog a dose of Pepto-Bismol to coat and soothe his stomach. As long as he continues to act well, he should be fine. If not, seek help from your vet.

Did your oral exam reveal any abnormal findings? Pale to white gums are immediate cause for concern and a visit with your vet. Pain alone, if dramatic enough, can cause a dog to regurgitate, so a broken tooth or signs of any other oral trauma or infection could explain the regurgitation. Be aware, though, that signs of trauma to the inside of your dog's mouth could also suggest that he swallowed something large and/or sharp that could be lodged somewhere further down his digestive tract.

When you feel your dog's throat, do you detect any lumps or swellings? If your dog's lymph nodes are swollen, you will feel them on either side of his throat, about where you would feel your own Adam's apple. These usually become enlarged when a dog has an oral or upper respiratory infection. If you find them to be enlarged, your vet should be consulted for possible antibiotic therapy.

Did you detect any discomfort or tenderness when you felt your dog's abdomen? Not every dog with an obstruction feels enough discomfort to flinch or cry out when pressure is applied to his abdomen. Likewise, not every dog that exhibits a painful response to palpation is obstructed; bowel loops distended with gas can cause the same response. Usually, however, a painful abdomen is what we look for to suggest an obstruction. Take your dog to the vet for abdominal X-rays.

Has your dog been suffering from congestive heart failure, a respiratory infection, or cough? Forceful coughing will often cause dogs to bring up whatever is in their stomachs at the time. Seek treatment for the source of the cough and the regurgitation should resolve in response.

When to Get the Vet

If you suspect that your dog has an obstruction of the digestive tract, rush him to the veterinary hospital at once!

My Dog Is
Vomiting

Dogs vomit quite easily. Believe it or not, this is actually a good thing. Given the number of inedible, rank, disgusting, and downright putrid things many dogs are willing to ingest, this capacity to evacuate such offal may actually protect them from repeat visits to the emergency clinic. When your dog vomits, there is usually a good reason for it. Sometimes, but not always, that reason can be identified and either simply acknowledged, corrected, or addressed in an attempt to solve a more serious underlying problem.

What to Look For

Unfortunately, your first step needs to be a one-on-one with the vomit. Look at it closely, observing its color, composition, and volume. Then move on to your dog and make an overall assessment of her health. Follow the directions in "My Dog Is Never Thirsty" on page 85 to evaluate her hydration status. Perform an abdominal exam like the one outlined in "My Dog Has a Swollen Belly" on page 142. Finish by offering your dog a few small sips of water.

What to Do

Ask yourself these questions to try to determine how to proceed:

Is the vomit primarily composed of undigested food? If so, this is actually a case of regurgitation, not vomiting. Refer to "My Dog Is Regurgitating His Food" on page 97 for advice.

Is there evidence of any foreign objects in the vomit? If you find foreign, indigestible objects in the vomit, try to identify them. If they seem to be intact or the pieces seem to add up to a whole, the act of vomiting may have solved the problem. Wait for thirty minutes and if no further vomiting occurs, try administering a weight-appropriate dose of Pepto-Bismol (check the dosage directions for humans to determine this) then wait a few hours before offering small amounts of bland food. (See "My Dog Is Pooping Everywhere" on page 254 for information on a bland diet.)

Is your dog dehydrated? Any time a vomiting dog is also found to be dehydrated, it's reasonable cause to see your vet. Without the ability to hold down fluids, it is highly likely that your dog will simply get progressively more dehydrated. This can lead to other complications. If you can get your dog to show interest, try giving small sips of water or an over-the-counter pediatric electrolyte solution such as Pedialyte. Ice cubes are another alternative that may be tolerated by a vomiting dog. Given repeatedly over time, this method of hydration may save you a visit

When to Get the Vet

- If you suspect that something in the vomit is a toxin, make an immediate call to the ASPCA National Animal Poison Control Center at 888-426-4435 for advice on how to proceed.

  Or, if you see blood in the vomit, seek help. Take any sign of frank, red blood; dark, brick-red blood; or granular blood seriously enough to consult your veterinarian.

- If your dog has recently suffered any form of head trauma, the combination of head trauma and vomiting is a serious one. If your dog's vomiting was preceded by head trauma within the last 24 hours, get her immediately to an emergency clinic.

to your vet. (See "My Dog's Treatment Strategies" on page 17.) The amount is never specific, but depends on your dog's tolerance.

Has your dog recently been stung or bitten by a bee, insect, spider, snake, scorpion, etc.? Any of these incidents could result in a solitary episode of vomiting or repetitious vomiting. If it continues for more than two episodes or if your dog is becoming dehydrated in the process, get her to a veterinary hospital.

My Dog Keeps
Smacking His Lips

Food is one of the most powerful motivators of dogs. When they smack their lips, we assume that it is simply a sign of hunger or anticipation of food. But when a dog is continually smacking his lips—unrelated to food, the smell of food, or even the thought of food—it is obviously the sign of something else. To find out what that something else is, examine your dog and ask a few questions, and you may be able to solve the problem.

My Dog Is
Smacking
His Lips

What to Look For

Your first step should be to put on a pair of rubber exam gloves and perform a thorough oral exam using the technique described in "My Dog Is Drooling Excessively" on page 90. Follow your oral exam with an assessment of your dog's recent dietary, urine, and bowel history.

Also check your dog for signs of dehydration. Grasp a handful of skin at the scruff of your dog's neck. Lift it up as far as it will stretch, then release it. A well-hydrated dog's skin will snap briskly back into place, while that of a dehydrated dog will return slowly to its original position, forming a "tent" in the process. (See an illustration of this on page 85.) If this test seems inconclusive, inspect his gums. (See "My Dog Is Drooling Excessively" on page 90 for instructions on how to do this.) Wet, slippery, reflective gums are healthy. Dull, sticky gums confirm dehydration.

What to Do

Once you have answered a few questions, you should be well on your way to explaining your dog's lip smacking behavior.

Did your dog have any evidence of oral disease or infection? Gingivitis and oral infections are both possible reasons for lip smacking behavior. If your dog has signs of these, enlist the help of your veterinarian to get them under control and the lip smacking should end. If it doesn't, your vet may find some other reason for the behavior.

Does your dog have a recent history of illness? Systemic illness, especially liver and kidney disease, can cause a dog to smack his lips. Your dog's vet can make these diagnoses by doing the appropriate blood testing. You can resolve the lip smacking behavior by treating the illness that brought it on.

Is your dog nauseated or in pain? If your physical exam indicated that your dog is either in pain or nauseated, there is a good chance that the nausea or pain is also the reason for the lip smacking. Once again, if you can resolve the nausea and pain, you will be likely to put an end to the lip smacking.

Is your dog dehydrated? If you notice the "tenting" of your dog's skin (described on page 101), and/or if his gums are dull and tacky, you are likely dealing with dehydration. Since dehydration will often cause a dog to smack his lips repeatedly, correct the dehydration by giving fluids aggressively and you may correct the lip smacking. Simply administer fluids either orally, subcutaneously, or intravenously. The first method, orally, is one you can accomplish at home.

The second method, subcutaneously, can also be accomplished at home, but you'll need to get the necessary equipment from a nurse, doctor, or veterinarian. The third method, intravenous hydration, should only be performed professionally, in a hospital setting.

When to Get the Vet

If your dog is dehydrated despite drinking excessively, he should be seen immediately by his veterinarian to determine why he is not meeting his body's hydration needs.

Has your dog recently gotten into any unusual chemicals or medications? Since many toxins have a direct effect on the nervous system, it is common for exposure to a variety of substances to result in abnormal behaviors or neurological symptoms. Some may even cause temporary blindness. If you know what chemicals or medications your dog has possibly ingested or inhaled, call the ASPCA National Animal Poison Control Center at 888-426-4435 for immediate advice. Plan to make a trip to the nearest animal emergency facility as well.

My Dog Just
Ate Some Chocolate

Dogs appear to like chocolate just about as much as humans do. Unfortunately for dogs, however, eating too much of it can kill them. Two ingredients in chocolate seem to act synergistically on dogs. The one that we're all familiar with is caffeine; the other is theobromine. In extreme cases, this combination causes death, but in lower doses and/or larger dogs, illness, vomiting, and diarrhea may be the only side effects. If your dog has eaten chocolate, a few quick actions may save you some major headaches and may also end up saving your dog's life.

What to Look For

No physical exam is of any use immediately after your dog has eaten chocolate. Don't waste the time.

What to Do

Quickly ask yourself the following questions:

How much does your dog weigh? Don't bother wasting the time to find a scale; a simple ballpark estimate will suffice.

What kind of chocolate did your dog eat and how much? If it was a chocolate donut or a few chocolate chip cookies, don't expect more than a little diarrhea or vomiting.

When to Get the Vet

If the amount your dog ate was anything approaching an ounce per pound of your dog's weight, try to get your dog to vomit immediately by following the advice in "How to Make Your Dog Vomit" on page 17. With that amount of chocolate in your dog's system, even if you are successful at getting him to vomit, you should get him to an emergency center for follow up treatment.

My Dog Just
Ate Some Plants

Dogs are not herbivores. They will, on occasion, as curious puppies, bored adults, or simply because a particular plant entices them, experiment by chewing and even swallowing plants. In today's world, with the advent of personal green-houses and gardens, private homes often house a variety of exotic and poten-tially dangerous plants and flowers. Fortunately for pets, most people who both collect unusual plant life and own animals are aware of the dangers specific to the plant species they cultivate and what to do in case of accidental ingestion.

What to Look For

Don't waste time with an exam here. Skip right to "What to Do."

What to Do

Here are a few courses of action you should consider taking if your dog has ingested a dangerous plant:

- Call your dog's vet for advice.

- Look up the potential toxicity of the plant your dog has eaten in a plant encyclopedia or on the Internet and take the suggested course of action.

- Call the 24-hour ASPCA National Animal Poison Control Center Hotline at 888-426-4435 for immediate advice.

- Immediately induce vomiting by administering hydrogen peroxide as directed in "How to Make Your Dog Vomit" on page 17.

It's just not feasible to include a compre-hensive list of toxic plants and flowers in a book like this, but just for the sake of pro-viding you with a few helpful tips, here is a short, noncomprehensive list of fruits, plants, vegetables, and flowers commonly found in people's homes that also present dangers to their dogs:

- **APRICOT PITS** are cyanide producers.

- **AZALEAS** (all parts) cause gastroin-testinal problems.

- **BITTER ALMOND** (bark, leaves, and especially seeds) are cyanide producers.

- **BOXWOOD** (all parts, especially berries) causes cardiac, gastrointestinal, and neurological problems.

- **BUTTERCUP** (meadow) top growth can cause gastrointestinal, neurological, and renal problems.

- **COMMON BEAN** (Green, uncooked pods and tendrils) cause gastrointestinal and neurological problems.

- **CROCUS BULBS** can cause gastrointestinal, renal, and cardiac problems.

- **CYCLAMEN** (tuberous rhizomes and sap) can cause gastrointestinal, neurological, and dermatological problems.

- **DAFFODILS** can cause gastrointestinal problems.

- **FOXGLOVE** (all parts) can cause cardiac problems.

- **GRAPES AND RAISINS,** eaten in abundance, can cause serious kidney problems.

- **HOLLY SEEDS** can cause gastrointestinal and neurological problems.

- **IVY** (English) causes gastrointestinal and neurological problems.

- **LARKSPUR FLOWERS AND SEEDS** can cause gastrointestinal, cardiac, and neurological problems and death.

- **LILY OF THE VALLEY** can cause cardiac and renal problems.

- **MISTLETOE BERRIES** can cause gastrointestinal problems.

- **MORNING GLORY SEEDS** can cause neurological problems.

- **PEACH AND PLUM PITS** are both cyanide producers.

- **POINSETTIA** (all parts) cause gastrointestinal problems.

- **POTATO GREENS** and top parts are toxic and cause gastrointestinal and cardiac problems.

- **ONIONS,** raw or cooked, can cause hemolytic anemia, especially in small dogs.

- **RHODODENDRON FLOWERS AND LEAVES** can cause gastrointestinal problems.

- **RHUBARB LEAVES** can cause oral ulcers and gastrointestinal problems.

- **SWEET PEA FOLIAGE AND SEEDS** can cause neurological problems.

- **TULIP BULBS** can cause gastrointestinal and neurological problems.

- **WOLF'S BANE** can cause gastrointestinal, neurological, and cardiac problems, and even death.

My Dog
Just Ate
Some Plants

My Dog Just
Ate Another Dog's Feces

As mentioned elsewhere, and much to their owners chagrin, all bodily secretions, discharges, and excreta seem to be ambrosia to dogs. If your dog has eaten another dog's feces, go ahead and be disgusted, but don't bother trying to do anything about it, other than getting a powerful deworming medication from your vet and a pleasant-smelling canine toothpaste from your pet supply store. Brush her teeth and forget about it, but try to pull her away before she gets the next shot at a similar "treat."

My Dog
Just Ate
Another
Dog's Feces

My Dog Just
Ate a Tampon

Dogs love the smell and taste of just about all bodily secretions. This includes blood, pus, urine, feces, and sweat. This is why they are forever stealing dirty socks and underwear, used tissues, and even dirty diapers.

Used tampons appear to be a particular delicacy for dogs and because of their capacity for absorption and subsequent expansion, they pose an obstructive threat. Fortunately, because tampons are soft, they pose little threat on their way up and out, if you can get your dog to vomit right after he has swallowed one.

What to Look For

Your examination should be directed solely at confirming that a used tampon has been swallowed and determining about how long it has been since it happened.

What to Do

Follow the directions in "How to Make Your Dog Vomit" on page 17 for getting your dog to vomit. If he proceeds to vomit it up, congratulations! Your work is done.

When to Get the Vet

If your dog starts to act ill, take him in to a nearby animal hospital.

If you are certain that he has recently swallowed a tampon and you haven't succeeded in getting him to vomit it up, feed him starchy foods like bread, rice, or potatoes to keep the tampon company without adding lots of fluid, which would promote the expansion of the tampon. As long as the dog behaves normally, don't worry too much.

My Dog
Just Ate a
Tampon

My Patient's Story

When Steven called me on a Saturday night at around 11:00 pm, I could tell from the sound in his voice that I was probably going to be visiting his home shortly. "Doc," he pleaded, "You gotta help me. My wife's out of town and I think her little Tootsie is about to die. She's been straining for about an hour and just now there's this god-awful thing coming outta her behind like you wouldn't believe! I don't know whether it's a tumor or a poop or what, but it's covered with blood and slime and she's so tired with the effort and all that I think she's about to have a heart attack or something." This was all said in one breath and ended with a gasp for air.

I knew Tootsie (named that because he was originally mistaken for a female as a puppy) had a taste for scavenging and I suspected this was probably something he had swallowed inappropriately. Sure enough, some rubber gloves, a little K-Y jelly, and a gentle tug were all that were needed to remove a tampon from Tootsie's rectum.

"Can we keep this our secret?" was Steven's plea as I wished him a restful night.

My Dog Has Been
Gaining Weight

My Dog
Has Been
Gaining
Weight

There are plenty of overweight dogs in the world. Many of their owners are either unaware or don't let it bother them in the least. Those of you who do worry about your dog's weight will probably become quite alarmed if you notice your dog experience a sudden, unexplained weight gain. Even if the weight gain is not so sudden, if it's noticeable, it should be investigated.

What to Look For

An examination of your dog, under the premise of establishing a reason for the recent weight gain, should also include self scrutiny. Try to analyze whether your dog's feeding schedule or amount has contributed to the weight gain. Look closely at her behavior for clues. Ask all the members of your household what they have been contributing to your dog's diet. Leave no aspect of caloric intake out. Go as far as actually quantifying the number of calories your dog takes in each day of the week and balance it against the amount of exercise she gets. Don't put this aspect of weight gain to rest until you have firmly established that an imbalance does not exist.

Your next step should be a simple comparison of your dog's actual weight to the recommended breed standard for a dog of her stature. Check the American Kennel Club's *The Complete Dog Book*. If your dog is free of enormous weighty growths or tumors, and her weight is greater than five pounds above the breed standard, you've got some work ahead. If she is more than fifteen pounds over, there is a major problem, as well as a health risk, to deal with.

What to Do

Next, ask yourself a few questions:

Did your investigation reveal that the reason for the weight gain is simply too much food and too little exercise? If so, take comfort in the fact that this is the case for most overweight dogs. Certainly an increase in exercise combined with a decrease in dietary calories will help, but there are many ways to solve the problem. Here are a few to try:

- Try feeding your dog a lower calorie dog food.

- Replace your dog's usual treats with either lower calorie treats or frozen vegetables or carrots.

- Replace one-third of your dog's meals with canned pumpkin. At first you may need to heat it to make it more appetizing, but eventually most dogs will respond and accept this high fiber, filling food.

Does your dog seem lethargic most of the time? Being overweight may often contribute to lethargy, but there remains the possibility that your dog's lethargy is due to an endocrine disorder such as hypothyroidism. Ask your veterinarian about it. If blood tests confirm this diagnosis, daily medication may result in an energy boost as well as substantial weight loss.

Does your dog seem to suffer from more than the expected number of infections? Dogs that are both overweight and suffer from more than their fair share of infections, or seem to be drinking excessively, may well be suffering from another endocrine disorder known as hyperadrenocorticism, or Cushing's disease. Your veterinarian can perform the necessary blood tests to confirm this. Appropriate treatment is available to manage this disease.

Is your dog diabetic? Diabetes sometimes goes along with weight gain. Increased water intake is usually present as well. Your dog's veterinarian can investigate the possibility of diabetes and Cushing's disease at the same time.

My Dog Has Been
Losing Weight

Most dog owners spend a significant amount of time worrying about ways to prevent their dogs from gaining weight. The opposite problem is rarely the case. When a dog does appear to be losing weight inexplicably, it is always cause for concern.

The first step toward a resolution is to go over your dog's eating and exercise schedule. Question all members of the family about their responsibilities related to the dog's care and feeding. Go as far as making a chart that quantifies amounts of food offered and actually consumed, and duration of and exertion during the various walks the dog is taken on. Not until the logic of this part of your dog's daily routine has been established should you move on to further investigation.

What to Look For

Weight loss is weight loss. When it represents a threat to your dog's health, however, it is much more of a concern. Of course, any time significant weight loss is mentioned, a thorough physical exam is called for.

For your current purposes, though, let's focus on your dog's immediate issues. Start evaluating your dog as a whole. Analyze his levels of energy and enthusiasm. Check his fur to see if it is sparse, coarse, or dull. Look for any loss of muscle mass. If you observe such a loss, see if it occurred in a symmetric fashion or if it is limited to certain parts of his anatomy. Check for evidence of protruding bones, especially the ridges of his skull, his shoulder blades, spinal vertebrae, ribs, and hips.

What to Do

Now go through the following questions to figure out what to do next:

Has your dog been ill recently? Chronic illness, especially organ system failure of the pancreas, kidney, or liver can result in long term nausea and vomiting, often leading to dramatic weight loss. If any of these conditions affect your dog, weight loss is to be expected, but not irreversible if the prognosis for the disease is optimistic.

Is your dog's coat sparse, coarse, or dull? If so, it could be due to the same cause as the weight loss. If your dog's appetite has remained healthy throughout the weight loss, intestinal parasites may be the problem. Warn your family members to practice strict personal hygiene and submit a fecal sample from your dog to your veterinarian.

Is your dog currently taking any medication? Either the illness your dog is being treated for or the medication he is taking for it could be a factor in his weight loss. If your veterinarian approves, try reducing or even eliminating your dog's chronic medication to see if that helps him regain his appetite and the weight he has lost.

Has your dog recently suffered from any form of head trauma? If so, there is the possibility of a concussion, as well as the dizziness and nausea that go with it. These symptoms could very well result in noticeable weight loss over a relatively short period of time. Seek your vet's help for a neurology consult.

When to Get the Vet

Has your dog recently gotten into any unusual chemicals or medications? Since many toxins have a direct effect on the nervous system, it is common for exposure to to result in abnormal behaviors or neurological symptoms. This could include nausea or loss of appetite. If you know what chemicals or medications your dog has possibly ingested or inhaled, call the ASPCA National Animal Poison Control Center at 888-426-4435 for immediate advice. Plan to make a trip to the nearest animal emergency facility as well.

My Dog Has a
Discharge from Her Eye

At some time or another, almost every dog has a bit of material collect in the corner of the eye. When this happens, it's not considered a discharge so much as a normal response to the day-to-day foreign matter a dog is exposed to. When a dog leads a healthy, active life, she is bound to get dust and debris in her eyes on occasion, and tearing is an expected, appropriate means of clearing that material, flushing the eye in the process. Once that accumulated material is cleared, the healthy eye will return to its normal appearance.

But if the accumulated material recurs repeatedly, the collected material is yellowish to green, and/or the surrounding tissues are red and irritated, your dog needs further attention and action.

What to Look For

Put on your rubber gloves to avoid introducing additional foreign matter to your dog's eyes. Go slowly to give your dog confidence that there will be no surprises, and speak soothingly to keep her calm. Take a close look at your dog's eyes. Take note of the color of the discharge and check for any injury or mass near the eyes.

What to Do

Ask yourself the following questions:

When to Get the Vet

Any dog with an eye problem that causes repeated rubbing or scratching of the eye should be seen immediately by a veterinarian, preferably a veterinary ophthalmologist.

What breed is your dog? Exophthalmic dogs (those with naturally bulging eyes, such as pugs and Boston terriers) are more likely to have eye problems than other breeds of dogs. Because their eyes are more exposed and accumulate foreign material at a greater rate, they're also more likely to have eye discharge than other dogs. And because their eyes protrude more, they are more likely to seriously injure their eyes. Combine this with a narrowed drainage angle, and you have a greater tendency for increased intraocular pressure, which can lead to glaucoma. In short, if you own one of these breeds, be knowledgeable concerning your particular dog's eyes and be prepared to act swiftly if you notice even a slight cause for concern. Your dog and your vet will appreciate it!

Is your dog behaving normally in every other way? Dogs with eye discharges and no other symptoms are usually safe to treat at home. Clean the eye, flush it with a sterile saline solution, and observe it for a few days to see if it improves. (See "How to Flush and Treat Your Dog's Itchy, Irritated Eyes" on page 21 for complete instructions.) If it doesn't improve, call your vet.

Is your dog bothered by the affected eye? Dogs that are annoyed enough by a discharging eye to rub or scratch it are in danger of doing themselves serious harm through repeated trauma. Call your vet right away if the rubbing and irritation persists after you have cleaned and flushed the eye.

Can you see any injury or mass in or near the eye? Injuries to the eyes will invariably result in irritation, tearing, and discharge. Flush the eye gently with a sterile saline solution to get a better look at the injury and determine how serious it is. Masses within the eyes or associated with the surrounding conjunctival tissues and those of the eyelids can also result in irritation and discharge. Once again, thorough yet gentle cleansing with sterile saline will help clear away extraneous material and help gain a clearer picture of the extent of the problem.

My Patient's Story

Charlie and Betsy are friends of mine with a Jack Russell terrier. One night Betsy called to say that Charlie had pulled his car into their driveway and inadvertently hit Spike, the dog.

"Jake," she said, "I'm not sure, but I think there is something really wrong with Spike's eye. There's a lot of blood and he keep's trying to rub it with his paw. Oh my God, I think there's something coming out of it, can we bring him right over?"

When they arrived, Charlie was sitting in the back seat with Spike wrapped in a towel, with one eyeball hanging about two inches below his eye socket!

While Spike managed to live many more feisty, productive years, the eye did not. This sort of injury, though more likely to occur in exophthalmic breeds, can happen to any dog and immediate action can, in some instances, save the eye.

My Dog Has a
Discharge from His Ear

Your dog's ears are critical to his daily routine. Of course, they're an important source of auditory information, but they also help maintain normal body temperature by radiating excess body heat. When a dog's ears become clogged with wax or discharge, they function poorly and become uncomfortable and often smelly. The good news is that most ear problems can be managed, and sometimes even cured, at home using commercially available products.

What to Look For

A quick examination of the ear flap and the auditory canal it protects will give you most of the information you need. Start by observing the external ear flap, or pinna, for abnormalities such as puncture wounds, hair loss, and irritations. Next, gently lift the flap up, flattening it against the top of your dog's skull to expose the ear canal beneath. This will give you a clear look at the inside of your dog's ear flap and into the entry to your dog's vertical ear canal. (See the illustration on page 31 for a cross section of a dog's ear.)

If you need to get a sample of the discharge in your dog's ear, get a cotton swab. Using your nondominant hand, hook your

dog's collar with your pinky and ring finger. Grab the tip of the flapped-over ear between your nondominant thumb and index finger. Now use your dominant hand to place the cotton swab in the entry of your dog's ear canal, using a gentle twirling motion. Don't go in further than half an inch, then slowly withdraw the swab while lightly swiping the sides of the canal.

What to Do

The following questions will help you identify the type of problem you are dealing with and, in turn, dictate the type of treatment you need to begin:

Did you see any wounds, hair loss, or irritation to the ear flap? If so, refer to the chapters directed at these specific issues.

What does the discharge look like? Normal ear wax may vary from slightly yellowish to tan in color, but with some dirt mixed in may end up looking darker. The normal amount shouldn't be copious. Anything more than $1/8$ teaspoon for small dogs, $1/4$ teaspoon for medium-sized dogs, and $1/2$ teaspoon for large-breed dogs should be considered suspicious. Often, the appearance of the material in the ear canal is enough to suggest a diagnosis:

- **BLACK AND GRANULAR DIS-CHARGE,** like coffee grounds, usually means your dog's ears are infested with ear mites. To treat them at home, purchase an ear flush, an ear mite medication, cotton balls, rubber gloves, and cotton swabs. Take your dog to a safe area where spatter will be easy to clean up afterward. Plan on treating the ears twice daily. Wear clothing that is easily laundered.

Now here's what to do:

1 Squirt a generous amount of the ear flush directly into the affected ear canal and quickly (before your dog has a chance to shake the flush out all over you and the room) flap the pinna back down over the ear canal. Massage the ear thoroughly so the debris in the ear canal mixes with the flush you have just put in.

2 Lift the pinna and swiftly (you know why) insert one of the cotton balls right down into the ear canal, packing it in until you feel that you might not be able to get it back out. Once again, massage the ear canal thoroughly to get as much of the debris-laden flush as possible to soak into the cotton.

3 Lift the pinna and remove the soiled cotton ball. If the cotton ball appears to be too deep within the ear canal, try grasping the ear at its base, right where it meets your dog's head, and pinching it between your fingers, working it out like you would try to get that last bit of toothpaste out of an almost empty tube.

4 Repeat the cotton ball maneuver until you are getting no more moisture and little to no more debris from the ear canal.

5 Clean the outermost portion of the ear canal and the inside of the pinna with cotton swabs for more precision.

6 Apply the recommended amount of medication deep into the ear canal and quickly (ditto) flap the pinna

back over and massage the ear thoroughly to distribute the medication evenly throughout the ear canal.

7 Use whatever means necessary to distract your dog for a few minutes to allow the medication to get absorbed by the ear canal before he has a chance to shake it out.

Usually the successful treatment of an ear mite infestation requires one daily flush/cleansing and twice daily medication. The trick to preventing a recurrence is to treat for one week, stop for the second week, then repeat the treatment for the third week. This coincides with the life cycle of the mites. However, different medications may come with different treatment recommendations.

- **YELLOW TO GREEN, PASTY, AND SMELLY DISCHARGE** usually means your dog has a bacterial ear infection. You may be successful treating it topically at home, but many dogs with bacterial ear infections may need antibiotics, so if your dog seems sick in any way other than the obvious ear problem, consult his vet. To treat a bacterial ear infection at home, follow the above directions exactly, except substitute an antibiotic ear lotion or ointment for the ear mite medication. Also, keep in mind that in some cases the reason why the pus discharge is noticed is because an inner ear infection has caused a perforation in your dog's ear drum, releasing the pus from behind it into his outer ear. Because of this, your treatment of the bacterially infected ear should be very gentle.

This treatment does not require the week on, week off, week on treatment. Instead a ten- to twelve-day treatment course should do. If you don't notice any progress after three days, however, you should see your vet.

- **BROWN TO DARK BROWN DISCHARGE WITH A DISTINCT, PUNGENT, "FERMENTING" ODOR** usually means that your dog has a fungal ear infection. These infections, which are caused by yeast organisms, usually arise after exposure to moisture while swimming or being bathed. They can usually be corrected using the treatment outlined on page 114, but substituting an antifungal lotion or ointment for the ear mite medication. This could include any of the human vaginal yeast infection medications, such as Monistat. Like a bacterial infection, the treatment should only be necessary for about ten to twelve days.

My Dog Has a Discharge from His Ear

When to Get the Vet

If your dog has a discharge that appears to be a mixture of some or all of the above and when your dog's rubbing, shaking, and scratching cause additional, more serious problems, call your vet. Some medications are effective in treating multiple symptoms simultaneously, and your veterinarian is the best source for these medications, particularly when the symptoms are complicated by self-induced trauma.

My Dog Has a
Discharge from Her Nose

A clear, runny nose without other signs of illness is a common problem, usually dealt with by watching and waiting for time to allow the signs to abate or for some underlying problem to make itself more obvious. Every other type of nasal discharge is worth being concerned about, however. Bloody, purulent, gray, and viscous discharges should all be regarded as signs of a problem.

What to Look For

With your dog comfortably seated or lying down, take a peek at her nose. Look at the discharge and note if it's coming from one nostril or two. Go slowly as you gently wipe the discharge away with a clean, white towel or paper towel to see how quickly more comes out.

What to Do

Once you've gotten a good look at your dog's nose, ask yourself the following questions:

What does the discharge look like? As mentioned above, a clear, watery discharge is certainly cause for closer observation, but never an emergency unless it is accompanied by other, more serious symptoms.

Any nasal discharge that has a thick, creamy, or gelatinous consistency and/or appears yellow, green, or gray and/or con-

tains blood is a more immediate concern. This type of nasal discharge could be a symptom of many problems, ranging from relatively benign respiratory allergies to life-threatening forms of cancer.

Is the discharge coming from one nostril or both? Unilateral (one-sided) discharges are less likely to be viral in origin, but should be taken no less seriously. If they persist for more than a day, see your vet.

Is your dog up to date on his vaccines? Upper respiratory viruses are often the cause of nasal discharges. Once your dog's immune system is challenged by one of those viruses, opportunistic bacterial organisms move in, causing discharge.

Vaccinations against distemper, parainfluenza, and bordetella provide protection against the most common upper respiratory pathogens. If your dog is either overdue for his boosters or you have no record of his having received them, an immediate veterinary visit is important, not only to maximize your dog's chances for recovery, but also to prevent your dog from spreading the disease to others.

Does your dog have other symptoms as well? Dogs with mild viral infections or allergies often have watery eyes and occasional sneezing in addition to their clear nasal discharge. As long as these symptoms occur in an otherwise active, energetic dog with a good appetite, you can just watch and wait for further developments. Fever, lethargy, vomiting, and diarrhea combined with a nasal discharge, however, should be addressed immediately. See your dog's vet to have these symptoms evaluated.

When to Get the Vet

Puppies with nasal discharges of the thick or colorful variety are an immediate worry, especially if they have yet to be vaccinated. The canine distemper virus is a primary concern. If the discharge is from both nostrils, get your puppy to a hospital immediately!

My Dog Has a
Discharge from His Skin

The substances that typically arise from your dog's skin are oils and waxes, which help to maintain the health of his skin and coat. While some dogs normally have slightly oily or waxy skin, it is never normal for a dog's skin to noticeably discharge any substance. So if there appears to be an unusual substance arising from your dog's skin, something is wrong.

What to Look For

Your first priority is to assess exactly what you are dealing with and how extensively your dog is affected. Any time a significant area of your dog's skin looks different than usual, there is bound to be some discomfort. You should therefore be gentle as well as cautious in your efforts to examine the region more closely. Comfort your dog first by petting or rubbing a separate area of his body from the location of the problem, particularly in a place you know he likes. Once your dog is calm and his attention has been diverted from the affected area, try to position him so that you have a clear view of the problem.

If your dog can tolerate it, use a wide-toothed comb to separate the hair covering the site to get a better view. Look for abnormal signs, such as changes in color, texture, and integrity of the skin, i.e., is the skin healthy and intact or does it seem to be thin, scratched, torn, or otherwise damaged? Pay particular attention to the discharge itself and where it seems to be coming from. Also try to identify the precise extent of the region that seems abnormal.

If your dog is too uncomfortable to allow this type of examination, you can either have your vet see him as soon as possible or you can try to ease the discomfort with cold compresses before resuming your efforts. This latter approach may also be necessary (combined with additional aggressive cleaning and combing) if there is enough discharge to have accumulated in the surrounding fur, creating a nasty mess!

What to Do

After you've gotten a good look at your dog, the following questions will help you decide how serious his symptoms are:

Does your dog appear to be uncomfortable? If your dog is restless and irritable, or if he is rubbing, scratching, licking, or chewing the area in question, you'll need to do something quickly before he does himself any further harm. In the process of your exam, you will already have gotten a pretty good idea of how much attention to the area your dog is willing to tolerate. Using that as a guide, and possibly by recruiting a few helpful hands, alternate using cold compresses with clearing the area of excess hair, accumulated discharge, and any crusts that may have formed in response to the problem. This may be enough to noticeably improve your dog's affect. If so, that's great!

Next, disinfect the area with a 50/50 hydrogen peroxide/water solution. Then, to prevent your dog from going right back to attacking the area, put an Elizabethan collar on him, which are available at most pet supply stores.

It's possible that this cleaning and disinfecting may draw your attention to a much more serious issue than you originally expected. In that case, call your vet.

What does the discharge look like? If the discharge is bloody, there is bound to be some injury or excoriation involved. This could be the only problem or it could be the result of self-trauma by your dog in

When to Get the Vet

Consult your dog's veterinarian if your dog is in acute pain or scratching uncontrollably, or if more than 25 percent of his body is affected by the discharge.

response to the discomfort from some other source. That source may or may not be identifiable.

If the discharge is yellow or green, sticky, and foul-smelling, it is probably pus, meaning that there is a bacterial infection present. This could be the primary problem or it could be in response to some breakdown in the integrity of the skin. Cleansing with an antibacterial solution such as a 50/50 hydrogen peroxide/water mixture is called for, followed by topical and possibly systemic antibiotics. Also place a call to the vet.

If the discharge is yellow and waxy, it may just be sebum, a waxy discharge that appears in excess when dogs have seborrhea, a chronic, manageable skin disorder that can often be successfully treated with medicated shampoos that contain chlorhexidine. You can buy these products at pet supply stores. Follow the instructions on the package.

Is the skin red and angry looking? Whenever there is a discharge related to red, irritated skin, you'll want to relieve the source of the irritation so that whatever therapy is needed to promote resolution and healing will be successful. Sometimes self-induced trauma is so extensive that the source of the problem is impossible to identify. (See "My Dog Has a Hot Spot" on page 72.)

Is there any evidence of parasites? The chronic, sometimes overwhelming discomfort caused by ectoparasites such as fleas, mites, and lice can lead to discharge from the skin. However, you'd also be noticing a lot of scratching, licking, biting, or chewing. (See pages 22–23 for advice on how to deal with these skin parasites.)

My Dog Has a
Discharge from Her Anus

Anything coming from your dog's anus other than feces should be considered a discharge. The only normal discharge that comes out of a dog's anus is the pungent-smelling material produced by the scent glands, or anal sacs, located on either side of the rectum. Because it is not always easy to distinguish between this normal anal sac discharge, feces, and the other abnormal types of rectal discharge, the following tips and questions may help.

What to Look For

To examine your dog's anus properly, choose a place and time that provide comfort, low stress, and excellent lighting. To safely avoid any chance contact with fecal matter or any of the discharge in question, it would be wise to don rubber gloves, protective lab goggles (or your own glasses), and a surgical mask. Once these are in place, gently lift your dog's tail straight up in the air. This should give you full view of her rectum, unless she happens to be a long-haired dog, in which case you will have to push the hair aside to get a better look. If the discharge has been copious, you may have to trim or comb away enough hair and/or crusted material to get a better look.

Once this has been accomplished, look at the anus like you would a clock. From this perspective, your dog's genitals will be at six o'clock and her tail at twelve o'clock. Look first for evidence of the discharge that alarmed you in the first place. Get a good idea of what it looks like and see if you can identify from where specifically it is arising.

Next, look for any swelling or puffiness of the tissues surrounding the anus, specifically in the lower quadrants, between three and six o'clock and six and nine o'clock. These are the areas usually affected by problems with your dog's anal sacs. In many cases, there will be a noticeable bulge in these regions, indicating full, inflamed, and maybe even infected anal sacs. In extreme cases, the sacs may have ruptured, resulting in an inflamed hole at approximately three or nine o'clock.

What to Do

Ask yourself the following questions to figure out what to do next:

What does the discharge look like? As described above, fecal matter doesn't count as a discharge, but anal sac material may be visually difficult to distinguish from loose stool. The way it smells should help you identify it, since the scent of the material produced by your dog's anal sacs is very pungent. Most people describe it as smelling like sweaty gym mats, dirty socks left in a locker for a few weeks, crankcase oil. Regardless of how you describe it, it is unlikely that you will confuse its smell with the smell of your dog's bowel movements.

Other types of discharge you may encounter could range from bloody to purulent and could actually originate from the rectum or the anal sacs.

It might be helpful to collect a sample in a ziploc pouch and have a veterinarian look at it under a microscope. This will be doubly useful in that it will both identify the contents of the discharge and supply some sense of the nature of the problem.

Is it painful for your dog when you lift her tail? If the pain is enough to cause your dog to cry out or snap at you, an injury may be responsible for the discharge and it may be better to leave the exam up to your veterinarian. If your dog exhibits signs of pain but is able to endure the exam, be especially aware of the possible presence of trauma to the area, including puncture wounds, open cuts, or dramatic bruising and/or swelling.

Is there an obvious area of swelling or irritation? If the lower quadrants mentioned earlier are bulging with no other evidence of a problem, your dog's anal sacs may simply need to be expressed. While this is generally something left to the experienced hands of your groomer or veterinarian, many a brave owner have successfully, albeit cautiously, expressed those sacs, to the great relief of their dogs. (See "How to Empty Your Dog's Anal Sacs" on page 23.)

When to Get the Vet

Any time an anal discharge is composed predominantly of frank, red blood and lots of it, your dog should be rushed to a veterinary hospital!

PART 6: MY DOG HAS A GROWTH

My Dog Has a
Growth on His Face

If you spend a substantial amount of time with your dog, you probably have just about every crease and whorl of hair on his face memorized. As soon as something new crops up, then, you will most certainly notice it, right? Honestly, you'd be surprised at how many "growths" seem to crop up out of nowhere and develop overnight into fairly substantial masses in dogs belonging to the most devoted dog owners! If this has happened to your dog, don't jump to any conclusion before closely examining the growth and getting a better idea of what you are dealing with. If you are overwhelmed by the prospect of doing any of this, consult your vet, who may likely suggest a biopsy to definitively identify the growth as benign or something more grave.

What to Look For

Put on rubber gloves to protect your skin. Choose a well-lit room and put your glasses on if you wear them. Even if you don't, try using a magnifying glass for a better look. Start by performing a thorough investigation of your dog's head, from nose to neck. First check for other growths like the one that has you worried. If you notice others, check for symmetry in their location. Pay attention to their size, texture, color, and sensitivity. When you observe them under the magnifier be sure to check for legs, since the majority of the facial "growths" that I get called for end up being ticks!

Look each growth over closely and don't be afraid to touch it and even squeeze it gently to see how it behaves and how your dog reacts to the sensation of having it touched and manipulated.

What to Do

Next, ask yourself a few questions:

Does the "growth" move at all when you scrutinize it? If so, you are probably dealing with a tick. You can confirm this by identifying the legs, which will be located at the end closest to the tick's mouth, where it is attached to your dog's face. Remove the tick either directly with a pair of tweezers or by covering it with Vaseline.

The Vaseline will cause the tick to suffocate and back out of your dog's skin within a few days in an attempt to survive.

Does the growth have a pebbly, rough texture with a normal skin color? This could most likely be either a wart or a benign tumor of one or more of your dog's sebaceous glands. These rarely represent a threat to your dog's health, but they may be a source of local infection, particularly if they get traumatized by scratching. If they are growing at an alarming rate or they are getting repeatedly traumatized, have your veterinarian evaluate them.

How large a base of attachment is there from the growth to the skin? Growths with broad bases of attachment are generally more worrisome than those with small attachment bases. The latter of these are easier to remove and are less likely to be a threat to your dog's overall health. The larger, broad-based growths are usually best tested by fine needle aspirate or excisional biopsy, just to be sure what they are and what, if anything, needs to be done about them.

Is there bleeding and/or infection associated with the growth or growths? Either or both of these would be enough reason to get your veterinarian involved and to seek immediate treatment.

My Dog Has a
Growth on Her Eyelid

Eyelid growths vary tremendously. Some dog owners insist that the growth you ask them about has existed ever since the dog was a puppy, while others will report that the marble-sized mass that is dragging their dog's lower lid downward enough to alter her expression was definitely not there yesterday. Both stories are possible, but the truth is that tumors of the upper and lower eyelid don't necessarily fit into one specific category. Some are benign and, once removed, do not return. Others may return or, more accurately, new growths of similar cell origin may appear, in close proximity to the original site. Others may have potential to spread, or metastasize, but if removed early and completely, will never reoccur or spread. Still others may be aggressive enough to spread rapidly to nearby locations and/or metastasize to distant sites.

What to Look For

Put on a pair of rubber gloves. Look the growth over closely and don't be afraid to touch it and even squeeze it gently to see how it behaves and how your dog reacts to the sensation of having it touched and manipulated. However, never wait long to have your vet look at one of these growths, unless your close-up examination reveals legs—if it does, remove the tick at once and be relieved!

What to Do

Ask yourself just one important question:

Does the "growth" move at all when you scrutinize it? If so, you are probably dealing with a tick. You can confirm this by identifying the legs, which will be located at the end closest to the tick's mouth, where it is attached to your dog's face. Remove the tick either directly with a pair of tweezers or by covering it with Vaseline. The Vaseline will cause it to suffocate and back out of your dog's skin within a few days in an attempt to survive.

If you don't think the growth is a tick and if you have a trusting relationship with your dog's veterinarian, this is a time when you have to put that trust to the test. Your vet has probably seen many growths just like the one on your dog's eyelid and can give you an honest opinion about what to do. The choices will include radical excisional biopsy, punch biopsy, fine needle aspirate with cytological examination, simple excision, freezing, cauterization, or topical therapy. Sometimes the response, or lack of response, will lead from one conservative course of therapy to one that's a bit more aggressive. The ultimate goal is to prevent the growth from becoming a threat to either your dog's health or level of comfort.

My Dog Has a
Growth on His Third Eyelid

Your dog's third eyelid is a specialized structure that serves a strictly protective function. It is not under your dog's control, and therefore only rises to where it can be seen when there is something wrong. The sorts of things that might cause the third eyelid to rise include, but are not limited to: dehydration, head trauma, diseases of the eye and/or the muscles that control the eye, and growths of the eye itself or its surrounding structures, including the third eyelid. If the reason for the emergence of your dog's third eyelid is the presence of a growth of some sort, be concerned, but don't panic.

What to Look For

Under close light and using a magnifying glass if necessary, look at the growth closely and try to determine whether there is a distinct growth present or whether what you thought was a growth is actually a swelling.

Since you are probably not accustomed to seeing this third eyelid, what you think is a growth on it may actually be the lid itself without any abnormal growth present at all. See the illustration on page 29 for an idea of what the normal lid looks like.

What to Do

If your dog is younger than two-years-old and the lid is present with a distinct, angry-looking redness to it, but no clearly defined growth apparent, you may be dealing with something known as cherry eye, a protrusion of the secretory gland of the third eyelid. This will probably require a simple surgical procedure to correct. (See "My Dog Has a Problem with His Third Eyelid" on page 181.)

(See "My Dog Has a Problem with His Third Eyelid" on page 181.)

When to Get the Vet

If you are pretty clear that what you are concerned about is indeed your dog's third eyelid with some sort of growth on it, there is little you can do to correct the situation without the help or your veterinarian, or better yet, a veterinary ophthalmologist. Consult one right away.

My Dog Has a
Growth on Her Ear

Your dog's ears are interesting structures in that they are composed of a number of different types of tissue. On the outer portion they are covered with fairly thick-haired skin, while the inner portion is lined with thinner, almost hairless skin that is significantly more sensitive. The shape of the ear is provided mostly by cartilage. Except for the smaller ones contained within the skin of your dog's ears, the blood vessels and nerves are sandwiched in between the inner and outer layers of skin. Because of the variety of functions your dog's ears serve, the different types of tissue they are made of contain a variety of specialized glands and nerve endings which can represent sources of a variety of abnormal growth types.

If you notice a growth on your dog's ear, use your common sense knowledge of your dog's normal anatomy (the opposite ear will serve as a perfect model for comparison) and your best judgment to determine whether to consult your veterinarian. Usually, unless you find that the "growth" is moving or has legs (probably a tick and therefore removable), calling your vet is the best course of action.

What to Look For

Grab a flashlight, rubber gloves, and a magnifying glass and bring your dog to a room that is well lit. Start by facing your dog directly and observe the way she carries her ears, checking specifically for asymmetry or swelling. Note any evidence of head tilt, excessive drooling, or repetitive blinking. Move on to the ear flaps, or pinnae. Examine them for unusual heat or sensitivity. Look inside the ears and down into the canals of each ear using your flashlight. Check for evidence of infection. Finally, use your magnifying glass to carefully investigate the growths you have noticed, observing all aspects, including color, size, texture, shape, and sensitivity.

What to Do

Asking yourself a few questions should point you in the right direction of what to do next:

Does the "growth" move at all when you scrutinize it? If so, you are probably dealing with a tick. You can confirm this by identifying the legs, which will be located at the end closest to the tick's mouth, where it is attached to your dog's ear. Remove the tick either directly with a pair of tweezers or by covering it with Vaseline. The Vaseline will cause it to suffocate and back out of your dog's skin within a few days in an attempt to survive.

Are you sure that what you are concerned about is a growth of some sort? If you are certain that a growth is what you are dealing with, you should probably have it seen by your veterinarian. In general, the only growths that clients should feel comfortable observing over time without veterinary intervention are growths that look like warts. These may very well be warts, or they could be benign masses of the sebaceous, or wax-producing, glands. Either way, they present little to no health risk to your dog, with the exception being when trauma to one of these masses causes it to bleed and get infected. In such cases, a visit to the vet is in order.

My Dog Has a
Growth on His Nose

Your dog's nose is an important part of his anatomy. It is composed of specialized cells that normally remain supple and moist and contribute to the gathering of useful information from his environment. If the architecture of your dog's nose is changed in any way whatsoever, it should be cause for concern. Conduct a thorough examination of the area and the surrounding tissues.

What to Look For

Don a pair of rubber gloves. Start by choosing a room with good lighting. Stand your dog squarely in front of you and look him straight in the eyes. Observe his breathing pattern and how he uses his nose in the process. Go slowly and cautiously so as not to alarm, frighten, or anger him. Check for signs of asymmetry and any evidence of color or texture changes from what you are accustomed to. Pay close attention to the areas immediately adjacent to the growth as well as the growth itself. Look for signs of irritation or sensitivity. Gently touch those areas around the growth and then the growth itself to get an idea of how tender it is and what its surface texture is like.

What to Do

Asking yourself the following questions should point you either to your first-aid kit or to your veterinarian:

Is the growth well-defined or more diffuse in shape? If a growth on the nose is well-defined and appears to be confined to the superficial tissue of the nose, chances are good that it may be something benign, such as a wart, or something very treatable like a cyst or small abscess. In any case, if it seems to be growing or at least not improving, see your veterinarian. If it lacks clear, clean edges, it should be seen by your veterinarian sooner rather than later.

Does the growth have a specific texture to its surface? The texture of any growth is often key in making an accurate diagnosis. Pebbly, verrucous (wart-like), crusty, horny, leathery, scaly, and smooth are all possibile textures. Share this information with your vet to get an opinion on how soon you should bring your dog in.

Is the growth tender or itchy? If the lesion is warm and tender, it is possible that it represents some form of localized infection and may respond quickly to antibiotics. If it is especially itchy, it could be the result of some form of insect bite or allergy. Try calming down the itchiness with cold compresses and topical steroids, such as Cortaid or Corticin. If that doesn't help, see your vet.

Is there swelling, bleeding, or discharge associated with the growth? These signs can all be evidence of injury, infection, or underlying problems. In such instances, first try localized home treatment of these symptoms with the items in your first-aid kit. (See "How to Control Bleeding" on page 18, "How to Clean a Wound" on page 18, and "How to Dress a Wound" on page 19.) If your home therapy doesn't appear to work within a few days, consult your veterinarian.

My Dog Has a Growth Near Her Mouth

My Dog Has a
Growth Near Her Mouth

The tissues of your dog's mouth and those immediately surrounding it are prone to developing a variety of growths. Many of them are benign, but some are quite invasive and downright dangerous. That is why it is so important to identify them as early as possible. When in doubt, check with your vet. When your vet is in doubt, request a biopsy.

What to Look For

If you find a growth in or near your dog's mouth, always investigate further, looking for additional growths in the surrounding areas. Check the opposite side of your dog's lip, mouth, or face for symmetric structures. Be sure to take note of how well-defined or amorphous the growth is. Look closely at the size, color, and texture of the growth as well as how deep or superficial it is.

What to Do

Now, ask yourself a few questions:

Is the growth solitary or are there others like it in the surrounding regions? Multiple growths in and around the same region, especially the mouth, may be warts. If they are warts, they usually resolve on their own without treatment, within two months. If they are verrucous (wart-like) in appearance but are not warts, they are probably sebaceous gland tumors that are benign but will not go away without treatment and will often grow larger and messier with time. You should get your vet's help to deal with these. Solitary growths are usually more worrisome.

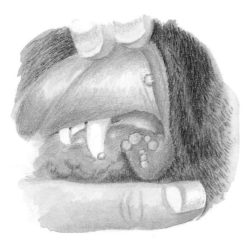

Oral Warts

Does there appear to be bilateral symmetry to the growths? If so, be sure that what you are worried about are actually growths and not some normal structures that you have simply failed to notice previously.

Is the growth tender or itchy? If the lesion is warm and tender, it is possible that it represents some form of localized infection and may respond quickly to antibiotics. If it is especially itchy, it could be the result of some form of insect bite or allergy. Try calming down the itchiness with cold compresses and topical steroids, such as Cortaid or Corticin. If that doesn't help, get your vet's help.

Is there swelling, bleeding, or discharge associated with the growth? These signs can all be evidence of injury, infection, or underlying problems. In such instances, it is often acceptable to first try localized home treatment of these symptoms with items in your first-aid kit. (See "How to Control Bleeding" and "How to Clean a Wound" on page 18, and "How to Dress a Wound" on page 19.) If your home therapy doesn't appear to be working in a few days, consult your veterinarian.

My Dog Has a Growth Near Her Mouth

My Dog Has a
Growth on His Skin

My Dog Has
a Growth on
His Skin

Your dog's skin surface is his largest organ and therefore the most likely place to develop abnormal growths. Because the skin is also anatomically positioned as a barrier against threats from the environment, it is likely to be exposed to more parasites and foreign matter than any other part of your dog. Because of this, approach every unusual, suspicious object attached to your dog with caution, care, and an open mind.

What to Look For

Once you have established that there is an unusual object growing from, or at least attached to, your dog, try to figure out whether that object is unique or if there are others like it present. If there are others, check closely for bilateral symmetry in case they are normal structures that either appear unusual due to swelling or irritation or that you simply have never noticed before. Check closely to see whether the growth is related to any specific part of your dog's anatomy. If it is, check the appropriate chapter title for that location (see pages 121–134).

What to Do

Try to answer the following questions:

Does the "growth" move? If so, it is probably a tick. Remove it with tweezers, making sure that you get the entire tick. If you feel that you have not successfully gotten all of it out, keep trying until all of the tick is gone. If this process is more than you're willing to deal with, try covering the tick with Vaseline, then watch it back out of your dog within a few days as it begins to suffocate.

Is the growth pigmented? Pigmented growths are usually more worrisome than flesh-toned ones because whenever we see one, we have to concern ourselves with the possibility of melanoma, a deadly form of skin cancer.

Is the surface of the growth smooth or rough? Growths that are rough in texture may be safe to wait on because there are many of them that are benign, such as warts and sebaceous gland adenomas. There are many smooth benign growths too, but these are usually cysts, papules, or pustules. When in doubt, ask your veterinarian, because unless the growth suddenly disappears, you are going to have to make the call sooner or later.

My Dog Has a
Growth in Her Armpit

Your dog's armpits are a sensitive area of her body. Although they are difficult to reach, a very determined dog can get close with her mouth and tongue and actually do herself substantial damage with her hind paws while in a standing position. To reduce the potential for such self-mutilation, take the necessary steps toward gaining a diagnosis any time you discover something unusual in your dog's axillae, or armpits.

What to Look For

Grab a flashlight and magnifying glass. First, try your best to guarantee that what you are noticing is indeed a growth or swelling and not a foreign body, parasite, or nipple! Next, look over your dog's entire body, checking for other growths like the one you have discovered in her armpit. Take note of their locations and whether their distribution seems to be in any particular pattern. If you notice one, always look for a bilaterally symmetric counterpart just in case what you have found is a normal anatomical structure. (In other words, check to see whether your dog has a matching growth on the other side of her body.) For each growth, use whatever means necessary to check its size, color, texture, and sensitivity. Here's where your flashlight and magnifying glass may be helpful.

What to Do

Now ask yourself the following questions:

Did your examination reveal any movement, smell, or stickiness to your growth? If you can answer no to all three of those questions, you should feel confident that your concerns are not unfounded.

Is there any symmetry to other growths on your dog's body? Symmetry makes it more likely that you're dealing with a normal part of your dog's body, such as a nipple.

Is the growth you were originally concerned about solitary or paired? As mentioned above, paired growths may suggest normal structures, but they may also suggest multiple or spreading growths.

When to Get the Vet

If the growth is bothering your dog, get your vet's help right away. The masses that bother dogs are often the most worrisome because they result in the dog acting out, and sometimes attacking the bothersome area enough to create a bloody mess. Quickly get your vet's help to figure it out and do something about it right away.

Is the growth large or small, isolated to the skin or deep and possibly involving other subcutaneous structures? This information will help you and your vet determine the next step.

My Dog Has a
Growth in His Groin

The term *groin* is a broad one, covering much of the urogenital area of your dog and including both inner thighs and lower abdomen. When and if you discover any sort of unusual growth in this region of your dog's body, first make sure that it is not a parasite of some sort (check for movement or legs) and then be certain that it isn't a nipple (look for another one on the other side of your dog's midline). This will avoid the embarrassment of hearing your vet explain that your "growth" is one of the above.

Once you have established that you are actually dealing with a growth, try to determine how serious it is by examining it more closely, using a magnifying glass and a flashlight if needed.

What to Look For

Start your investigation by looking carefully for evidence of any other similar growths elsewhere on your dog's body as well as in the general vicinity of the original one. Be on the watch for any pattern to their location. Check them for size, color, texture, and sensitivity. Get an idea of how much of each growth appears to be attached to your dog's skin versus how much is not attached.

What to Do

Ask yourself a few questions to determine how to proceed:

Is the growth solitary or are there many?
If there are many growths in your dog's groin, especially if they seem to have arisen spontaneously and are reddish to pink, they may be a rash, pustules, or very irritated insect bites. Try applying a cold compress and distracting your dog from licking or chewing at them for a day or two before rushing to see your vet. Be sure to go over your dog's entire body again,

just to make sure there are no parasites responsible. Mites, which are microscopic, could also be responsible.

Is the location or the size of the growth irritating to your dog? Growths in this general area are easy for your dog to reach. If they bother your dog, he is sure to make a mess of them in short order. Put an Elizabethan collar on your dog to protect him from himself, and then arrange for your veterinarian to have a look. Growths in this area are easy for your vet to figure out and the chance of you doing anything beneficial in a situation like this is minute.

My Dog Has a Growth on Her Leg

My Dog Has a
Growth on Her Leg

Your dog's legs are designed to support her weight, transport her wherever she needs to go, and to pump furiously if you ever try to trim her nails! Most dogs' legs are fairly slim and—except for the furry covering—smooth in contour. This makes detecting any sort of abnormal swelling or growth fairly easy to identify. If you notice any such inconsistency in the normal silhouette of your dog's legs, investigate right away.

What to Look For

Start with the leg opposite the one that concerns you. Follow the directions for examining your dog's legs as outlined in "My Dog Has a Swollen Leg" on page 146 to examine first the unaffected limb, then the worrisome one opposite it.

What to Do

Next ask yourself a few questions:

Has the growth appeared suddenly or gradually? A sudden unexplained growth may actually be something simple like an attached tick or some type of foreign object. If it isn't painful, try experimenting with the growth by pulling it gently, stretching it to its limits to get an idea if it is removable.

Is the growth painful? Any growths, swellings, lumps, or bumps that are painful to your dog should be seen by a veterinarian. In such cases, a professional is needed to determine what they actually are, what needs to be done about them, and whether they are threatening to your dog's ongoing health. If it is not painful, scrutinize it closely, feel it, stretch it, squeeze it gently to get an idea of its density and how broad its base of attachment is.

Is the growth a different color than the surrounding tissue? Although this information won't change whether you choose to investigate on your own or with your vet's help, it will help if you are trying to explain it to your vet on the phone.

My Patient's Story

Some years ago I had a client call me urgently, saying "Doctor, I know it's late, but I think Kramer has come down with some awful form of cancer. He has this horrid growth coming out of his side and it's oozing blood and pus and it's absolutely awful." The client, Jody, described where it was on his body and that it seemed to have cropped up over night.

"How could this have happened? Do you think it was something we fed him or that he got into in the garbage?," she asked. Knowing Jody as well as I did, I prepared myself for something unusual. What I found when I arrived was a frightened, timid Kramer and a totally frantic Jody, wearing a pair of bright yellow lobstering gloves and a night-gown. Once I had had a moment to look, feel, and smell the "lesion," however, it only took me a moment to make the diagnosis. Kramer had managed to acquire a new accessory—a menthol cough drop! This should serve as a reminder to look closely and use all your senses, including your common sense, before panicking.

My Dog Has
a Swollen Face

Unless your dog's facial swelling occurs in a gradual, perfectly symmetrical fashion, the swelling should be obvious. The reasons for a dog's face to swell up are varied, but they're not difficult to decipher with the proper guidance.

PART

7

MY DOG HAS
A SWELLING

What to Look For

To properly examine your dog's face, choose a comfortable area with good lighting. Start with your dog standing so that no wrinkles or skin folds prevent an accurate assessment of her facial swelling. Look your dog straight in the face, comparing your current evaluation with your memory of what is normal for her. Move your dog's head side to side and up and down to get an accurate look at all aspects of her head, including the eyes, chin, muzzle, jaw line, and the base of her ears.

Apply gentle pressure to the areas that appear swollen, checking for signs of injury, tenderness, and heat. Finally, follow the directions in "My Dog Is Drooling Excessively" on page 90 to properly examine your dog's mouth.

What to Do

Ask yourself these questions:

Did the swelling appear to occur spontaneously rather than gradually?
Spontaneous swelling of the face is usually the result of some form of trauma, infection, or allergic response. The latter could be due to ingesting a certain food or chemical, or to an insect bite or sting. In either instance, as long as your dog continues to breathe comfortably and you notice no blood, pus, or dramatic injury to any of the specific areas of the face mentioned above, start applying cold compresses. Giving your dog a weight-appropriate dose of an antihistamine such as Benadryl may help reduce the swelling significantly. See "How to Treat Your Dog's Allergic Symptoms" on page 25.

Did the swelling come on slowly? Slow swelling of the canine muzzle/face is worrisome because it may suggest various forms of cancer or a systemic disease such as chronic renal failure. Dental disease can cause this type of gradual swelling as well, so be sure to have your veterinarian conduct a thorough workup of your dog, including blood testing, if this is the case. This should be done within a few days of noticing the swelling, if possible.

Is there evidence of injury to the area? Bruising, punctures, and lacerations can all cause swelling. If any of these are present, treat them as aggressively as you feel comfortable doing. Be sure to ensure against infection by disinfecting and using an antibiotic ointment, such as Bacitracin, Neosporin, etc.

Is there blood and/or pus in the area? Blood alone should be cleaned and evaluated for ongoing blood loss and controlled as appropriate. (See "How to Control Bleeding" on page 18.) If there is pus present, the swelling may be an accumulation of more pus under your dog's skin, which is called an abscess. In this case, the use of a warm compress and gentle but steady pressure may allow you to drain the bulk of the pus from the site and thus reduce the size of the swelling. Antibiotics will still be necessary, however, so chances are you will need to see your vet for further treatment and a prescription.

Did your oral exam reveal any dental issues? Chronic dental disease is a fairly common cause of facial swelling. Any time it is severe enough to result in noticeable facial swelling, it is enough to merit a visit with your vet. Without your vet's help, your dog could end up losing some teeth and developing more serious systemic illnesses due to the entry of oral bacteria into her bloodstream.

My Patient's Story

A few years ago, my neighbor Bill called on a Saturday afternoon in July. Bill and I coached baseball together but we had cancelled practice that day because of rain. "Jake, Lola's face is swollen to about twice its normal size and I can see traces of blood on her lip. I'm hesitant to touch it, though, because it looks like it must be killing her."

Since I was home and he lived within a short walk of my house, I headed right over to have a look. Lola greeted me with her tail wagging and a big, swollen, bloody lip. As Bill and I calmed her, I lifted the lip to reveal a completely sheared off canine tooth and a number of tears on the inside of her lip and cheek. At that point, Bill's son, Alex, one of our outfielders, came running around the side of the house in tears. "I'm sorry, Dad, but she ran right in front of me while I was already swinging!" Lola was trying to steal the baseball off the tee that Alex was using to work on his batting technique and she learned a very unfortunate lesson.

Today Lola, has two broken canines—the second one was fractured when she tried to bite Alex's bicycle tire while he was riding down the driveway!

My Dog Has
a Swollen Ear

Your dog's ears are a very sensitive part of his anatomy. Not only do they provide him with a constant source of valuable auditory information, but they also serve as a way to dissipate body heat, detect air currents and temperature changes, and convey changes in attitude and mood. Because your dog's ears are so sensitive, if they are swollen or irritated they will certainly become a preoccupation to him. As a result, it is critical that a swollen ear be accurately diagnosed and correctly treated to avoid symptom progression.

What to Look For

Start by observing the way your dog carries the affected ear when he is still. Try to evaluate whether the ear seems enlarged throughout its length or just at the base, tip, front, or back.

Next, carefully grasp the base of the healthy ear and run the length of it through your hand, between the palm of your hand and your thumb. Note its thickness, weight, and flexibility. Now repeat the process on the swollen ear, noting any differences. Finally, check inside both ears, looking for evidence of irritation or infection.

What to Do

Answering these questions should help you figure out what to do next:

Did you detect any signs of infection inside the affected ear? Evidence of pus or excessive wax might be consistent with, and a possible reason for, the swelling. If, from past experience, you know how to treat the type of infection you notice, proceed with that treatment in the hope that your efforts may again solve the problem. If they don't, get your vet's help.

Is the swelling superficial and confined to one well-defined area? These types of swellings are often the result of some sort of insect bite, sting, or the site of a recent tick attachment. Such swellings can be treated safely with a simple disinfectant (hydrogen peroxide) and topical antibiotic (Bacitracin) therapy.

Does the swelling seem to be creating a balloon-like effect with the ear? This usually means that your dog is suffering from something known as an aural hematoma. (See the related illustration on page 287.) This results when a blood vessel within the ear begins to ooze, filling the hollow structure of the ear flap with blood.

This is very uncomfortable for dogs and will often cause them to shake their heads repeatedly, exacerbating the symptoms. If left alone, the pressure inside the ear may eventually cause the bleeding to stop, but the blood inside the ear will take time to congeal, and only some of it will be resorbed. It will eventually heal, but the result will be a thickened, heavy, wrinkled "cauliflower" ear.

A better solution is to seek your veterinarian's help. There is a surgical procedure that will correct the problem with much more attractive results.

Did the swelling seem to occur spontaneously? If it seems to have happened rapidly and doesn't have that balloon-like appearance, it is probably allergic in nature. Try following the directions for the use of antihistamines in "How to Treat Your Dog's Allergic Symptoms" on page 25.

My Dog Has
a Swollen Nose

If you have owned your dog for any significant amount of time, you should have a pretty good idea of what the normal size of her nose is. It is never normal for that size to increase to the point of being noticeably larger. If it does, you should be worried enough to find out why and decide on a course of action.

What to Look For

A good look at your dog's nose involves scrutinizing its color, texture, symmetry, and moistness. Use a flashlight to get a peek into your dog's nasal passages.

What to Do

Next, ask yourself the following questions:

Is the swelling confined to one portion of the nose or is it an overall swelling? When nasal swelling is restricted to a focal area, it is likely to be the result of an insect bite or sting or some other form of traumatic injury. Try applying a cold compress to see whether it reduces the swelling. The compress may help reduce any pain as well.

If the swelling seems to take up the entire nose, the possibilities increase to include blunt trauma, infectious disease, serious illness, and parasitism.

Is there any discharge from the nose? If you notice pus or blood coming from your dog's nose, there is little you can do to solve the problem without the help of your vet. If the discharge is clear to slightly gray, it may just be the result of a respiratory virus or allergies. (See "My Dog Has a Discharge from Her Nose" on page 116 or "My Dog Is Bleeding from Her Nose" on page 32.) As long as your dog's behavior is otherwise normal, you can try the cold compress and wait a day or two to see if the swelling subsides.

Do you notice any changes in the texture of the nose itself? When a dog's nose takes on a distinctly different texture, becoming coarser and harder, pebbly or dry with fissures or cracks, it often signifies immune system problems or nutritional deficiencies. External parasites such as flies and mites can cause such problems as well. If the dog is otherwise healthy, try giving her a multivitamin and apply a moisturizing vitamin-enriched salve, such as A & D ointment or Bag Balm. If this is still unsuccessful after a few days, consult your veterinarian.

Does your dog show any other signs of illness? If your dog is acting weak or lethargic, if she is losing hair in unusual places, or if she is scratching or rubbing herself more than usual, she may be suffering from some systemic illness like kidney failure or an immune-mediated disease like Lupus or pemphigus. Seek your vet's help to check your dog if this seems to be the case.

My Dog Has
a Swollen Neck

Your dog's neck needs to be comfortable, flexible, and pain free to perform all of the many functions demanded of it on a daily basis.

If there is even a mild swelling of just about any portion of your dog's neck, he should have a difficult time hiding it from you. You may notice the actual swelling first, but many times the initial clue will be that your dog is holding his head at a funny angle or experiencing difficulties eating and/or drinking.

Some dogs will try to scratch at the swollen area, either because it hurts or because the heaviness of the area is quite annoying. Diagnosing the actual cause of a neck swelling can be a bit tricky, but if you are patient and gentle you may be able to figure it out, or at least get a good idea of how serious it is.

What to Look For

In a comfortable room with good lighting, stand your dog squarely on all four legs and face him. Using both your hands, smooth the fur on his face and back, from nose to neck, as you would if you were just beginning a friendly petting session. By initially scratching the fur behind your dog's ears, you can first relax him. Then work your hands forward, toward his throat, then down to the base of his neck and chest, and finally around his sides and up to the back of his neck where it joins his spine.

Throughout the exam, use your fingers to gently but firmly probe in slow, circular patterns, checking for any swellings, lumps, or areas of heat or tenderness.

What to Do

Next, ask yourself these questions:

Are there areas of heat or tenderness associated with the swelling? These signs are often present when an infection is responsible for the swelling. Check the area more closely for evidence of a punc-

ture or other injury. If you find one, follow the directions for "How to Treat an Abscess" on page 25.

Is the swelling solitary or does it cover more than one area? Solitary swellings can be treated based on their location and the way they feel. The soft superficial ones are usually less worrisome than the hard, fibrous, or deep ones. If your vet is convinced that you are not dealing with an abscess, he or she may suggest a biopsy. This would be performed as a fine needle aspirate, a punch, a core, or an excisional biopsy. Which one is performed will be dictated by the size, location, and texture of the mass. If there is more than one swelling, determine whether they seem to be bilaterally symmetric, which means they are the same on both sides of your dog's body. If so, they may actually be enlarged lymph nodes, often a sign that your dog is fighting either a bacterial or viral infection. Alternatively, this could be a bilateral enlargement of your dog's thyroid gland. In all of these cases, it would be good to see your vet.

Has your dog recently been vaccinated or received any other injections? Soft, non-painful swellings of the area at the back of the neck closest to the shoulders often occur following vaccinations or reactions to injectable medications. These situations are usually treated by simply waiting for them to resolve on their own. If the area begins to bother the dog, many vets will suggest the use of an antihistamine, such as Benadryl.

My Dog Has
a Swollen Belly

**My Dog Has a
Swollen Belly**

Most dogs are known to be fairly enthusiastic when it comes to their food. It probably won't surprise you, then, if you happen to notice your dog with a full belly, especially following a recent successful scavenging expedition or after a family barbeque. Overeating is, in fact, the most common reason for dogs' bellies to become distended. Unfortunately, a distended abdomen can also be a sign of much more serious—and even deadly—problem, so it is crucial that dog owners know how to tell the difference.

What to Look For

If your dog exhibits that characteristic "look at me, I just swallowed a watermelon" look, try to assess her overall attitude. Obviously, a lethargic, sedentary dog is of much more concern than a happy, mobile one with her tail wagging.

The next step should be a quick look in her mouth. Carefully examine the areas of her gums that are typically a healthy pink color, checking for any changes to that normal color. Once you've seen the color, pick a spot that is uniform in hue and press it firmly with your thumb, then release it. The original pink color should blanch with the pressure, then return to its original color within two seconds. If your dog is darkly pigmented in these areas, you may need to base your assessment on tongue color instead.

Next, gently run your hands over your dog's abdomen, applying light pressure to check for any points of tenderness. If your dog is standing, straddle her and then, starting just behind and under her rib cage, use both hands to slowly and carefully lift upward to the point of almost lifting her off the ground. Repeat this maneuver, working your way down toward her tail, one hand width at a time, as many times as your dog's size requires. If your dog is on her side, perform this maneuver using one hand, pressing downward, toward the surface on which she is resting. This procedure is designed to again assess discomfort, but also to get a better sense of the nature and specific location of the distension. Finally, from the same position, keep one hand flat against one side of your dog's abdomen while you use the other to perform a quick press-and-release form of pressure on the other side, maintaining contact with both hands all the while. If your dog is on her side, the surface beneath her will serve as the stabilizing surface. The purpose of this test is to check for fluid in the abdomen. If it is the reason for the distension, you should feel a distinct "return wave" of fluid come back to the pressing hand a moment after the press-and-release has been performed.

What to Do

Ask yourself the following questions:

Is your dog uncomfortable? If your dog appears to be absolutely unaware of her increased girth, it is unlikely to be anything other than the aforementioned dietary indiscretion that has caused it. Watch and wait but be sure to keep her away from any source of food for at least twelve hours. If, on the other hand, she is weak and listless or making attempts at vomiting, immediately try to evaluate her predicament. In some instances a dog that has recently suffered some form of blunt trauma, such as being hit by a car or a baseball bat, will exhibit a swollen and tender abdomen. If you pay strict attention to your dog's behavior and conduct a safe, level-headed evaluation, you will be able to determine how serious the problem is and whether immediate action is necessary.

What breed is your dog? Large, deep-chested dogs—such as Great Danes, greyhounds, and German shepherds—are more prone to developing a life-threatening form of abdominal distension known as gastric dilatation and volvulus (GDV). While an exact cause is not currently known, it appears to happen more frequently in dogs that are fed one large meal per day or have recently endured some trauma or stress, such as surgery or long distance transport. If your exam reveals a drum-tight abdomen and ghost-white gums, head directly to a veterinary emergency facility. Dogs with GDV that are not treated within a small window of time often die as a result.

Is your dog panting rapidly? Dogs that are uncomfortable will often breathe rapidly, particularly if they have just gorged themselves to the point of distension. This behavior may also be a prelude to a vomiting episode. If the gums are pink and healthy, you can watch and wait for a short while to see what develops. If failed attempts at vomiting occur and your dog appears to be getting worse, get him right to the veterinarian.

When to Get the Vet

- If your dog is in acute pain and you can't isolate it, veterinary care is critical. Use a large blanket to help protect you and the dog in your attempts to transport her. If the pain is present but it can be isolated and her color is good, you have a little more time to plan your next move. Let your dog have thirty to sixty minutes to recover, monitoring her behavior throughout, then conduct your exam once again.

- Any dog, especially deep-chested breeds, with a swollen abdomen and pale gums should be rushed to an emergency facility!

Does your examination lead you to suspect fluid or masses in your dog's abdomen? If so, your veterinarian's help is in order, since X-rays and blood work are probably necessary.

Does your examination reveal any distinct large masses? Dog owners are often embarrassed to tell their vets that they suddenly noticed their dog's increased girth, fearing that they may have been guilty of some form of negligence. In fact, there are some masses that can literally grow from nothing to the size of a softball within a few hours. Abscesses can behave this way as well. The point is, if it appears to be abnormal, it is always wiser to have it looked at than to wait and worry.

My Dog Has a Swollen Back

My Dog Has a Swollen Back

Dogs, like most mammals, have a distinct fight or flight mechanism that results in a number of chemical and subsequent physical changes. Among these is the constriction of the piloerector muscles, which causes the hairs on certain parts of the body to stand up. We humans feel this as a tingling at the back of our necks or what we describe as a "hair-raising" event. In dogs, we call it having their "hackles" up. This is perfectly normal.

However, if you notice an elevated section of hair on your dog's back without any external threat or stimulus involved, or if your dog's back bulges without any raised hair at all, it is not normal. Conduct a more thorough examination to figure out how serious a problem you have.

What to Look For

Start by conducting a comprehensive exam like the one outlined on the following page. Pay particular attention to the portion of the spine closest to the area that is swollen. Be sure to examine all the areas that you are palpating and probing with your fingers, checking for changes in color, texture, temperature, and sensitivity.

What to Do

Answering the following questions should help you figure out how serious a problem you have:

Has your dog recently received any vaccinations or other injections? Swelling at the site of any injection, but especially after vaccinations, is a common, usually painless occurrence. As long as your dog is demonstrating no obvious discomfort, these types of swelling are okay to monitor at home. They usually resolve within two weeks.

Has your dog recently suffered any form of trauma to the area? Blunt trauma to the back, when it results in noticeable swelling, is worth having your dog's vet evaluate, unless there appears to be no discomfort associated with it at all. In such cases, watch closely for further developments.

Is the area of swelling soft or hard, warm or cool? Soft, warm swellings can be infectious in origin. If you suspect a local infection or abscess, try following the directions included in "How to Treat an Abscess" on page 25. If the swelling is cool and/or hard, have your dog's vet evaluate it to determine whether a biopsy is recommended.

When to Get the Vet

If your dog demonstrates obvious signs of discomfort during your back exam, take it seriously. If the swelling on your dog's back is painful when it is touched, don't waste time getting to the vet for a more thorough workup, probably including X-rays.

How to Ace Your (Dog) Exam

Think of this exam as a slow, elaborate body massage, and it will be fun for you and your dog. While your dog is lying on his side, cradle his head in your hands and begin scratching his ears. Next, work your way down the length of his throat and neck; circular, rubbing motions (edging toward slight probing) are the best way to comfort and relax him while testing for discomfort and sensitivity.

Once you have reached your dog's shoulders, isolate his upper front leg (the one not against the floor) and work the same circular, rubbing-to-probing motions, using both hands for leverage, control, and support, from his shoulder all the way to the tips of his toes. Resume the process by returning to his chest and side, working backward toward his hind legs. Once there, repeat the process of examining his rear leg the same way you did the front.

When you have reached the tips of your dog's toes, move on to the head of his tail. Lift the tail gently with one hand and slowly use your other hand to encircle and sequentially squeeze sections of the tail until you reach the tip.

Now carefully roll your dog over to his other side and repeat all the steps, starting with his shoulder. Once this is completed, get your dog into a comfortable, stable, standing position. Again cradling his head in your hands, slowly move it up and down, and then side to side, checking for any sign of resistance or discomfort. Finally, beginning at the base of his skull, apply cautious but firm pressure while walking the index and middle fingers of one hand down his spine, all the way to his tail, noting any sign of a flinch or other complaint.

My Dog Has
a Swollen Leg

The comfort and function of all four of your dog's legs are essential to her everyday existence. Because a dog's mobility is one of her most valued attributes, the compromise of any aspect of the complex of vessels, nerves, muscles, and bones that function as one to facilitate the ability to move can be devastating. If you notice a swelling of one of your dog's legs, examine it immediately in an attempt to identify the exact cause and avoid the development of additional symptoms and potential disaster.

What to Look For

Before placing your dog in any specific position, observe her at rest, looking for signs of discomfort or asymmetry.

Identify the leg that is swollen, but start your exam by manipulating the contralateral, or opposite, leg. This will test your dog's ability to bear weight on the affected limb while giving you a baseline for comparison once you get down to examining it.

In each instance, begin by examining the toes one at a time, extending and stretching them individually, squeezing the bones and bending the joints and eventually feeling the spaces between them while stretching the interdigital webbing. Next, move on to the carpal, or "wrist" joint if it is the front limb, tarsal or "ankle" joint if it is the rear. The move itself should be performed by encircling the limb with your hand and sliding upward while squeezing. The joint should then be put through its full range of motion to check for discomfort or stiffness while listening for any cracking or grinding sounds. Now move on to the next joint, using the same encircling maneuver as before, eventually arriving at the elbow (front) or stifle (rear). Put this joint through its full range of motion just as you did the previous joint, checking for the same things. Ultimately you will arrive at either her shoulder (front limb) or hip (rear limb). Once you have manipulated this joint, checking its range of motion while looking for any signs of discomfort or any cracking or grinding sounds, you will have completed your exam.

What to Do

Next, ask yourself these questions:

Has your dog recently been in any sort of accident or fallen? Traumatic incidents are a common reason for leg swelling in dogs. Your exam should have pinpointed the location of the injury, and your dog's response to manipulation may have given you a good idea of its severity. If at any point in this process your dog begins to cry out, struggle, or snap, stop immediately and let your vet do the rest!

Did you see any bleeding or discharge? If closer scrutiny of the area reveals a puncture or laceration and there is bleeding or pus without severe pain, you may have a local infection to deal with. Try following the directions for treating an abscess in "How to Treat an Abscess" on page 25.

Is the swelling generalized and associated with one of the major joints mentioned? Injuries that result in diffuse swelling of major joints of the legs are often serious. They may involve ligament, tendon, vessel, or nerve damage or some combination of them. The resulting joint instability predisposes it to further damage, and the swelling actually serves to prevent the joint from moving about and further harming itself. This is the type of injury that requires the help of a veterinarian experienced in orthopedics.

Is there swelling and pain associated with one or more of the toes? Injured toes, although they are quite painful, are often left to heal on their own without a cast or splint, sometimes even when they are fractured. The reason behind this is that the pain is usually enough to prevent the dog from putting much weight on it. In addition, the splint or cast might actually be so bothersome that the dog could do more damage in her efforts to rid herself of it than if she were never to have been placed in a splint or cast in the first place.

However, if you noticed that the swelling felt like an overall sponginess that remains indented after you stop pressing, rush your dog to an ER. This condition is known as pitting edema and is quite serious. It could mean that your dog has vascular or lymphatic disease. In either case, a major animal hospital is where you should take her right away.

When to Get the Vet

- If your dog seems to be in a great deal of pain, skip the exam and follow the directions for transporting an injured dog included in "How to Transport an Injured Dog" on page 20. Get her to a veterinary emergency facility immediately.

- If your exam revealed a distinct coldness of any portion of the limb, get your dog to an emergency clinic immediately. Sometimes circulatory difficulties will result in poor venous return from the limbs and blood will pool in them, causing dramatic, puffy swelling. These legs may get quite cold.

My Dog Has a Swollen Leg

PART
8

MY DOG
IS ITCHY

My Dog Is
Scratching or Rubbing His Eyes

Your dog's eyes, like your own, are sensitive to even the mildest of irritations. It is understandable, then, that for your dog to not only have something bothering his eyes, but to also lack the tools to do something about it with precision, must be quite frustrating! This is why the intense scratching and/or rubbing come into play, occasionally to the point of creating more trouble than there was to begin with. What you do about it could very well determine whether the problem persists and develops into a chronic condition or gets resolved quickly and efficiently. Your first action in all such cases is to take steps toward restricting your dog's ability to traumatize himself. Start by applying an Elizabethan collar. Your dog's initial annoyance will distract him while you trim his nails (to prevent further injury). Then you can get to work on figuring out what the problem is.

What to Look For

Start by conducting a thorough examination of your dog's eyes, like the one outlined in "My Dog's Eyes Are Red" on page 167. Be aware that some, if not all of your abnormal findings could be due to the effects of the rubbing and scratching you noticed. Look for evidence of foreign matter, masses, redness, irritated areas, and injuries. Make note of any asymmetry of the eyes and/or their surrounding structures.

What to Do

Now ask yourself the following questions:

Did you notice any foreign body or material in your dog's eyes? Unless the object is something penetrating your dog's eye, it is possible that you may be capable of solving the problem yourself. Try employing the technique for flushing your dog's itchy, irritated eyes in "How to Flush and Treat Your Dog's Itchy, Irritated Eyes" on page 21.

Did you notice any growths in or near your dog's eyes? A number of types of masses can develop within the eye and its surrounding structures. Any growth that bothers your dog enough to prompt scratching or rubbing is enough to merit a consult with your regular vet or, ideally, a veterinary ophthalmologist. This should be accomplished as soon as possible.

When to Get the Vet

If you notice any bleeding in or around the eyes, get your dog to the vet. An injury or disease of the eyes is not something to fool around with, and timing may be important.

My Dog Is
Scratching or Rubbing Her Ears

Itchy ears are one of the most annoying and common complaints of all dogs and their owners! Not only are itchy ears uncomfortable, but they are quite easy for dogs to reach, permitting them to make a mess of things without ever achieving much in the way of solving the initial problem. Your prompt action may save you some money and a great deal of aggravation.

My Dog Is Scratching or Rubbing Her Ears

What to Look For

Start with a thorough examination of your dog's head and ears, paying strict attention to signs of asymmetry in the way she holds her head and moves her ears and the angles that her ears adopt at rest. Look at each ear both outside and in, using a flashlight if needed. (See the illustration of the anatomy of the ear on page 31.) Finally, watch your dog walk both toward you and away from you, checking for signs of clumsiness or imbalance.

What to Do

Asking yourself a few questions should help you figure out what to do next:

Does your dog display signs of imbalance? A head tilt, imbalance, or even clumsiness can be signs of an ear infection. As mentioned, some ear infections are quite painful and if your dog is anxious to begin with, she may snap at you. If you are comfortable enough to proceed after you have finished your exam, try to clean and even medicate your dog's ears following the directions provided in "How to Clean and Treat Your Dog's Dirty and/or Infected Ears" on page 24. Keep in mind that when an ear infection is serious enough to cause a head tilt and imbalance, it is often necessary to treat the infection with oral antibiotics. In such an instance, your veterinarian is the one to provide you with the proper strategy and protocol.

Does your dog have any wounds or lesions on or in her ears? If you discover any minor wounds or other superficial lesions of the ears and you are comfortable treating them, do so by following the directions for wound management outlined in "How to Clean a Wound" on page 18 and "How to Dress a Wound" on page 19. Be sure to use an Elizabethan collar in conjunction with your treatment plan to ensure that your dog doesn't go right back to her self-destructive scratching.

Does your dog suffer from allergies? If so, your dog's scratching may be in response to the discomfort arising from some environmental or food allergy. Check your dog's recent meal and exposure history for the introduction of any new foods, cleaning products, fabrics, air fresheners, or perfumes. If you are strongly suspicious that the scratching is due to one of these potential allergens, try the combination of a weight-appropriate dose of Benadryl, cold compresses, and the trusty Elizabethan collar to put an end to the immediate scratching problem. (See "Treating Your Dog with Anti-Inflammatories" on page 24 for dose information.)

Does your dog have evidence of any parasites? This could take the form of little red spots, black flea "dirt," reddish-brown droppings, and/or actual fleas or ticks. Fleas, mites, and flies can all be responsible for making your dog's ears itchy. Use the combination of a weight-appropriate dose of Benadryl, cold com-presses, and an Elizabethan collar to soothe your dog's ears while you devise the appropriate strategy for treating the parasites. (Check "How to Treat Your Dog's Fleas" and "How to Treat Your Dog's Mites" on page 22.)

My Patient's Story

Melba lives in Roxbury, MA in a somewhat dicey neighborhood. When she called me late on a Thursday night, I was hesitant to travel there, but her voice made me reconsider. "Doctor, my Sally's ear is bleeding and she won't leave it alone. She looks a little weak and, you know Sally, she's very delicate to begin with, and I'm worried she might bleed to death before morning! Please, doctor, I'll do anything just to get you to come. You know she and Brutus are all I have."

What do you say to that? Of course I was questioning my sanity as I drove up to her house, fearing for my safety and wondering what to expect inside. As I climbed the stairs, my fears were realized when, at the same moment that I saw streaks of blood on the walls, I heard a gunshot in the street. Instinctively, I dropped to my knees and crawled into her apartment. Melba laughed a bit, but was so relieved to see me she hugged me and brought me in to see Sally.

It was immediately obvious that Brutus, Melba's crazy German Shepherd, had bitten Sally's ear and it was still bleeding. I was able to stop the bleeding by applying an encircling bandage and trapping her ears, one over the other with some gauze in between, on top of her head, still leaving enough "play" so that she could eat and drink. Two weeks later, the ear was good as new.

My Dog Is

Scratching, Rubbing, or Licking His Nose

If your dog is pestering his nose, your obvious assumption is that something is bothering him enough to tickle or itch him in that region and that he is simply doing something to satisfy the stimulation. Of course you are right, but you might be surprised by the number of different stimuli that could induce your dog to begin the scratching, rubbing, or licking. To get to the bottom of the dilemma, you'll need to do some investigating.

What to Look For

Start your investigation by performing a thorough examination of your dog's entire nose, muzzle, and mouth, like the one described in "My Dog Is Drooling Excessively" on page 90. Look for any evidence of the four I's: inflammation, irritation, infection, or injury. While you're at it, check for foreign objects stuck in any of those parts of your dog's anatomy.

What to Do

Now ask yourself a few questions to figure out what to do next:

Does your dog suffer from allergies of any kind? Allergic dogs are generally highly susceptible to dramatic responses (like frantic scratching, rubbing, or licking) to allergen exposure, particularly when that exposure is through the kind of direct contact your dog would experience with his nose. If your exam revealed no obvious evidence of injury or foreign body, there is a strong possibility that allergies may be responsible. Try using cold compresses, a weight-appropriate dose of Benadryl, and an Elizabethan collar to solve the problem. (See below for more information.)

Did your examination reveal any foreign objects? If you find any foreign bodies lodged in or penetrating any of the structures of your dog's nose, muzzle, or mouth, attempt to remove them only if you are able to accurately identify them and at the same time feel certain that there is no danger of causing any further damage.

Does your dog have a recent history of exposure to any new foods or household products? If so, prevent further exposure and try using cold compresses, a weight-appropriate dose of Benadryl, and an Elizabethan collar to solve the existing problem.

When to Get the Vet

If your dog has recently experienced any blunt trauma to the head, that trauma can cause intracranial side effects that would induce nose scratching, rubbing, and licking. If you suspect that your dog's behavior is secondary to head trauma, get him to an emergency veterinarian right away.

Treating Your Dog's Allergies

If your dog shows signs of an allergic response, your first priority should always be to ensure an open airway without any respiratory difficulties whatsoever. If there is even a hint of a struggle to breathe, get your dog to an emergency facility immediately.

If breathing is normal and your dog's allergy symptoms are topical itching or local swelling, try applying cold compresses. If this doesn't help significantly, try an over-the-counter human antihistamine, such as Benadryl, Tavist, or Claritin. These can also be used to effectively treat allergy-related coughing and sneezing, but it is better to consult your veterinarian before going ahead with treatment, as the dosage and frequency will depend on more than just the size of your dog.

Most antihistamine medications are available as either liquid, chewable tablets, or capsules. The tablets and capsules can be given by emptying the capsule contents into a food that your dog finds delicious. The liquid form is best given through a dosing syringe, which can be teased in between your dog's teeth and carefully squirted into his mouth, but not too forcefully. An overly aggressive squirt might cause your dog to aspirate the medication, which could result in other problems.

My Dog Is
Scratching or Rubbing Her Mouth

When a dog persistently scratches or rubs at her mouth, it is usually an indication that something is wrong, but not always that it is an emergency. There are, in fact, a number of reasons for such behavior that you may be capable of solving yourself. The trick is to identify whether or not that is possible.

What to Look For

Conduct a thorough oral exam like the one described in "My Dog Is Drooling Excessively" on page 90. Direct your investigation toward discovering any of the four I's: infection, irritation, inflammation, and injury. Also check for growths, as well as any foreign matter that might have penetrated your dog's oral tissues or become lodged between her teeth.

What to Do

Now ask yourself a few questions to try to puzzle out what to do next:

Is your dog an allergy sufferer? Any dog that has a history of allergies could very well scratch or rub at her mouth when exposed to the right allergens. As mentioned in the other chapters about scratching and rubbing, Benadryl and cold compresses might provide some dramatic relief although the longevity of the improvement is often difficult to predict. (See "How to Treat Your Dog's Allergic Symptoms" on page 25.) If the symptoms do not significantly improve in a few days, get your vet to help.

Has your dog recently had any head trauma? If so, the aftereffects of a concussive force could possibly cause the signs you are witnessing. Your veterinarian should be consulted immediately and will probably refer your dog to a neurologist.

Did your exam reveal any injury, foreign body, or other possible source of the problem? If you are able to identify that source and then go on to effectively resolve it, the allergy treatments listed above may have saved you the trouble and expense of going in to take care of it at a hospital. They are not designed to replace the care of your veterinarian, but simply to augment the successful therapy of the cause by reducing the itch.

My Dog Is
Scratching or Rubbing His Neck

Your dog's neck, like so many other sensitive areas associated with his head, is quite easy to reach and therefore predisposed to self-inflicted trauma. For this reason, it is one of the most common sites for hot spots and all sorts of infections and irritations associated with the wearing of a variety of collars.

What to Look For

Take a close look at all aspects of your dog's head and neck, from his nose to his shoulders, including his ears—and especially at their base, where they attach to his head. Look for the four I's: injury, infection, irritation, and inflammation. Be aware of the possibility that there could be a sharp foreign body penetrating your dog's skin that might be causing the problem. Go slowly and gently to reduce your dog's anxiety—and your own.

What to Do

Take a moment to answer a few questions to ascertain what to do:

Does your dog have an ear infection?
Many dogs with ear infections will scratch aggressively at their own necks because that is an area they can reach more easily than the spot that is causing the problem. By treating the dog's neck and skin at the same, you stand the best chance of resolving both at the same time.

Does your dog suffer from allergies? If so, and if the scratching appears to be in response to allergen exposure, try treating the neck like you would a hot spot, as described in "My Dog Has a Hot Spot" on page 72.

Does your dog's neck appear to have any superficial injuries and irritations? If so, try employing the strategy outlined in the box below. Try to prevent further trauma to your dog's neck. Remove all collars except an Elizabethan one or one of the turtleneck variety.

Are there any parasites on your dog's neck? If so, treat them immediately. (See "How to Treat Your Dog's Fleas" on page 22 and "How to Treat Your Dog's Mites" on page 22.) Then move on to your dog's neck skin and treat the injuries or irritations by following the directions mentioned in the box below.

My Dog Is Scratching or Rubbing His Neck

Treating Your Dog's Superficial Injuries and Irritations

To take care of superficial, or surface, problems, start by trimming away any excess hair. Next, blot and eventually scrub the area with your 50/50 hydrogen peroxide and water mixture until you have succeeded in clearing away all crusts, discharge, and debris. Now apply a cold compress. Ideally such a compress should be flexible, so create one by taking an appropriately sized towel, soaking it in water, ringing it out, and putting it in the freezer for about 15 minutes or until it is cold but only slightly stiff. Apply the compress by wrapping it completely around your dog's neck for about 10 minutes.

After removing the compress, apply the appropriate medication (antibacterial, antifungal, steroid, etc.) and protect the neck from further scratching by using a modified turtleneck. This can be one of your own winter neck warmers if your dog is large, a cut out turtleneck if your dog is small to medium in size, or a sweat band or gauze bandage if your dog is small. Just be sure it isn't too tight!

My Dog Is
Scratching, Rubbing, or Licking Her Back

When a dog focuses her attention on scratching, rubbing, or licking her back, the incentive must be a strong one because there are many more easily accessed parts of her anatomy to reach. Fortunately, your dog's back is readily accessible to you, her caring owner, making your attempts at diagnosis less difficult.

What to Look For

To thoroughly examine your dog's back, start from the point directly behind her head and work your way down her spine, all the way to the point where her back ends and her tail begins. Your evaluation should include a complete assessment of her hair, skin, muscles, spine, ribs, and the space between her vertebrae. You can accomplish the latter by using the index and middle fingers of one hand to slowly "walk" the length of her spine, applying cautious but firm pressure to each intervertebral space, checking for even the slightest flinch or complaint.

What to Do

Ask yourself these questions to help determine what to do next:

Does your dog have any noticeable parasites present? Fleas would be the most likely parasites to be visible to the naked eye. Treat them immediately, either by yourself or with the help of your dog's groomer or veterinarian.

Does your dog suffer from allergies? If your dog has had allergic skin problems in the past and you are suspicious that this may be a new, yet similar episode, try the therapy that appears to have worked in the past.

Does your dog have any distinct, identifiable skin lesions, such as abnormal scabs, scratches, wounds, ulcerations or growths? They could be infectious—of fungal, viral or bacterial origin—or they could be endocrine-driven. In most such cases, it is best to get help from your veterinarian.

Is your dog a Rhodesian ridgeback? If so, there is a possibility that a lesion in the middle of your dog's back may be a dermoid or pilonidal cyst. This lesion, common to this breed, is likely to require surgical intervention and should be evaluated as soon as possible.

My Dog Is Scratching, Rubbing, or Licking His Armpits or Groin

Your dog's ventrum, or underside, is easy to overlook when it comes to the four I's (irritation, inflammation, injury, and infection) solely because it is usually hidden from sight. As a result, when these problems are finally discovered, they are often dramatic. Don't feel guilty, just get to work right away to figure out the source of the problem and get your dog some relief.

What to Look For

Before focusing your attention on the specific areas of concern, look at your dog's entire body. Check his coat for signs of dryness or loss of luster. Review his recent history concerning appetite, thirst, bowel, and urinary habits. In short, give him a good "once over." Returning to his axillae (armpits) and inguinal (groin) area, look closely for signs of lumps, bumps, rashes, blisters, wounds, scratches, dry patches, and infection. Remember that if your dog has been pestering the area for any significant amount of time, what you see may simply be the results of his efforts—namely a hot spot.

What to Do

Now ask yourself these questions:

Does your dog suffer from allergies? If so, be suspicious of any new foods or household products as possible sources of irritation. Eliminate any such items from his environment immediately, and try administering an appropriate dose of Benadryl. (See "How to Treat Your Dog's Allergic Symptoms" on page 25.)

Did your examination reveal any evidence of parasites? Fleas and/or their reddish-brown droppings are usually easy to identify, but other parasites, such as mites and lice, are more difficult. They are not identifiable by direct observation, but suspected based on the lesions they cause.

While an attached tick may be easy to spot, once it has dropped off, all you may see is a swollen, crusted blemish or just the aftermath of your dog's furious efforts to rid himself of the nuisance. If you identify parasites, use the appropriate treatment to eradicate them while you simultaneously treat the results of your dog's efforts. (See "How to Treat Your Dog's Fleas," "How to Treat Your Dog's Mites," and "How to Treat Remove a Tick from Your Dog" on page 22 and "How to Dress a Wound" on page 19.)

Does your dog appear to have dry, flaky patches of skin in the area? If so, they may simply be due to increased dryness from home heating or weather. Try adding omega-3 fatty acids to his diet. Do so cautiously; too much of this good thing can result in soft stools or diarrhea. Omega-3s are currently included in many commercially available diets, as well as in liquids or capsules. Check with your vet for dosage recommendations.

Did your exam reveal any distinct, identifiable lesions? These would be any abnormalities or irregularities in the skin surface, including wounds, growths, and irritations. A call to your vet may help rule out—or confirm—the need for a visit.

Did you see an angry, raw, irritated, possibly bloody or infected mess? This sounds like a classic hot spot, and it can be treated (if you're comfortable trying) by following the directions and advice in "My Dog Has a Hot Spot" on page 72.

My Dog Is
Rubbing or Licking Her Anus

Part of most dogs' repertoire of unsavory habits is the routine of licking their rectal region. Regardless of our disgust in having to observe the event, or even worse, hear it, it does serve a purpose. It enables our dogs to keep themselves relatively clean without the use of tissues. It also gives veterinarians a reason to lecture children on the dangers of letting dogs lick their faces!

If you find that your dog is spending an unusually great amount of time licking her anus or the area around it or even rubbing her bottom on the floor repeatedly, it should get your attention.

What to Look For

To perform an effective perianal (the technical term for that particular region of your dog's body) examination, follow the directions in "My Dog Is Dragging Her Bottom" on page 256. Look for anything unusual, including but not limited to foreign matter, crusts, residual feces, wounds, bleeding, and discharge.

What to Do

Now ask yourself these questions to determine what to do next:

Did your exam reveal any evidence of parasites? Typically, intestinal parasites will appear as dried worms or rice-like deposits around the edges of your dog's anus. If you see these, get your dog treated right away before there is a chance of spreading the parasites to other animals or members of your family. You can confirm the existence of parasites just by submitting a stool sample to your vet. If family members complain of intestinal cramping and/or diarrhea at this time, they should submit stool samples to their physicians as well.

Did you notice any bulging around your dog's anus in the five o'clock and/or seven o'clock regions? This would suggest that your dog's behavior has been prompted by the discomfort of her full anal sacs. These scent glands are often the source of incredible annoyance to dogs. You can help solve the problem at home if you're up to the task and have a strong stomach. (See "How to Empty Your Dog's Anal Sacs" on page 23.)

Did your examination reveal any open wounds in the area? Open wounds, typically in the three o'clock and/or nine o'clock regions, are often the result of an anal sac rupture. This can happen when the sacs become full to the point of bursting, and this area appears to be the point of least resistance. Your veterinarian is the best one to resolve this problem, which may require sedation and in extreme circumstances, surgical intervention. Get this taken care of right away.

Are there any unusual tissue masses in the area? Your dog's perianal region is a common location for a variety of tumors, both benign and malignant. Have your veterinarian examine any such growths to help decide whether a biopsy or surgical excision is appropriate.

My Dog Has

Something Stuck in His Ear

The ears are two of your dog's most sensitive anatomical structures. Always treat them with the utmost care and caution in the interest of both you and your dog's comfort and safety.

Warning

In the unusual event that you discover something apparently stuck in your dog's ear, do not lose your composure, but do proceed with caution! This is bound to be a very uncomfortable situation for your dog, and he is quite likely to be upset if he perceives any threat to the area around his head. Get a friend to help distract your dog with treats, toys, or anything that will keep his attention while you get a better look at his ear.

What to Look For

Your sole purpose is to identify the object and the severity of whatever damage it has caused. This is not a time for heroics. It is a time for efficient, level-headed assessment and resolution. With your helper keeping up an endless stream of treats, entertainment, etc., try to get a good look at the object and an idea of how uncomfortable its presence is to your dog. Sometimes just knowing exactly what the object is can give you a realistic idea of whether it is something that you might reasonably expect to remove yourself.

What to Do

Ask yourself the following questions:

Is the object large enough to identify from a distance? If so, and if you are absolutely certain that any attempt to remove it will result in no further trauma to your dog, you may wish to give it a try. Be sure to have clean towels or cloths to clean the area afterward. They can also be used to apply pressure to stop bleeding if necessary. (See "How to Control Bleeding" and "How to Clean a Wound" on page 18, and "How to Dress a Wound" on page 19.)

Is the object too small to identify from a distance, but seems to cause your dog little, if any, discomfort? If this is the case, cautiously try to manipulate the ear enough to get a closer look at the object. If it appears to be something familiar and reasonable to remove without incident (such as a tick, a burr, or a plastic toy) go ahead and give it a try. Have antiseptic and clean towels handy to treat it afterward. (See "How to Control Bleeding" on page 18, "How to Clean a Wound" on page 18, and "How to Dress a Wound" on page 19.)

My Dog Has
Something Stuck in Her Throat

Dogs are not rocket scientists. They are also, under ordinary circumstances, not likely to try to swallow something larger than their heads! As every Labrador retriever on the planet will attest to, there are many gray areas when it comes to food and toys, and the world is full of extraordinary circumstances.

If you think your dog has literally bit off more than she can chew, try to identify the object or substance. Many instances of items stuck in dogs' throats are false alarms, so before you rush to the emergency clinic, try to figure out whether your assessment is an accurate one.

What to Look For

Look, listen, and investigate should be the order of priority when it comes to a possible esophageal obstruction. Look at your dog first for signs of severe discomfort or overt panic. Listen for sounds that indicate a partially obstructed throat. This would sound like either a restricted wheeze on exhale, or a sharp, staccato cough (like what you would expect if blasts of air were being forced around a piece of hard plastic or wood). If you are still convinced that there is something lodged in your dog's throat, cautiously attempt to open her mouth and see for yourself. It may help to have a helper hold a flashlight for you while you peer in as far as your dog will permit.

What to Do

Ask yourself a few questions to determine what to do next:

Did your examination confirm the presence of a foreign object lodged in your dog's throat? If so, and if you are certain that you can get it out without further traumatizing your dog, go ahead and try. Otherwise, see your veterinarian, who can sedate your dog and remove the object without a struggle.

Did your examination reveal no evidence of a foreign body? This could mean that there is nothing stuck in your dog's throat, it could mean that whatever is there is just too far down to visualize, or it could mean that the choking attempts are the effects of some viral or bacterial infection. In each of these cases, the ultimate resolution will depend on either your dog's powers of recovery or your veterinarian's skills as a doctor. Don't wait until your dog is uncomfortable to consult your veterinarian.

My Dog Has Something Stuck in Her Throat

My Dog Has
Something Stuck in His Paw

Your dog's ability to function as an independent member of your household is directly related to his ability to move around on his own. If he manages to get something stuck in his paw, it is more than likely to hamper that ability dramatically. In many instances, you may be able to solve the problem on your own with the proper advice and direction.

What to Look For

Since your dog is probably already holding the affected paw in the air, take the opportunity to grasp his limb well above the paw and just hold it for a few moments, speaking soothingly to calm him. Once he is relaxed enough to proceed, slowly work your hand down the length of the limb, closing in on the carpus (wrist) if it is a front limb or the tarsus (ankle) if it is a rear limb. Your hand movements should approximate the action of a massage—rubbing, kneading, and pressing, slowly and gently. After crossing the carpal or tarsal joint, cautiously work your fingers between the digits, feeling for the foreign object while gauging your dog's tenderness. Finally, supinate (place the paw so the pads face upward, toward the ceiling) the paw. Look closely for any flaws in the pad surfaces, where the foreign body might be or have been lodged.

What to Do

Now ask yourself a few questions:

Were you able to identify the object during your exam? If so, and if it is something you feel comfortable removing yourself, put on your rubber gloves, grab some cotton gauze and disinfectant, and go for it. Find additional advice on wound treatment in "How to Clean a Wound" on page 18 and "How to Dress a Wound" on page 19.

Warning

As you conduct your exam, be alert to the fact that the object that's stuck in your dog's paw could be sharp enough to cut or penetrate your own skin, so go slowly!

Did your dog become too uncomfortable during your attempts to examine his paw? If so, and you still really want to try to solve this on your own, give your dog a weight-appropriate dose of an anti-inflammatory such as aspirin, Rimadyl, or Deramaxx (these last two are only available through your vet's office). Wait about 45 minutes, and try again. (See "How to Treat Your Dog with Anti-Inflammatories" on page 24.) Otherwise, have your vet take a look.

When to Get the Vet

If the amount of blood and/or pus is substantial, get your veterinarian involved right away.

Did your examination reveal any blood and/or pus? If it did, try dipping the entire paw in a cup of a 50/50 mix of water and hydrogen peroxide, drying it gently with cotton, and then attempting your exam again.

My Dog Has
Something Stuck in Her Rectum

Because dogs are literally incapable of inserting things into their rectums, there are only four ways an object can become lodged there. Foreign objects that your dog has swallowed or tumors that have grown in or near your dog's rectum can both appear to be stuck there. Objects that your dog has sat on could get stuck to the skin near your dog's rectum, or someone could have maliciously placed an object there. In any case, if any abnormal appearance in your dog's rectal region looks like a stuck object, your dog will need some help.

What to Look For

Choose a well-lit room, grab some tasty treats, don a pair of rubber gloves, and get a friend to help you. While your friend distracts your dog by feeding her treats, lift up her tail and look closely at her rectum. First assess whether the object is stuck to the skin surrounding the rectum or if it is actually emerging from inside the rectum. Next, check for blood and pus and signs of injury or infection. Finally, try to identify exactly what the object is and if it seems like something that you might be able to remove without harming your dog.

What to Do

Armed with the information from your exam, ask yourself the following questions:

Is there any blood present? In cases of rectal bleeding, determine the source of the blood. Does it appear to be coming from within your dog's rectum, from the skin or tissues surrounding the rectum, or from the object itself? Foreign objects that penetrate the skin around a dog's rectum are best removed by a veterinarian. If bleeding appears to actually be coming from the object, it is possible that the object is either a tumor or some sort of swollen tissue or blood-sucking parasite. These situations, too, should be evaluated by your veterinarian. If the bleeding is coming from the tissues around the rectum, get a better idea of the severity of the bleeding and the nature of its source by blotting the area with a hydrogen peroxide-soaked cloth or towel. If the source is insignificant, like a scratch or superficial cut, and has caused a scab to form (which you thought was a stuck

object), apply Bacitracin and see how the dog responds. (See "My Dog Is Bleeding from His Anus" on page 43.)

Is the object obviously something that your dog swallowed? You can remove soft, non-traumatizing objects such as socks, tampons, and plastic wrap by gently tugging on them with a gloved hand. If the object is something of a difficult or traumatic shape or material, it is probably best left for your veterinarian to remove once your dog is sedated.

My Dog Has Something Stuck in Her Rectum

When to Get the Vet

If you can't identify the object, take your dog to the vet. Unidentifiable objects are always best left for your veterinarian to see, identify, and treat or remove. As mentioned previously, these could be tumors, enlarged or impacted anal sacs, prolapsed rectal tissue, parasites, or simply some foreign object you don't recognize. (Passage through the entire digestive tract can change the appearance of many normal household items.)

My Dog's
Eyes Are Red

Many pet owners feel queasy just talking about their dogs' eyes. As a result, reports on eye problems may be questionably accurate! When describing redness, therefore, it is important to distinguish where the red is. (See the illustration on page 29.) Is it in the anterior chamber, (the portion between the cornea and the iris), the iris (the colored part of the eye), the sclera (the white part of the eye), or the conjunctiva (the tissue surrounding the globe and lining the eyelids)?

What to Look For

Place your dog in an area that affords enough light and space for his comfort and your ability to examine him. Get a flashlight with a bright beam. Cradle your dog's head in both your hands and look straight into his eyes. Observe the upper and lower lids, the tissues surrounding the eyes, and the part of his head that spans the area between his eyes.

Lift each upper lid and tug down on each lower lid to observe the tissues beneath them. Using the flashlight, shine it directly into each eye to check the way your dog's pupils respond. Also shine the flashlight from the side of your dog's eyes to see how it illuminates the clear portion at the front of each globe.

Place your thumb on the upper lid of each eye and press gently down on your dog's eyes in order to assess how hard the eyes feel underneath. By forcing the globes back slightly in their sockets, you will also allow your dog's third eyelids to rise passively, giving you a look at them as well.

Check your dog's ability to see by testing his menace reflex. With the palm of your hand facing your dog, move your hand swiftly from a position about eighteen inches from your dog's eye to within about three inches of your dog's eye. If your dog can see, he'll blink. The absence of that response is a strong indication of reduced or absent vision. Repeat the maneuver a few times to check your result, since some blind dogs may actually blink in response to the movement of air created by your hand.

What to Do

To figure out what to do next, ask yourself the following questions:

Did you notice any discoloration or swelling of the areas around your dog's eyes? This could represent the effects of some type of blunt trauma and explain the redness. It could also be an infection or a mass of some sort. If it is warm and tender, but your dog is acting fine, try applying cold compresses to reduce the swelling and discomfort. If it begins to drain fluid, blood, or pus, see your vet for help.

Are your dog's pupils equal in size and do they both get smaller when you shine the flashlight into them? If so, then your dog's eyes are behaving normally, and the redness should be treated as just an eye symptom. If they are unequal in size or they behave unequally when exposed to direct light, then there is something affecting part of your dog's nervous system. Watch this closely and if no improvement is noted within 24 hours consult a veterinary ophthalmologist.

Is the redness associated with the conjunctival tissues that surround the eye? If so, and there is no blood present, but an overall, angry redness, your dog has conjunctivitis. See "My Dog Has a 'Stye'" on page 183.

Does the redness look like a bulging pink growth coming from the lower corner of the eye closest to your dog's muzzle? If you see something like this and your dog is under two years of age, he probably has protrusion of the gland of the third eyelid, otherwise known as cherry eye. See "My Dog Has a Problem with His Third Eyelid" on page 181.

Does the redness appear to be confined to the whites of your dog's eyes? If so, and if the redness is in the form of streaks of red from the iris and radiating out toward the lids, your dog's eyes are bloodshot. See "My Dog's Eyes Are Bloodshot" on page 169.

Is the redness contained within the colored iris? If so, and if the redness moves with the iris when the pupil reacts to light, then it is probably a normal pigment variation. If the redness seems independent of the actions of the iris, it may be blood in the eye. If this is the case, it may gradually get resorbed. If your dog is not suffering, wait a day or two to see if there appears to be some improvement. If not, have your vet take a look. If, when you shine a light from the side of the eyes, the redness appears to be in the anterior chamber, it may be associated with an inflammatory process called uveitis. This could be serious and should be examined by a veterinary ophthalmologist.

Do your dog's eyes appear to be bulging more than usual? Refer to "My Dog's Eyes Are Bulging" on page 171.

My Dog's Eyes Are Red

Eyes Are Bloodshot

If the whites of your dog's eyes are streaked with red like she has been swimming with her eyes open in a heavily chlorinated pool for the last hour, they are indeed bloodshot. But how they got that way may be tricky to identify. The most important thing to figure out is whether there are any other symptoms in conjunction with your dog's red-streaked eyes.

My Dog's
Eyes Are
Bloodshot

What to Look For

Follow the same procedure outlined in "My Dog's Eyes Are Red" on page 167. Pay particular attention to any evidence of conjunctivitis, such as extreme redness, blood in the eye itself, or increased hardness to one or both eyes.

Also, check your dog for other signs of bruising, especially in the mouth. Broken blood vessels in this area will look like little sunbursts of red to dark red color.

What to Do

Now ask yourself these questions:

When pressing down on the upper lids, do the globes beneath feel surprisingly hard? If so, your dog's bloodshot eyes may be a result of a serious disease called glaucoma. This is a problem that often responds well to aggressive, immediate treatment and, consequently, should be evaluated by a veterinarian as soon as possible.

Do you notice any pus in your dog's eyes? Pus always appears when there is bacterial infection present, such as bacterial conjunctivitis. This condition often occurs in conjunction with bloodshot eyes and can be quite contagious, so handle the situation carefully. Wear gloves, throw away or wash thoroughly any materials you use to treat your dog's eyes, and keep her away from other dogs until the symptoms have resolved. Flush her eyes repeatedly with sterile saline and treat them with any of the many commercially available soothing eye drops, such as Visine. If this doesn't seem to be helping within two days, see your vet.

My Dog's Eyes Are Bloodshot | 169

Is your dog rubbing or scratching at her eyes? Dogs with allergies to their food or environment may develop very itchy eyes. The constant rubbing usually causes their eyes to become bloodshot. If you suspect that this is your dog's only symptom, try giving a weight-appropriate dose of Benadryl. (See "How to Treat Your Dog's Allergic Symptoms" on page 25.) While this may only be a temporary help, it will at least give you an idea if you're right about the reason for the eyes being bloodshot.

Since Benadryl has a mild sedative quality, you can use the time that your dog is affected to flush the eyes and use some soothing eye drops. If this helps, try continuing the flushing and soothing drops while reducing the frequency of the Benadryl until the redness is completely gone and the rubbing and/or scratching has stopped. If you don't succeed, you may need your vet to prescribe the appropriate medications.

Do you notice any cloudiness to your dog's eyes? Cloudy eyes in any dog are always worrisome. This could be a sign of corneal ulceration, developing cataracts, uveitis, glaucoma, or other serious disease processes. Have your vet take a look.

Is there any blood in the eyes? Blood in the eyes without other symptoms could be the result of some trauma and may resorb on its own. If it doesn't begin to resolve within two days, see your vet.

My Dog's Eyes Are Bloodshot

When to Get the Vet

- Any sign of cloudiness, particularly in a young dog, should prompt an immediate visit to your veterinarian.

- Did you notice any other signs of bruising that resulted from trauma, especially in the mouth? If so, get your dog to the vet immediately. This kind of inappropriate bruising could be the sign of a blood clotting problem.

My Dog's
Eyes Are Bulging

If you are the proud owner of one of the many brachycephalic breeds, such as the pug, Pekingese, Boston terrier, or shih tzu, you are quite familiar with bulging eyes! These dogs are distinguished by their protruding exposed eyes, extremely short pushed-in noses, and small nostrils. You are also likely to be all too familiar with what a nuisance it can be to treat the problems that go along with those exposed eyeballs.

When your dog's eyes appear to be bulging more than you are accustomed to, it is always a reason to be concerned. Take some time to examine both eyes carefully and pay special attention to how willing your dog is to tolerate the examination process.

What to Look For

Put on a pair of rubber gloves. With your dog in a comfortable position in a well-lit room, cradle his head in your hands and look him straight in the eyes. Pay strict attention to the symmetry of his eyes, looking for differences in shape, position, color, sensitivity, and response to light. Look at all of the structures associated with the eyes, including the upper and lower lids, the conjunctiva, or soft pink tissue immediately surrounding the eyeball, the sclera, or white of the eye, iris, pupil, and the third eyelid. The last of these will be difficult to view in a bulging-eyed dog.

To get a look at it, place your thumb on the upper lid and, by placing gentle pressure on that lid, force the globe of the eye back into its socket. In the process, the third eyelid should rise passively from the lower corner of the eye closest to the muzzle. Use a bright flashlight to check your dog's pupils' response to light.

In addition, check the anterior chambers of your dog's eyes by shining the flashlight beam from the side, checking for any cloudiness in the forward-most portion (anterior chamber) of each globe. Finally, evaluate your dog's ability to see out of each eye. This test is to check his menace reflex. With the palm of your hand facing your dog, move your hand swiftly from a position about eighteen inches from your dog's eye to within about three inches of your dog's eye. A sighted dog will exhibit a menace reflex by blinking. The absence of that response is a strong indication of reduced or absent vision. Repeat the maneuver a few times to check your result, since some blind dogs may actually blink in response to the movement of air created by your hand. Be cautious, however, as most dogs do not find this procedure easy to tolerate.

Bulging Eyes

What to Do

Next, ask yourself these questions:

Has your dog recently suffered any blunt trauma? Any type of solid blow to the head or body of a dog can cause enough intracranial pressure to result in a bulging eye or eyes. In some extreme cases, the eye will actually pop right out of its socket! If you think trauma is the reason for the bulging, but your dog appears to be other-

wise healthy, try applying a cold compress to the affected side of your dog's face and give the eye some time to return to its normal position. Give this some time, but no more than a week, for improvement. See your vet if the situation does not resolve.

Has your dog been scratching or rubbing at his eyes? Dogs with painful, irritated, or itchy eyes are likely to scratch or rub them aggressively. Over time this can cause swelling and bulging. In such cases it is important to correct the source of the discomfort in order to get them to stop the self trauma before you can expect the eye position to resolve. Initially, use an Elizabethan collar, which you can buy at pet supply stores, to protect the eyes from further trauma. Then follow the directions in "My Dog Has a 'Stye'" on page 183. If this doesn't dramatically improve the problem within a day, see your vet. Corneal abrasions and ulcerations will often seem just like simple irritations, but they won't respond as well to simple at-home therapy.

When you pressed down on your dog's upper lids, did his eyeballs feel unusually hard? Rises in intraocular pressure usually occur as a result of the disease called glaucoma. Immediate veterinary care for such a case may save the dog's sight, so don't waste any time if you notice this during your exam.

When you pressed down on your dog's upper lids, was it painful for him? This could also be due to glaucoma, which is often quite painful. Alternatively, it could be due to a retrobulbar abscess. See "My Dog Cries Out When She Tries to Open Her Mouth" on page 215.

Does your dog appear to be sensitive to light? See "My Dog's Eyes Are Squinting" below.

**My Dog's
Eyes Are
Squinting**

My Dog's
Eyes Are Squinting

It may be cute when your dog appears to be letting you in on a secret by winking in your direction, but winking is not a normal part of dogs' social repertoire. What you're seeing is known medically as blepharospasm. This squinting behavior is usually due to either irritation or photosensitivity—sensitivity to light. While squinting may be corrected using at-home means, it is never something that should be ignored or overlooked.

What to Look For

Follow the directions for examining your dog's eyes in "My Dog's Eyes Are Red" on page 167.

What to Do

Answering the questions in "My Dogs Eyes Are Red" on page 167 and the ones that follow here should help you figure out why your dog is squinting and what you can and should do about it:

Does your dog stop squinting in the darkness or shade? If so, then your dog is photosensitive. This could be due to any irritation that might cause abnormally dilated pupils, such as a retrobulbar abscess or a corneal ulcer. Regardless of the source of the photosensitivity, it is always a symptom that requires veterinary intervention.

Is your dog trying to scratch or rub the affected eyes? Start by applying an Elizabethan collar to prevent any further trauma to the eye. Next, employ the techniques for flushing your dog's eyes in "How to Flush and Treat Your Dog's Itchy, Irritated Eyes" on page 21. Don't

assume that this is the end of the story. If your dog has an injury or damage to any of the tissues associated with the eye, the flushing will only serve as a temporary, pain-reducing measure. A variety of eye problems—including corneal ulcers, bacterial conjunctivitis, and periorbital masses—may cause enough discomfort to prompt scratching and/or rubbing. Plan on seeing your vet if the simple flush and soothe technique doesn't solve the problem within a few days.

My Dog's
Pupils Are Large

Enlarged or dilated pupils are normal in dogs when they are in dim lighting or shade, or if they are highly stimulated, either positively or negatively. But if your dog's pupils are widely dilated all the time, regardless of the lighting or his level of excitement, it is abnormal and should be further investigated.

What to Look For

Follow the directions for examining your dog's eyes as outlined in "My Dog's Eyes Are Bulging" on page 171.

What to Do

Ask yourself these questions to figure out why your dog's pupils are large:

Is your dog blind? If your dog shows no menace reflex (see "My Dog's Eyes Are Red" on page 167 for instructions on how to test this), or if the pupils fail to respond to bright, direct light, there is the distinct possibility that blindness is the reason for your dog's dilated pupils. Without the ability to perceive the influx of light through the widely dilated pupil, your dog's nervous system will be unable to respond and contract the iridal muscles responsible for narrowing down those pupils. Don't resign yourself to your dog's blindness, however, without a thorough exam by a veterinary ophthalmologist. Some forms of blindness can be transient and/or correctable.

Does your dog appear to be excited or agitated? Excitement, pain, or agitation could be the reason for the dilation of your dog's pupils. If so, the pupils may fail to respond to light even though the dog's menace reflex remains effective. Try removing your dog from whatever source of excitement or irritation may be present and then re-examine his eyes. Also examine the possibility that your dog may be experiencing some form of pain. If pain is the reason, treating it successfully should resolve the pupillary problem.

Does your dog show other behavioral or neurological signs such as imbalance, disorientation, or failure to recognize certain people familiar to him? Dogs with abnormally dilated pupils, especially when the pupils are of unequal size, should undergo a thorough neurological evaluation. Signs of cranial nerve damage are often enough to raise suspicion of an intracranial tumor. In this case, your vet might suggest a CAT scan.

When to Get the Vet

- If your dog has recently suffered head trauma, the resultant swelling of parts of the brain can result in the neurological symptoms we are describing. If your dog has no other symptoms, watch him closely over the next twenty-four hours. The symptoms may resolve spontaneously within that period. If they don't, or if they worsen, take your dog to your veterinarian.

- Has your dog recently gotten into any unusual chemicals or medications? Since many toxins have a direct effect on the nervous system, it is common for exposure to result in abnormal behaviors or neurological symptoms. Some products may even cause temporary blindness. If you know what chemicals or medications your dog has possibly ingested or inhaled, call the ASPCA National Animal Poison Control Center at 888-426-4435 for immediate advice. Plan to make a trip to the nearest animal emergency facility as well.

My Dog's Pupils Are Large

My Dog's Pupils Are Small

My Dog's
Pupils Are
Small

Similar to the situation when your dog's pupils are abnormally large, you should be just as concerned if you suddenly notice that her pupils are unusually small. The pupils act like the aperture of a camera. Normally, like the operation of an aperture, the pupils constrict under conditions of bright light. This is the brain's way of protecting the sensitive photoreceptive cells of the retina. Constriction of the pupils under any condition other than bright light is immediately considered a problem.

What to Look For

Employ the examination techniques in "My Dog's Eyes Are Red" on page 167.

What to Do

Next, ask yourself these questions:

Has your dog recently suffered blunt trauma to the head? Constricted or "pin-point" pupils following blunt trauma is never a good sign. The good news, though, is it will often resolve with time. But if your dog's pupils change from small to non-reactive to light, the prognosis is grave.

Has your dog recently been acting differently? If so, suspect some type of poisoning or intracranial problem, such as a tumor, a stroke, or a bleed. See your vet immediately in any instance when small pupils coexist with other symptoms.

When to Get the Vet

- Has your dog recently ingested any chemicals or medications? Toxins can cause a variety of neurological abnormalities. If your dog has swallowed or inhaled something that you can identify, immediately call the ASPCA National Animal Poison Control Center at 888-426-4435 for advice. If you don't know what the substance was, head directly to the emergency facility.

- See your veterinarian if the pupils don't return to their normal size and ability to respond to light within twenty-four hours.

My Dog's

Pupils Are of Different Sizes

Mammals (this includes both you and your dog) are all about bilateral symmetry. This includes every aspect of your dog's eyes, and specifically, in this case, his pupils. A particularly interesting aspect of the mammalian oculomotor system is that it responds equally to stimulation. This means that if you shine a light in one of your dog's eyes, both pupils will constrict equally. This is known as the consensual response. So, if you ever notice that your dog's pupils are of unequal size, regardless of the lighting, something is seriously wrong.

What to Look For

Follow the examination techniques outlined in "My Dog's Eyes Are Bulging" on page 171.

What to Do

Now ask yourself the following questions:

Has your dog recently suffered any form of head trauma? Trauma to the head is probably the most common reason for anisocoria, or unequal pupil size. It means that there is something affecting the nerves that travel between the eyes and the brain. If the trauma occurred recently and your dog is showing no other negative or worrisome signs, it is reasonable to wait for up to twenty-four hours to see if the pupils return to normal. If you don't notice any improvement, have your dog seen by a veterinary ophthalmologist.

Do you notice any other symptoms associated with either eye? Other symptoms that occur in just one eye could cause either eye to respond by exhibiting pupillary dilation or constriction. Check closely for discolorations, growths, and unusual sagging or tightening of the structures of, and associated with, both eyes. Other findings, depending on their severity, may dictate your course of action. If there is any doubt about what to do when it comes to your dog's eyes, always opt to have your vet take a look.

Has your dog been scratching or rubbing either one of his eyes? Repeated trauma to one eye could result in either pupillary dilation or constriction, but it's more likely that the reason behind the scratching or rubbing would also be the cause of the change in the size of the pupil. Try using an Elizabethan collar, which you can buy at pet supplies stores, to prevent your dog from continuing to traumatize the eye for the time being. Also try following the techniques for flushing and soothing the eye that are outlined in "How to Flush and Treat Your Dog's Itchy, Irritated Eyes" on page 21. If that doesn't help within a day or two, call your dog's vet.

Has your dog recently gotten into any plants, chemicals, or medications? It is unlikely that an inhaled or ingested plant, chemical, or medication would cause a uni-

When to Get the Vet

If your dog was exposed to a plant, chemical, or medication and you flush his eyes repeatedly, but you don't notice improvement within twenty-four hours, seek the help of a veterinary ophthalmologist.

lateral change in one of your dog's eyes, but it could cause a pre-existing condition to become obvious. Alternatively, direct exposure of one eye to a plant, chemical, or medication could easily result in a direct effect on that eye. Try flushing both eyes repeatedly with sterile saline solution until you are sure that anything that might have been trapped in any portion of either eye has probably been dislodged and flooded away.

My Dog's Pupils Are of Different Sizes

My Dog Has
Dark Pigment
in Her Eye

Except in cases of true albinism, dogs' irises—the colored part of the eye—range in color from pale blue to dark brown. However, variations in development before a puppy is born can cause color variations within the iris resulting in multiple colors within one eye. Normal variations usually appear as wedge-shaped, streaks, or bursts of a different color within an iris, such as a streak of brown in a blue eye. Abnormal pigment can often be easily identified and is not always dangerous.

What to Look For

You likely don't have to get too close to your dog to see an unusual spot in one or both of her eyes. Simply take a look at both of her eyes and note where the pigment is and what shape it is.

Next, you want to see if the pigment is fixed or moves around. Observe your dog first while she is standing looking directly at you. Note the location of the area of pigment. Next, place your dog on her side and again note the position of the pigment. Finally, place your dog on her back with her head on the ground and her throat facing the sky and examine the placement of the pigment. If the pigmented area is fixed, it will remain in the same location regardless of your dog's position. If it is a mass of some sort, its point of origin will remain fixed but its body may shift with your dog's position. (Think of a bean bag stapled to the face of a clock. The bag will tend to droop with the pull of gravity, toward the number six on the dial. If you then rotated the clock face so that another number was facing downward, the bag would droop toward it.)

What to Do

Now that you've gotten a good look at what's going on, ask yourself the following questions:

How old is your dog? If your dog is a puppy or if she is an adult that you just purchased or adopted, the pigment you are noticing may be a perfectly normal congenital trait. However, if your dog is an adult and this is a new development, it is more likely cause for concern.

Is the pigment confined to the iris, or colored part of the eye, or is it elsewhere within the globe? Normal pigmentation within the eye is always associated with the iris. If the pigment you are questioning appears to be separate from or only partially within the iris, it is worth investigating with your vet. If the pigment is entirely within the iris and your dog seems unaffected by it, keep a close watch on it either until changes in size, shape, or color are noticed or until your dog's next veterinary visit, whichever comes first.

Is the pigment well-defined with clear, crisp edges or are the boundaries amorphous, fading into the surrounding, colored part of the iris? While rough, poorly defined edges to an area of pigment are more worrisome than those with clear outlines, not all such lesions are dangerous. Many pigments in the iris are simply areas of different color, similar to freckles on the skin, called iris nevi. Some iris nevi remain the same throughout a dog's life, never causing a problem. However, others can become dangerous, and eventually be identified as melanocytomas or malignant melanomas.

If the edges are rough, have it seen. If they are crisp and clean, monitor them closely for changes or until your next veterinary appointment.

When to Get the Vet

All intraocular, or implanted, masses should be evaluated by a veterinarian, preferably a veterinary ophthalmologist.

Is the pigment the only problem with your dog's eye? Dogs with tumors in their eyes will often have other symptoms, such as glaucoma or inflammation of the eye, which is called chronic uveitis. If your dog seems to have more than one symptom relating to his eye, it is always best to have him seen by a veterinary ophthalmologist who has the instruments to make more precise, accurate diagnoses than a general practitioner.

Is the pigment fixed or does it move within the eye? If it is an iridal cyst, it may be free floating, in which case it will fall to the bottom of your dog's eye regardless of his position. These are benign and only require intervention if they become large enough, numerous enough, or fixed in a position to obstruct vision.

My Dog Has a
Problem with His
Third Eyelid

One major difference between your eyes and those of your dog is that your dog has a third, protective lid. Under normal circumstances that membrane, referred to as the third eyelid, rests passively beneath your dog's lower lid. It should rise to cover the globe of the eye only under extreme circumstances when the eyeball retracts or gets pushed back in its socket. So, if you ever notice that third lid rising above the rim of your dog's lower eyelid, consider it an indication that something is wrong.

That third eyelid also contains a secretory a gland that helps lubricate the eye. Usually the gland is hidden beneath your dog's lower eyelid. But if it protrudes and you can see it, that's called cherry eye. This usually looks like a red, bulbous swelling arising from the lower corner of your dog's eye, closest to his muzzle. It's most common in the brachycephalic breeds like the pug, Pekingese, shih tzu, etc., because of their bulging eyes. These breeds tend to have less physical space for the gland, forcing it up and out.

Cherry Eye

What to Look For

Start by conducting a typical eye examination like the one outlined in "My Dog's Eyes Are Red" on page 167. Be as thorough as possible, looking for signs of irritation, asymmetry, or abnormal structures or appearance. As part of this exam, you will force the third eyelid of your dog's other eye to rise passively and you can use it for comparative purposes.

What to Do

Now, ask yourself the following questions to figure out how to proceed:

Has your dog recently suffered any blunt trauma to the head? If a blow to the head has resulted in a protruding third eyelid, there is a good chance that bruising and/or inflammation are responsible for the problem. Try applying a cold compress for a few minutes up to thirty minutes then check the eye again. This may solve the problem.

Applying Cold Compress

When to Get the Vet

If *both* of your dog's third eyelids are showing, you will need to see your veterinarian right away.

Does the eye appear to be fine in every other respect? If it does and the other eye is healthy, try a closer examination of the way your dog's eyes respond to light. See if both eyes react similarly to light. If they don't, there may be some form of cranial lesion responsible for the abnormality. This would be an appropriate time to seek the advice of a veterinary ophthalmologist.

Is your dog having a difficult time keeping that eye open? If your dog is squinting with the affected eye, particularly in direct light, it could mean that the eye has been injured and the third lid is doing its best to cover the injury and promote healing. This will work to promote scar tissue formation, but also cause a resulting blind spot. An ophthalmologist will be much more likely to solve the problem and to preserve your dog's full vision.

Is there any discharge from the eye? An accumulation of yellowish to green material in the eye periodically each day is a good indication that your dog's eye is infected. Try treating the eye by following the directions outlined in "How to Flush and Treat Your Dog's Itchy, Irritated Eyes" on page 21 (see also "My Dog Has a Discharge from Her Eye" on page 111). If your treatment is not successful within three days, see your vet for a thorough eye exam or a referral.

Is the exposed portion of the third eyelid bulbous and angry red in color? If so, your dog probably has cherry eye, a common problem in young dogs of a number of breeds. The solution is usually a simple surgical procedure.

Occasionally, however, when cherry eye results from chronic inflammation, giving your dog ophthalmic antibiotics and/or steroids will clear it up. More often than not, cherry eye is a permanent problem that occurs for the first time before the dog reaches two years of age. After a few weeks of unsuccessful attempts at treatment, surgical correction is the solution. This is not a dangerous procedure, though, and in the hands of a skilled surgeon your dog will be comfortable and fully functioning a short while after surgery.

Although many veterinarians are comfortable performing the procedure, a veterinary ophthalmologist is best equipped and probably the most experienced. He or she will also be good to establish a relationship with, since breeds that get cherry eye are usually prone to other eye problems later in life.

My Dog Has
a "Stye"

If your dog is looking at you sadly with droopy, red-rimmed, uncomfortable-looking eyes that you know have her scratching and rubbing, you might think she has what's commonly called a stye. But actually, she's probably dealing with a nasty case of conjunctivitis, which is simply inflammation of the mucous membranes that line the inner surface of the eyelids.

Conjunctivitis can be caused by five major things: trauma, bacteria, viruses, foreign matter, and allergies.

My Dog Has a "Stye"

What to Look For

Wearing rubber gloves, under good light or with the help of someone holding a flashlight, take a good look at both of your dog's eyes. Check for any foreign material that may be irritating your dog's eyes and look for pus and mucus.

The important immediate distinction to make is whether there is any injury to the cornea. Unfortunately, without the aid of your veterinarian, you probably won't be able to determine whether your dog has a corneal injury. What you can do is treat your dog's problem in a way that may solve the problem if there isn't an injury, and then if it doesn't respond, get your vet's help.

When to Get the Vet

After cleaning your dog's eyes two to three times a day for two days, if you don't notice improvement, you will need your vet's help.

What to Do

Here's what to ask and do to get your dog on the road to recovery:

Did you see any foreign material, pus, or mucus? Use a squirt bottle filled with sterile saline solution to liberally flush out your dog's eyes. Once you're confident that any matter that might have been irritating your dog has been flooded out of her eyes, use a cotton swab to clear out any pus, mucus, or other tenacious material that could have remained behind.

Following this process, place a few drops of one of the commercially available soothing eye drops, such as Artificial Tears or Visine, in your dog's eyes to reduce any residual discomfort. Repeat this process two to three times a day. Most cases of conjunctivitis will respond at least partially to this treatment alone. Some will resolve completely within a few days.

My Dog

Is Limping

When a dog limps, he is usually doing so because one or more of his limbs hurt or because his normal range of motion has somehow been altered. The most important initial distinction to make is whether the limp is bad enough to prevent the dog from bearing any weight on the affected limb.

What to Look For

The next step is to try to first identify which limb has the problem and then to pinpoint exactly where the source of the problem is. To figure out which limb is bothering your dog, watch him walk for a while. Usually a dog will come down heavier on his healthy limb and avoid putting substantial weight on the limb that is bothering him. You can identify this by observing your dog's head when he walks. The comfortable limb will be placed on the ground and his head will go down at the same time. His head will tend to come up when the uncomfortable limb is on the ground.

Next, you'll need to examine the limb that's bothering your dog. I like to start by examining a limb that I'm pretty sure is uninjured, starting at the toes and work-

Warning

Always proceed with caution when examining a dog suspected of being in pain. Extreme pain will cause a dog to revert to his most primitive instincts, which include biting any creature that approaches, even his beloved owners! With that in mind, a thorough yet cautious exam will usually reveal the reason for the limp. If at any time during the exam your dog indicates discomfort or pain, stop immediately.

ing my way toward the body. This gives me an idea how the dog responds to pressure he is not accustomed to so I can compare it to his response to similar pressure on the affected limb. It may also instill some trust in a dog, who might otherwise think I'm trying to take advantage of his injury.

Examine each of the following areas:

TOES: First check each of the toenails for cracking or splitting. A cracked or split nail will expose the sensitive tissue and blood vessels beneath and can be extremely painful. A simple crack with no bleeding and a mild limp usually does not require veterinary intervention, but any crack that results in bleeding could require sedation, thorough cleansing, trimming, and possibly cauterization and bandaging. Examine each toe individually and gently move and squeeze them to check for possible injury. Bruised and even fractured toes will cause a limp but don't always require intervention. X-rays, however, are usually necessary to evaluate a toe that remains painful even after a few days of rest.

WEBBING: The spaces between many dogs' toes are connected with soft skin that stretches and provides a large surface area for swimming. This skin is often sliced by sharp objects a dog is likely to walk on, such as glass and metal. If such a slice is bleeding, stitches and antibiotics are usually appropriate. In addition, foreign objects—such as gravel, tar, and thumbtacks—can get wedged in between a dog's toes, causing a limp that should resolve once they are removed. A variety of masses, cysts, and infections, however, can arise between a dog's toes and should be evaluated by your veterinarian.

PADS: Dogs have six protective pads on their front paws (this includes the one at the back of their carpi, or "wrists") and five on their hind paws. These are usually leathery in texture and are simply a thicker form of skin than exists elsewhere on a dog's body, with a higher percentage of hardened protein-rich tissue called keratin.

Like the rest of a dog's paw, these pads can be sliced by sharp objects and can bleed if cut through the outer "horny" layer. They can also develop warts, become sensitive from walking on hot surfaces, and can grow abnormally hard, dry, or irritated due to chemical exposure or dietary imbalances.

JOINTS: Any one of the many joints in a dog's limbs can be the source of enough discomfort to result in a limp. Discounting the multiple joints of the paws, there are three major joints in each limb of a dog. A dog's front limb consists of the carpus (or wrist), the elbow, and the shoulder. The hind limb includes the tarsus (or ankle), the stifle (or knee), and the hip. Check each of these joints by applying light pressure and then increasing the pressure to moderate. If no discomfort is noted, try gently lifting the limb and slowly duplicate a normal range of motion. By supporting the entire limb, you can examine each joint in isolation and hopefully identify the source of the limp.

BONES: There are approximately 321 bones in a dog's body. Bruising or fracturing of many of them could cause enough discomfort to result in a limp. Check the leg bones by visual observation first. Look for swelling, bleeding, or other signs of injury or asymmetry. Similar to examining the joints, examine the long bones of the limbs by applying mild to moderate pressure along their entire length. You can verify any suspected irregularity or abnormality by comparing it to the other healthy limb.

What to Do

Exam complete, ask yourself the following questions:

Could your dog have suffered any trauma over the previous few hours? If the dog has been out of your sight, is it possible that he was involved in an accident of some sort, jumped or fell from a height, was bitten by another animal, or stung by an insect? If that's the case, refer to "My Dog Was Hit by a Car or Heavy Object" on page 268, "My Dog Fell from a Height" on page 266 or "How to Treat Your Dog's Allergic Symptoms" on page 25.

How old is your dog? Your dog's age is important in trying to get to the bottom of the problem. Young dogs can experience limb discomfort from developmental issues that older dogs wouldn't have, and older dogs can suffer from various cancers and forms of arthritis that puppies would be less likely to experience.

Did you notice a cracked toenail? Refer to "My Dog Has a Broken Toenail" on page 79.

Do you suspect a fracture? If there is significant swelling and pain and your dog refuses to bear any weight on the affected limb, assume there is a fracture and get your dog to a veterinary hospital, following the advice in "How to Transport an Injured Dog" on page 20.

Are your dog's footpads dry or cracked? If so, see the chapter "My Dog Has Cracked Footpads" on page 63.

Does the pain appear to be isolated to a specific joint? If so, try treating with a weight-appropriate dose of a buffered or enteric-coated aspirin product. If that doesn't help within a day, see your vet for a more thorough evaluation.

My Patient's Story

When Ned called me one Saturday afternoon, he sounded distraught. "Doc, I know you haven't been out here to see the girls in a while, and I know it's a Saturday, but Nellie has broken her back leg real bad and can't stand up. Could you please come take a look? She seems like she's in a lot of pain."

After asking him a few questions I had a pretty good idea that the leg was not broken, but knew she needed some attention nonetheless.

When I examined her, Nellie was quite enthusiastic, but didn't like it when I approached her tail end. While she was on her side, though, she allowed me to manipulate all four of her legs without a complaint. While putting her hind legs through their full range of motion, I noticed that her anus appeared irritated. With Ned distracting Nellie with a never-ending stream of sliced hot dogs, I was able to empty her remarkably full anal sacs, after which she bounded away, quite pleased with herself!

If none of the above questions help you to figure out the cause of the limp, give it a little time. Many limps are temporary and will disappear within an hour of being noticed. Others are the result of serious disease or injury and will require dramatic intervention, including surgery and possibly even the placement of supportive, corrective hardware such as pins, plates, screws or artificial joints. In general, a limp that causes a dog to hold a limb in the air and/or cry out in pain is one needing immediate attention. When a dog is favoring a limb by putting cautious pres-sure on it, less immediate action is required, but continued observation is important and professional help should be sought if the limp persists.

When to Get the Vet

If your dog won't bear any weight on the affected limb, get him to the vet-erinarian immediately.

My Dog
Keeps Falling Down

Although most of us who own aging dogs are accustomed to seeing our dogs lounging on their sides, dogs are, in fact, designed to support their own weight for lengthy periods of time. Their four sturdy legs serve them well in this respect, and their musculoskeletal system is structured to withstand a great deal of wear and tear.

With this in mind, it should be both a surprise and a concern when a dog repeatedly stumbles and/or falls down. You need to figure out whether the stumbling or falling is due to weakness, pain, or loss of balance. Further investigation may reveal whether the cause is musculoskeletal, neurological, or cardiologic in nature.

What to Look For

Start by placing your dog in a balanced standing position on a flat, even surface. Sit or stand facing her and observe her closely. Look at the way she holds her body, paying particular attention to the carriage of her head and neck, the position of her tail, and the symmetry of her four limbs.

To begin your closer examination, cradle your dog's head in your hands and look closely at her eyes for any unusual movements or differences in pupil size or response to light. Move her head gently in all directions to check for stiffness or pain. Examine her ears for heat, pain, and discharge. Open her mouth to check for evidence of pain, growths, or infection.

Next, move on to your dog's spine. Using your fingers in a "walking" manner, apply gentle but firm pressure to each sequential intervertebral space, checking for discomfort or weakness. Finally, examine each of your dog's limbs, first by lifting it up and placing it down with the top of the paw "knuckled" under. Check for your dog's reaction to this incorrect placement.

Next, lift each limb and put it through a normal range of motion, checking for discomfort, grinding, or cracking. If your dog is so unsteady on her feet that she has trouble maintaining an upright position during this part of the exam, lay her on her side and conduct the limb exams in that position. If, during the "knuckling" exercise, your dog fails to correct the position you have forced her paw into, pinch the toes of that paw and watch to see if she pulls her paw back.

What to Do

Next, ask yourself the following questions:

Does your dog's head tilt to one side? If so, your dog may be off balance due to an ear infection or some other process that is affecting her inner ear, resulting in vestibular syndrome. Take your dog to the vet to be evaluated and treated. Only in very few cases do such presentations resolve spontaneously.

Are your dog's eyes moving in a rapid, repetitious, side-to-side or up-and-down pattern? This is called nystagmus, and it is often associated with vestibular disease.

Does your dog complain, flinch, or drop to the floor when you palpate her intervertebral spaces? If so, there is a strong likelihood that she has some form of spinal disease, such as intervertebral disk disease, spinal arthritis, or even some type of vertebral mass. Take her to your vet or a veterinary neurologist.

Is your dog's tail tucked up underneath her? This is usually a sign of fear, discomfort, or anxiety. It's the discomfort that is of the most concern, particularly if it is spinal in origin, as mentioned above.

A tucked tail can also be an indication that your dog's spine or anal sacs are bothering her. Be sure to be thorough when you examine her spine in the hopes of identifying the source of the problem. Any spinal pain should be evaluated by a veterinary neurologist. Anal sac discomfort, on the other hand, would be an incidental finding, correctable by following the advice in "How to Empty Your Dog's Anal Sacs" on page 23.

Does your dog fail to right her paws when you perform the "knuckling" maneuver? If so, she has a proprioceptive deficit. This means she doesn't know where her paw is, like your leg feels when it "falls asleep." This is a neurological problem and should be evaluated by a veterinary neurologist. If the "pinching" procedure doesn't cause your dog to withdraw the paw, you should see the neurologist right away. If the paw is briskly withdrawn, then the proprioceptive deficit may resolve on its own and it's all right to wait a day or two for improvement. Sometimes an inflammatory process can cause the problem with proprioception, and once the inflammation improves, so does the proprioception.

Did your exam reveal nothing abnormal? Your dog's problem may be due to weakness or circulatory problems. Make sure that your dog has had enough to eat over the last few hours. If she hasn't, try rubbing some Karo corn syrup or pancake syrup over her gums. This will get some glucose into her system and improve her strength. If this seems to happen repeatedly and she appears to be drinking excessively, have her tested for diabetes. If you notice that your dog's gums and the tissues lining her mouth are pale, her circulation may be poor due to heart disease or some internal bleeding. Have her evaluated.

My Dog
Keeps Losing His Balance

Most dogs are not drinkers, so they never have a good excuse for losing their balance, especially when you consider that they have four, not two, legs to stand on. If your dog's balance seems off, it is always worth looking into. The possible reasons that should be sought to explain the incoordination, or ataxia, are infection, systemic illness, toxin ingestion, dehydration, electrolyte imbalance, and head trauma or other intracranial problems such as hemorrhage, stroke, aneurysm, or tumors.

What to Look For

You'll need to conduct three separate exams. First, do an ocular/neurological exam like the one outlined in "My Dog's Eyes Are Bulging" on page 171. Second, perform a thorough ear exam, as described in "My Dog Has a Discharge Coming from His Ear" on page 113, looking for evidence of discharge of any kind, particularly if it is yellowish to greenish in color and foul-smelling. Finally, perform a spinal exam, like the one in "My Dog Is Stiff" on page 200.

What to Do

Next ask yourself the following questions to figure out what to do:

Has your dog been suffering from illness, infection, or high fever recently? If infection, generalized illness, and/or high fever are responsible for your dog's imbalance, the successful treatment of the cause should result in resolution of the symptoms.

Did your neurological exam reveal any abnormalities? Inconsistencies and asymmetries in the neurological exam often indicate serious intracranial reasons for ataxia. If this is your suspicion, have your veterinarian arrange a neurological consult for your dog.

Did your spinal check indicate evidence of vertebral or intervertebral discomfort? Pressure on your dog's spinal nerve roots as they emerge from his spinal cord and exit between his vertebrae can result in limb weakness, which looks like a loss of balance. These problems can often be treated medically and occasionally corrected through surgery. Once again, a veterinary neurologist can help you diagnose the cause.

When to Get the Vet

- Has your dog recently suffered any form of head trauma? Intracranial changes subsequent to head trauma can often cause ataxia. When the imbalance begins a significant time after the trauma, it is more worrisome than if the imbalance follows close on its heels (in which case eventual resolution is more likely). In either case, consult your veterinarian immediately.

- Has your dog recently gotten into any unusual chemicals or medications? Since many toxins have a direct effect on the nervous system, it is common for exposure to result in abnormal behaviors or neurological symptoms. Some products may even cause temporary blindness. If you know what chemicals or medications your dog has possibly ingested or inhaled, call the ASPCA National Animal Poison Control Center at 888-426-4435 for immediate advice. Plan to make a trip to the nearest animal emergency facility as well.

My Dog
Keeps Losing
His Balance

My Dog
Keeps Fainting

First off, a fainting dog is not a normal dog. By fainting I mean when a dog suddenly falls down unconscious and remains so for a few moments before regaining consciousness.

What to Look For

After you've called the vet, conduct a physical exam much like the one outlined in "My Dog's Head Is Tilted" on page 203.

What to Do

In addition, you should try to answer these important questions:

Does your dog tire easily? If your dog has to stop to rest after walking short distances or exerting herself in any way, there's a good possibility that she is suffering from heart disease, which could explain the fainting spells. You should arrange for an appointment with a veterinary cardiologist.

Has your dog suffered a recent head trauma? Frequent losses of consciousness can be brought on by head trauma that results in concussion or intracranial swelling or bleeding. Sometimes these symptoms will diminish and eventually disappear entirely with time, but seek veterinary attention in case treatment is needed.

Does your dog have other symptoms? If your dog is showing other signs of a problem—such as loss of balance, head tilt, seizures, strange behavior, or if her eyes seem abnormal in any way—she could have a brain lesion or she might have had a stroke. Immediate veterinary attention is appropriate and may save her ability to function.

- If your dog is fainting, get her to your veterinarian right away!

- Has your dog recently gotten into any unusual chemicals or medications? Because many toxins have a direct effect on the nervous system, it is common for exposure to result in abnormal behaviors or neurological symptoms. Some products may even cause temporary blindness. If you know what chemicals or medications your dog has possibly ingested or inhaled, call the ASPCA National Animal Poison Control Center at 888-426-4435 for immediate advice. Plan to make a trip to the nearest animal emergency facility as well.

My Dog
Can't Use His Front Legs

Any time a dog loses the ability to use a front limb, it is a very serious matter. If both limbs are involved, it could be devastating. Yes, there are a host of minor problems that might result in an inability for a dog to bear weight on his front limb. Because the more serious reasons for such an event to occur are sometimes time sensitive, you need to act immediately to avert the possibility of permanent crippling. As the problem may be pain-related, protect yourself first, but conduct the following examination as swiftly and efficiently as possible.

What to Look For

If your dog is still standing or attempting to stand, take the opportunity to perform a quick assessment of his cervical (neck) spine. You may need a friend to help support your dog's weight while you do this. Start by getting a sense of whether your dog is experiencing any neck pain. If he is, forget the rest and get him to the animal hospital using the directions for transporting an injured dog in "How to Transport an Injured Dog" on page 20.

If your dog isn't experiencing neck pain, carefully move his head up and down, then side to side, checking for resistance and discomfort. Move on to his spine and, starting at the base of his skull, apply firm but gentle pressure to each of his intervertebral spaces in sequence, moving from head to tail, using your index and middle fingers in a walking manner.

Next, carefully get your dog into a comfortable resting position on his side. If only one of his legs is affected, try to have that one be up, making it easier to examine. Quickly check your dog's hind legs by massaging them for a moment to check his muscle tone and sensitivity to your touch. Pinch one toe on each of his hind legs to confirm that he will retract each one normally in response to the discomfort. Move on to the front limbs, repeating the same steps, but a bit more slowly and cautiously.

Once you have completed this part, try putting the leg through a complete range of motion, checking for pain, resistance, and muscle tone. If at any time in the process of this sequence of maneuvers your dog shows signs of extreme distress or tries to fight you or snap at you, follow the directions for transporting an injured dog mentioned above.

What to Do

Ask yourself these few questions to determine how to proceed:

Has your dog had problems with his front leg before now? If so, you probably already have an idea what the problem is and also some clue as to what needs to be done. In some cases, this may mean altering his dose of arthritis medication or massaging his leg for a while. Try these previously successful tasks before despairing.

Did your exam reveal no abnormalities other than an inability to bear weight on the affected limb? If this is the case, try giving your dog some time and an appropriate dose of one of the anti-inflammatory medications you may have used at another time. After an hour, repeat your examination and compare the two results. If no improvement is noted, consult your vet.

When to Get the Vet

- If your dog has just been hit by a car, fallen from a height, suffered some blunt trauma, or been involved in an athletic accident of some sort, follow the directions mentioned above and get him to the animal hospital.

- If your exam revealed evidence of cervical spinal pain or discomfort, your dog's lameness may be the result of an intervertebral injury or disc problem. An immediate veterinary consult, preferably with a neurologist, is called for.

My Dog
Can't Use Her Hind Legs

If your dog's hind legs appear unable to bear any weight, it is an immediate and grave concern. Without the use of both of her hind legs, your dog loses her ability to move around, support her weight, and adopt the correct posture to urinate or defecate. This can be both frustrating and depressing to a dog, and your dog might succumb to other health issues as a result. To avoid such consequences, do your best to efficiently assess what the cause for the incapacity is and arrive at a reasonable course of action.

What to Look For

Start your exam with your dog in a standing position. Obviously, if both of her hind legs are affected, you will need the help of a friend to support your dog's weight while you conduct your evaluation. Begin by performing the same spinal assessment described in "My Dog Is Stiff" on page 200. Go further, though, when you palpate her hind legs, by attempting to put each of them through a full range of motion, mimicking a bicycling movement.

Follow this by testing your dog's proprioception (the ability to spatially locate her limbs). While she is standing, place each paw in a "knuckled under" position and see if she rights it. If not, go on to pinching a toe of each of her hind paws to test for reflex withdrawal.

What to Do

Now ask yourself the following questions to ascertain what to do next:

Has your dog had problems with her rear limbs before now? If so, you probably have an idea what the problem is already and also some clue as to what needs to be done. In some cases, this may mean altering her dose of arthritis medication or massaging her legs for a while. Try these previously successful tasks before despairing.

Are you aware of any traumatic injury that might have caused this problem? If your dog has just been hit by a car, fallen from a height, suffered some blunt trauma, or been involved in an athletic accident of some sort, follow the directions included in "How to Transport an Injured Dog" on page 20 and get her to the animal hospital.

Did your exam reveal no abnormalities other than an inability to bear weight on the affected limbs? If this is the case, try giving your dog some time and an appropriate dose of one of the anti-inflammatory medications you may have used at another time. (See "How to Treat Your Dog with Anti-Inflammatories" on page 24.) After an hour, repeat your examination and compare the two results. If no improvement is noted, consult your vet.

Did your exam reveal any specific points of tenderness? Sometimes one area of pain or tenderness on a dog's leg will prompt her to simply stop using it. This could result from something as simple as an infected puncture wound or something as grave as osteogenic sarcoma (bone cancer). When in doubt, check with your vet.

When to Get the Vet

If your exam revealed evidence of spinal pain or discomfort, your dog's lameness may be the result of an intervertebral injury or disc problem. An immediate veterinary consult, preferably with a neurologist, is called for.

My Dog
Can't Walk Up or Down Stairs

Whenever a dog appears unable to travel up or down stairs, the obvious question is whether he is unable or simply unwilling to do so. Since there are a good number of reasons why a dog would suddenly stop using the stairs, it is important to rule out as many of the simple ones as possible before worrying about the more serious ones.

What to Look For

Start the rule-out process by observing the way your dog carries himself while walking on flat surfaces. Observe him walking and running, moving toward you and away from you, looking for any evidence of asymmetry, imbalance, or a limp. Repeat this process on more than one type of surface, including carpeted, paved, and high gloss, such as hardwood or linoleum. If you notice a limp of any kind, refer to "My Dog Is Limping" on page 185.

If you notice an imbalance or you sense a degree of incoordination, proceed with your investigation by following the directions in "My Dog Keeps Losing His Balance" on page 190, which include an ocular and a neurological exam. The completion of all of these assessments should give you a pretty good idea of whether or not your dog's behavior is driven by any physical or medical issues.

What to Do

Next ask yourself a few questions:

Did your physical exam reveal a limp, imbalance, or other gait abnormality? If so, successful treatment of the source of the problem should help return your dog to his normal stair-tolerant self. Refer to "My Dog is Limping" on page 185, "My Dog Keeps Losing His Balance" on page 190, and/or "My Dog Is Walking in Circles" on page 198.

Did your gait observation reveal any reluctance to walk on a particular surface? Some dogs balk at the prospect of crossing particular surfaces, especially shiny, reflective ones such as marble, hardwood, or linoleum. If this is the case, and if your stairs are smooth without a runner, your dog may be suffering from a visual field deficiency and should be seen by a veterinary ophthalmologist. Alternatively, try temporarily installing an all-weather type of rubber-backed runner to test your dog's response.

Does your dog have a history of orthopedic difficulties such as osteoarthritis? If so, try a combination of anti-inflammatory medication and personal assistance to help your dog overcome his hesitancy. (See "How to Treat Your Dog with Anti-Inflammatories" on page 24.)

My Dog Is
Walking in Circles

Normal dogs don't typically walk in circles, except when they are either preparing to urinate or defecate, or their attention is drawn by a smell or another animal to the extent that they are forced to do so to avoid losing the scent or direct contact. If you discover your dog walking in circles without any such reason for it, be immediately suspicious and try to figure out what the cause is.

What to Look For

Dogs with neurological reasons for circling typically find it difficult to turn in the direction opposite the one they are circling in. Start your investigation by attempting to get your dog to turn away from the direction in which she is circling. Next, conduct a neurological exam like the one described in "My Dog Keeps Falling Down" on page 188. This should include an evaluation of her eyes, ears, spine, and limbs.

What to Do

Now ask yourself these few questions:

Did your exam reveal evidence of an ear infection? If so, the circling might be due, in part, to the imbalance that sometimes results from an acute middle ear infection. See your vet for the appropriate course of action and that should help resolve the circling behavior.

Did your exam uncover any eye asymmetry? Different pupil sizes often indicate neurological problems that are best handled by a veterinary neurologist. The sooner your dog sees one the better.

When to Get the Vet

A recent head trauma can easily be the cause of a dog's circling behavior. Because these effects may be the beginning of something significantly worse, it is always wise to seek the immediate attention of a veterinary neurologist any time your dog exhibits even the slightest behavioral abnormality following head trauma.

Was every aspect of your physical exam completely normal? If it was, there is a strong possibility that the circling behavior is just that; a behavioral issue only. If it persists for more than a few days, it might be worthwhile to consult an animal behaviorist.

My Dog
Keeps Walking into Things

**My Dog
Keeps Walking
into Things**

Different breeds of dogs are known for different skills, and individual dogs may possess distinctly different skill levels. Walking into things, while it may add a note of levity to the moment, is not one of those skills! An occasional moment of clumsiness is one thing, but repeated collisions with immobile objects should alert you to the fact that something is wrong with your dog. Before your dog has a chance to injure himself, try to determine why he is walking into things. Your immediate action may allow for a solution to the problem or at least prevent its further development.

What to Look For

Start by performing a thorough eye examination like the one described in "My Dog's Eyes Are Bulging" on page 171. Follow that with the neurological exam outlined in "My Dog Keeps Falling Down" on page 188.

What to Do

Take a moment to ask yourself these questions, which should point you in the right direction.

When to Get the Vet

If your exam revealed any eye anomalies, ask your vet to refer you to an ophthalmologist. See one immediately in case your dog's problem is curable or at least possible to stabilize.

Does your dog's problem appear to be related to his sense of balance? Since balance issues can be related to a number of possibilities, refer to "My Dog Keeps Losing His Balance" on page 190 for further advice.

Did your neurological exam reveal any abnormalities? Neurological difficulties that may be responsible for balance issues or collisions are worthy of a neurological consult. In some cases advanced diagnostics such as CAT scans may be suggested.

My Dog Is Stiff

Since dogs are generally not accused of being socially stiff, we usually think of a stiff dog as one that is old, sore, arthritic, or some combination of the three. But these are far from the only reasons for a dog to move in a way that is interpreted as stiff. "Stiffness" can be as simple as a dog's method of dealing with the pain of osteoarthritis, as complex as some difficult-to-identify viral or bacterial meningitis, or something in between, such as an immune-mediated discomfort such as rheumatoid arthritis. Your job is to figure out why your dog is stiff.

What to Look For

Think of this exam as a slow, elaborate body massage, and it will be fun for you and your dog. Start with your dog in whatever position she finds most comfortable. Begin by cradling her head in your hands. Start with an ocular exam like the one outlined in "My Dog's Eyes Are Red" on page 167. Next, speak soothingly and begin scratching her ears, working your

way down the length of her throat and neck. Circular, rubbing motions (edging toward slight probing) are the best way to comfort and relax her while testing for discomfort and sensitivity.

Once you have reached your dog's shoulders, lay her on her side. Isolate her upper front leg (the one not against the floor) and work the same circular, rubbing-to-probing motions—using both hands for leverage, control, and support—from her shoulder all the way to the tips of her toes. Resume the process by returning to her chest and side, working backward toward her hind legs. Once there, repeat the process of examining her rear leg the same way you did the front.

When you have reached the tips of your dog's toes, move on to the head of her tail. Lift the tail gently with one hand and slowly use your other hand to encircle and sequentially squeeze sections of the tail until you reach the tip.

Now carefully roll your dog over to her other side and repeat all the steps, starting with her shoulder. Once this is completed, get your dog into a comfortable, stable standing position. Again cradling her head in your hands, slowly move it up and down, and then side to side, checking for any sign of resistance or discomfort.

Finally, beginning at the base of her skull, apply cautious but firm pressure while walking the index and middle fingers of one hand down her spine, all the way to her tail, noting any sign of a flinch or other complaint.

What to Do

Ask yourself the following questions to ascertain what to do next:

Did your dog demonstrate signs of pain or resistance during the exam? If the discomfort was easily identified as a response to one part of the exam, focus on that area and explore further, either on your own or with the help of your vet, depending on the intensity of her response.

Did your dog demonstrate focal pain at any point during your spinal exam? That is, does there seem to be one specific spot that hurts? This sort of discomfort could

When to Get the Vet

Has your dog recently gotten into any unusual chemicals or medications? Since many toxins have a direct effect on the nervous system, it is common for exposure to result in abnormal behaviors or neurological symptoms. Some products may even cause temporary blindness. If you know what chemicals or medications your dog has possibly ingested or inhaled, call the ASPCA National Animal Poison Control Center at 888-426-4435 for immediate advice. Plan to make a trip to the nearest animal emergency facility as well.

indicate a disc problem or vertebral issue. Consult your vet for advice as to whether medical treatment or more diagnostics are appropriate.

Did your dog show signs of neurological abnormality during your ocular exam? Your description of stiffness may actually be your dog's way of maintaining her balance in the face of a neurological ataxia, or imbalance due to some spinal or brain problem. Your vet will probably recommend that you have your dog seen by a neurologist.

Did all this examining, massaging, and probing give you nothing to go on? If your dog tolerates the entire exam and seems to simply enjoy the extra attention, try administering a weight-appropriate dose of either a buffered or enteric-coated aspirin. (See "Treating Your Dog with Anti-Inflammatories" on page 24.) If it works, continue this therapy for no longer than two weeks, keeping in mind that you have a successful treatment for an as-yet undiagnosed problem. Depending on your dog's age and the severity and frequency of the stiffness, you may be best served getting to the bottom of the original problem.

My Dog Is
Dragging
the Tops of
His Paws

My Dog Is
Dragging the Tops of His Paws

Dogs don't shuffle. They don't even appreciate the concept of cool. Therefore, if your dog is dragging the tops of his paws when he walks, there is definitely something wrong. Usually this represents something known as a proprioceptive deficit. This is similar to the feeling we get when our legs "fall asleep." In dogs, it is always a sign of some form of neurological problem and should be evaluated by a veterinarian, preferably a neurologist.

What to Look For

Start by observing your dog closely as he walks toward you, then away from you. Look for evidence of unsteadiness or any unevenness of gait. Watch as each paw strikes the ground. Evaluate both your dog's way of carrying himself as a whole and, more specifically, the way he holds his head.

Next, stand him beside you and, one at a time, lift each paw and place it on the ground "knuckled under." His normal response should be to immediately lift the paw and replace it correctly, pads down. Finally, perform an ocular exam like the one outlined in "My Dog's Eyes Are Red" on page 167 and a spinal exam like the one included in "My Dog Is Stiff" on page 200.

What to Do

Answer the following questions to figure out what to do based upon what you found:

Does your dog's sense of balance seem abnormal? Paw dragging can be caused by poor balance. Refer to "My Dog Keeps Losing His Balance" on page 190 for advice on how to evaluate and deal with balance issues.

Does your dog appear to be favoring one limb in particular? If the favored limb is also the one that your dog is dragging, examine it more closely for signs of pain, starting at the toes and working your way up to the body. If you find any point of tenderness, deal with it appropriately, but if there is no evidence of pain or discomfort, the problem is probably neurological.

Did your ocular exam reveal any evidence of neurological damage? Paw dragging can result from a variety of intra- cranial events such as hemorrhage, stroke, or tumor growth. Seek help from your veterinarian if you suspect any of these.

Did your spinal exam show any evidence of abnormalities? Intervertebral disc disease and spinal column problems can be the source of proprioceptive deficits that may be treatable. See your vet for advice.

Has your dog recently gotten into any unusual chemicals or medications? Since many toxins have a direct effect on the nervous system, it is common for exposure to a variety of substances to result in abnormal behaviors or neurological symptoms. Some may even cause temporary blindness.

My Dog's Head Is Tilted

A dog with a head tilt is always a concern. It could mean something as simple as a mild to moderate ear infection, or it could be something as serious as a stroke. By gathering a little information through a physical exam and by answering a few questions, you should be able to ascertain why your dog's head is tilted.

What to Look For

Examine your dog carefully, paying closest attention to her ears, eyes, head, and neck. Look for any evidence of infection, including heat, redness, discharge, and foul odor. Feel for signs of tenderness and pain, and observe your dog's pupils for any unusual movement or asymmetry.

What to Do

Answer these questions to figure out what's going on with your dog's tilted head:

Does your dog appear to be off balance? Dogs that lose their balance do so either because their equilibrium is off or because their limbs can't support them evenly. Your dog's head tilt suggests the former, so it is important that you explore further.

Are your dog's eyes making rapid up and down or back and forth movements? These movements, known as nystagmus, are normal only after your dog has undergone some recent, rapid head movement (but not when she is at rest). If you notice these movements while your dog is at rest, there is a neurological problem that should be assessed at least by your veterinarian, but ideally by a veterinary neurologist.

Does your dog have an ear infection? An obvious infection of the external ear should be readily apparent and would lead you to the suspicion that your dog's inner ear might also be affected. Infections of the middle ear (this is behind your dog's eardrum, so you won't always be able to detect such an infection by simply looking in your dog's ear) often cause imbalance. This is because your dog's limbic system, which is responsible for her sense of balance, is located adjacent to the inner ear. Any swelling or inflammation of the tissues in that region may have a direct effect on your dog's sense of balance and, therefore, cause her to tilt her head.

When to Get the Vet

A recent head trauma can result in a variety of side effects that could be responsible for causing a head tilt. All of them are worthy of further investigation and certainly merit an immediate visit with your veterinarian.

My Dog's

Testicles Are Enlarged

Most owners of intact males are acutely aware of the normal size of their dogs' testes. At the first sign of testicular enlargement, your first thought should be as to whether it is possibly the result of some outside influence, such as trauma.

What to Look For

Slow and gentle is always the best approach when examining a dog's testicles! Additionally, enlarged testes have a strong potential for being painfully sensitive, so you should always be prepared with distractions for your dog while you examine him. Having a friend help with the distractions while you conduct the exam should help things go more smoothly.

First off, have an idea of what "normal" should look like. To compare what you see to what you envision as normal, evaluate both testicles together, then individually. Normally, one will be slightly larger than the other (it is also normal for one testis to hang slightly lower than the other). If this difference in size is significant, then one of two problems is present; either one testicle is abnormally enlarged, or the other is abnormally small.

If your visual exam indicates that one or both of the testes is abnormally enlarged, try to assess whether that enlargement seems to be in length, girth, or overall. Also, by carefully resting the entire scrotal sac in your hand, see if it seems excessively warm.

When to Get the Vet

If you don't think trauma caused the enlargement, get your dog to your veterinarian immediately.

What to Do

Once you have made a satisfactory evaluation of the actual enlargement, you should try to answer the following questions:

How old is your dog? If your dog is just reaching full maturity, the enlargement you have noticed may simply be his normal sexual development. Don't assume this to be the case, though, unless the testes are of normal temperature (actually slightly cooler than body temperature) and non-painful.

Does your dog seem bothered by his testicles? If your dog is paying an excessive amount of attention to his testicles and, in fact, appears to be on the verge of doing himself some damage, seek your vet's help.

Do your dog's testes feel hot? This is definitely abnormal and suggests infection or trauma to the genitals. If you feel comfortable checking your dog's temperature, do so to find out if he has a fever related to his genital enlargement. (See "How to Take Your Dog's Temperature" on page 17.) If his temperature is above 102°F, you should have him seen. If his temperature is normal (98°F to 102°F), the genital heat may just be from licking repeatedly. Try using an Elizabethan collar, which you can buy at pet supplies stores, to prevent him from licking himself for a few hours, and then re-evaluate.

Are you planning on using your dog for breeding? If not, and if your vet is suspicious that the enlargement is for any reason other than blunt trauma, infection, or allergic response, you should be prepared to have him castrated and the testicles examined by a pathologist. Since testicular cancers are quite common in dogs and their metastatic potential is fairly high, this is sound medicine and often a simple way to dramatically improve your dog's chances for a normal, healthy lifespan.

When to Get the Vet

If your dog has recently been neutered, a common post-surgical complication of an orchiectomy (castration) is scrotal swelling. In such cases, the scrotal sac will fill with enough fluid and/or blood to stretch even larger than before the surgery. If so, you should consult the surgeon immediately.

My Dog's
Nipples Are Enlarged

Every normal dog—whether male, female, intact, spayed, or neutered—has a full set of eight nipples, and each one is associated with a mammary gland.

In females, the nipples are designed to nurse their offspring. Consequently, the nipples will become enlarged during the female estrous cycle, or "heat," and continue to remain enlarged throughout pregnancy and until the puppies are weaned. Only then will their size diminish, but rarely all the way back to their original, pre-pregnancy dimensions. Because nipple size is regulated by the various hormones circulating in the female's bloodstream, any non-estrous, non-pregnancy driven fluctuations in these same hormone levels—such as fluctuations caused by a problem with the dog's endocrine system—may result in the same enlargement of your female's nipples.

With the exception of "heat" and pregnancy-associated fluctuations, the same hormones that cause nipple enlargement in a female also do so in a male. We are immediately more suspicious of nipple enlargements in males, however, since these fluctuations are much more likely to be abnormal and potentially dangerous.

What to Look For

This is easy. Get your dog to lie on her back or side in a relaxed and comfortable position. Look closely at each nipple. Try to compare them to how you remember them the last time you noticed. In so doing, try to evaluate color, texture, length, and girth. Place the palm of your hand over each nipple to check the superficial skin temperature of each mammary gland. Finally, trap each nipple between your thumb and index finger and apply very gentle pressure in a pinching motion to check for sensitivity.

What to Do

Next, answer these questions:

How many nipples appear to be enlarged? As a general rule of thumb, if all the nipples appear enlarged, there is some systemic, probably hormonal reason behind it, and your dog's vet should evaluate her endocrine status.

If only one or a few nipples beside one another are enlarged, the cause is more likely to be due to some disease process or from some outside source, such as trauma or contact exposure like an allergy. This is not an emergency, and treating the nipples directly may solve the problem.

Try cleaning the nipples with lukewarm water, and then apply a thin film of a mild hydrocortisone ointment or lotion, such as Cortaid or Corticin, directly to the nipples three times daily. If you don't notice improvement within three days, you should check with your vet.

Are the nipples bleeding? A little bit of blood coming from a nipple is not always a great danger, especially if the nipple has been traumatized. Dogs that are extremely itchy will often scratch their nipples raw and bloody with their hind paws in an attempt to relieve the itchiness. If this is the case, cleaning the area and then applying cooling compresses and some hydrocortisone (see above for suggestions) will help. If the trauma is dramatic enough to result in an obvious open, ragged-edged wound, use an antibiotic ointment, such as Bacitracin, instead. Repeat this cleaning and antibiotic ritual three times daily until the wound has healed.

Is there pus coming from the nipples? This means that there is a bacterial infection of the nipple, the mammary gland, or the skin around the nipple. Sometimes topical treatment is enough to achieve a cure. If the amount of pus is minimal and there is no heat radiating from the mammary gland, try cleaning the nipples with a 50/50 hydrogen peroxide/water mixture, and then apply some antibiotic ointment, such as Bacitracin. Repeat this process at least three times daily until the nipple is back to normal.

When to Get the Vet

If you notice that the mammary gland beneath the affected nipples is hot, your dog may have an infection of the mammary gland called mastitis. This is serious and should be handled immediately by your veterinarian.

My Dog Has a
Constant Erection

The adolescent humor surrounding a dog's erection can quickly change to concern if that erection fails to subside in a normal amount of time. If your dog has an erection for more than 30 minutes and there is no female in heat nearby, there is something wrong. It is important to find out what the problem is before your dog begins to do himself any harm by excessively licking or even gnawing at his penis in an attempt to solve the problem.

What to Look For

Conducting a comprehensive examination of your dog's penis is probably best left to the experienced hands of your veterinarian. Not only might you manage to injure your dog, but he could injure you during your attempts.

What to Do

Here's what to do, depending on what you saw:

Is your dog still a puppy? If your puppy is experiencing an erection for the first time, it is possible that his excitement will last for more than the aforementioned 30 minutes, so be patient and try to distract him from focusing on the erection. Food and water may be enough to accomplish this. If this doesn't work, try applying a cold compress to his groin. Sometimes contact with a cold surface will reduce the engorgement that maintains an erection. If this doesn't work, try applying a water soluble lubricant like K-Y jelly to his penis and the leading edge of his foreskin. This may permit the penis to slide back in if there was simply a mechanical problem related to dry skin and hair.

Is your dog sexually active? This may seem like an unusual question, but any sexual activity, including self-stimulation, excessive humping, or actual copulation—even if your dog is neutered—can result in a condition known as paraphimosis, in which the penis becomes stuck in an erectile position and cannot retract. In many cases, removing any hair and debris that might have become wrapped around the penis will solve the problem. Paraphimosis, though commonly associated with sexual activity, can also be caused by infections and other sources of inflammation.

In dogs suffering from this condition, the foreskin swells and is less likely to withdraw back into its sheath once an erection has been achieved. Once this happens, return blood flow is restricted, making the problem worse. Both conditions must be addressed immediately!

Has your dog recently been showing signs of a urinary tract infection (UTI)? Symptoms of a UTI—such as frequent urinations of little quantity, excessive licking of the genitals, dribbling between urinations, or any type of discharge from the penis—can cause the foreskin to become inflamed, leading to your dog's erectile problem. Seek treatment for the infection and inflammation and you may solve the problem.

Has your dog suffered a recent traumatic injury? Trauma to the spine can result in a condition known as priapism, a neurological dysfunction that results in a vascular problem. Under this condition, the engorgement of the blood vessels in the penis will not diminish and the penis will thus not retract. Sometimes this can resolve on its own, but you should take your dog to your vet to confirm the diagnosis and to get advice on how to protect the penis from injury.

When to Get the Vet

If your dog still has an erection after these attempts, veterinary assistance is critical to avoid permanent damage to the penis. He may have a condition known as phimosis, in which the opening of his foreskin is too small and needs to be surgically enlarged.

My Dog Has a Constant Erection

My Dog's
Vulva Is Enlarged

Enlargement of your dog's vulva, unless she is an intact female, should always be cause for concern. Normally, rises in estrogen at the beginning of the estrous cycle, or "heat," result in increased blood flow and subsequent engorgement of the vulva. With the subsequent drop in estrogen and rise in progesterone, a period of behavioral changes known as "standing heat" ensues. Bleeding may or may not be apparent. If your dog is successfully bred, the vulvar enlargement will continue through the gestation until her puppies are weaned.

If a spayed female shows signs of vulvar enlargement it is usually a sign of infection, irritation, or allergic reaction. In some cases, certain types of skin cancer and vaginal tumors may cause vulvar enlargement.

What to Look For

The vulva of most spayed females is fairly well hidden by hair. This is why it usually goes unnoticed unless it becomes abnormally enlarged. In order to examine it, place your dog on her side and lift her upper leg to gain visual access to her genitals. The vulva should look like a simple fold of hair-covered skin, like a fortune cookie resting on its side.

When enlarged, the vulva usually expands outward, showing more of the pink mucus membrane of the vaginal lining and causing the covering hair to be pushed aside.

By this point in the exam, you should already have a pretty good idea of how sensitive your dog's genitals are. This knowledge should influence how much further you are willing to go in your examination. If you (and your dog) are comfortable continuing, proceed gently, cautiously, and only after donning rubber gloves.

For the next part of the exam, all you're looking for is evidence of blood, pus, or any sort of abnormal tissue swelling. To do so, apply some K-Y jelly to the index and middle finger of your examining hand. By placing both fingers in the vulvar opening and spreading them slightly, you can get a look at the first inch or two of the vaginal entry, which is plenty for a reasonable evaluation.

What to Do

Ask yourself these questions to determine what to do next:

Has your dog been licking her genitals excessively? All female dogs lick their genitals regularly in order to keep them clean, but they tend to lick excessively when they are irritated, allergic, or infected. If you notice blood or pus in your examination, there is a good chance that one or more of these problems exist.

Your next course of action may be dictated by how uncomfortable your dog is. If she is growling at you when you try to examine her, or if she is whimpering with discomfort, see your veterinarian for help. If she tolerates your examination with little or no complaining, try using an Elizabethan collar for a few to twenty-four hours to prevent further licking. During that time continue to check for signs of blood, pus, or ongoing irritation of the vulva and vaginal lining.

Is your spayed female bleeding from her vagina? If your vulvar examination reveals blood coming from her vagina, your dog may have an injury, a growth, or an infection, each one of which should be seen and evaluated by your veterinarian.

Is there pus coming from your dog's vagina? Any evidence of pus coming from her vagina confirms the presence of infection. Even though it doesn't confirm the source of the infection, it is enough to merit a veterinary visit to try to figure that part out, as well as to begin antibiotic therapy.

Is there any abnormal swelling or growth associated with her genitals? Spayed females may develop genital tumors, warts, or allergy-related swellings. Even though most of these are not dangerous, especially since she will not run the risk of communicating any of them to a breeding partner, they are still of some concern. It is wise to closely monitor them for changes in color, size, texture, and irritation. If changes occur, your vet should be consulted.

With intact females, the same concerns exist but with the additional possibility of hormone-responsive swellings and tumors. While spaying these dogs usually solves the problem, if the owners are trying to breed their dog, more creative treatment will be called for. More than just your local veterinarian, a specialist in reproduction, known as a theriogenologist, may be needed to choose the most effective and safe solution.

When to Get the Vet

If your dog is intact and you notice pus coming from her vagina, get her to the veterinarian immediately. If your dog is suffering from a uterine infection, or pyometra, she could end up losing her litter if she is pregnant, or her uterus if she is not.

My Dog's Vulva Is Enlarged

My Dog Cries Out
When He Tries to Chew

Few things come close to food in their importance to the physical and emotional well-being of every dog on the planet. It stands to reason, then, that if a dog experiences enough discomfort in an attempt to chew that it causes him to cry out in pain, something must be done right away. What to do depends on what the source of the pain is, and how to figure that out depends mostly on how tolerant your dog is to having you examine his pained mouth.

What to Look For

Get a flashlight or take your dog to a spot with very good light. If you can, get someone else to help out. Here's what to do:

Begin by petting your dog the way you normally would. In a few minutes, start rubbing his ears and working your way to his muzzle. Sit beside your dog and place the palm of your hand that's closest to his nose beneath his chin. Place the palm of your other hand flat against his cheek. Use the thumb of that second hand to apply gentle pressure against the outside of his upper lip, sliding it up to reveal the teeth and gums beneath. Similarly, use the thumb of your lower hand to slide your

Warning

Not every dog likes to have his mouth pried open or even his lips lifted to expose the teeth and gums. This is especially true if your dog's mouth is clenched shut in an attempt to protect something painful inside. Go slowly and speak soothingly.

dog's lower lip down, revealing his lower teeth and gums. (See the illustration on page 35.)

Take your time. By shifting the position of your hands and patiently starting and stopping repeatedly, you should eventually be able to take a look at your dog's teeth and gums on that side of his face.

Now it's time to check out your dog's tongue and hard palate (the roof of his mouth). To do this, place your left thumb on the right side of your dog's upper lip, just behind the large canine teeth. Place your left index and middle fingers on the left side of your dog's upper lip, just behind the large canine teeth. Do the same with your right hand on his lower lip, and then open his mouth like a clam shell. Take a good look inside. Don't forget to check under the tongue.

Now repeat the side exam from the other side.

What to Do

What to do depends on what you found. Also ask yourself the following questions:

Is there any bleeding from the teeth, gums, or cheeks? Injuries to the inside of your dog's mouth may cause sharp pain while chewing. If the bleeding is mild and the source of the bleeding is not significant, offer your dog some water and see if he'll drink. If he does, wait an hour, then offer him some food. If your dog won't eat or if he cries out in pain when he eats, have your vet take a look.

Does your dog have any fractured or infected teeth? Many dogs will cry out if they try to chew with a cracked or infected tooth. Neither situation is one you can solve at home. Brushing an oral analgesic such as Anbesol on the affected area may make your dog feel better until you can get in to see your vet.

Does your dog seem to be light-sensitive? Dogs that show signs of pain when chewing and squint one eye either spontaneously or when exposed to direct light, may be suffering from a retrobulbar abscess. These usually occur after a dog has been chewing on something that penetrates the tissue at the back of his mouth and then migrates back to a position behind the eye. The subsequent infection, inflammation, and swelling cause pain and photosensitivity. This is definitely a reason to see your veterinarian for antibiotics and possibly even surgery

When to Get the Vet

Call your dog's veterinarian if:

- Your dog has a fractured or infected tooth.

- There's a foreign object in your dog's mouth that you can't safely remove.

- You suspect a retrobulbar abscess, or pocket of infection behind the eye.

Do you notice any foreign objects in your dog's mouth? Sometimes an object lodged across the roof of your dog's mouth, wedged in between his teeth or penetrating his gums or cheek, can cause a painful response upon chewing. Be cautious in any attempts at removing foreign objects. Unless it appears to be unquestionably simple to remove, leave it to your veterinarian. You can probably safely remove pieces of rawhide, plastic toys, items of clothing, and sometimes even chicken bones, but only if the position allows it and there is low potential for further harm to your dog.

Some things should never be removed at home because doing so could mean more serious harm to your dog or to you. These include metal objects such as sewing needles, fish hooks, and various forms of hardware, as well as the occasional porcupine quill!

My Dog Cries Out When She Tries to Open Her Mouth

A dog that can't open its mouth is like a fish that can't swim. Dogs rely heavily on their ability to bark, howl, bite, and chew in order to function. When it hurts for them to open their mouths, it can be quite debilitating. Fortunately, by answering just a few logical questions you can usually figure out the reason for the pain without much trouble.

What to Look For

Get a flashlight or take your dog to a spot with very good light. If you can, get someone else to help out. Here's what to do:

Begin by petting your dog the way you normally would. In a few minutes, begin rubbing her ears and working your way to her muzzle. Sit beside your dog and place the palm of your hand that's closest to her nose beneath her chin. Place the palm of your other hand flat against her cheek. Use the thumb of that second hand to apply gentle pressure against the outside of her upper lip, sliding it up to reveal the teeth and gums beneath. Similarly, use the thumb of your lower hand to slide your dog's lower lip down, revealing her lower teeth and gums. (See the illustration on page 35.)

Take your time. By shifting the position of your hands and patiently starting and stopping repeatedly, you should eventually be able to take a look at your dog's teeth and gums on that side of her face.

Now it's time to check out your dog's tongue and hard palate (the roof of her mouth). To do this, place your left thumb on the right side of your dog's upper lip, just behind the large canine teeth. Place your left index and middle fingers on the left side of your dog's upper lip, just behind the large canine teeth. Do the same with your right hand on her lower lip, and then open her mouth like a clam shell. Take a good look inside. Don't forget to check under the tongue.

Now repeat the side exam from the other side.

What to Do

As you examine your dog's mouth, check for foreign objects, injuries, infection, dental problems, growths, and pain. See "My Dog Is Drooling Excessively" on page 90 for what to do in these circumstances. Also ask yourself the following questions:

Does your dog continue to have a normal appetite? Dogs that maintain a good appetite despite pain when they open their mouths are unlikely to be experiencing the discomfort for some purely dental reason.

Does your dog appear to be sensitive to light? If your dog is squinting or even blinking her eyes when facing any light, she may be suffering from something known as a retrobulbar abscess. This is an infection of the tissues behind the eyeball and usually caused by some foreign body that your dog chewed on, a small piece of which broke off and migrated up into the tissue behind your dog's eye.

Does the pain appear to be only sporadic? Anbesol, a topical oral analgesic, can be used to reduce oral pain that arises from gingival irritation and superficial injuries to many of the tissues in the mouth. Try using it to alleviate the discomfort and check your dog's response. If it isn't making a difference within two days, see your veterinarian.

Does your dog chew on a variety of large, hard objects? If so, your dog may have fractured a tooth in the process of bearing down on a hard object such as a soup bone or stone. If your exam reveals a broken tooth, have your dog's vet take a look at it to determine if the tooth can be saved.

My Dog
Cries Out When He Tries to Turn His Head

Pain demonstrated when moving the head and/or neck is always a serious concern. The most important issue to be concerned with is the possibility of causing any further injury to the spine and/or spinal cord. Don't be foolish! Your dog's veterinarian may wish to manipulate your dog's neck to examine it thoroughly, but don't you be the one to cause further injury to your dog.

What to Look For

First observe your dog for a while and try to assess whether it is all movement that causes pain or if there is a specific type of movement that brings on the complaint. Next, try to examine your dog's neck and shoulders by gently massaging the areas and applying light pressure to them all to check for point tenderness. Then, by answering the following questions, you should get a good idea of whether a veterinary visit or some rest and recovery is called for.

What to Do

Here's what to do, depending on what you saw:

Does your dog seem wobbly or unstable? If this is the case, your dog may be suffering from Wobbler's syndrome, instability of the spinal column at the base of the skull that results in loss of balance, weakness in the hind end, and often pain in the neck region. This syndrome rarely resolves without surgery.

Is your dog crying out with every little movement? Sometimes trauma to the head or neck will result in bruising that elicits pain on only the slightest motion. This is a situation that may resolve with rest and inactivity. Trauma could also cause a pinched nerve that would present as crying out on any kind of movement of the head and neck. Again, rest and decreased activity might solve the problem.

On occasion, Lyme disease can present as severe head and neck pain. In this situation, rest may improve the symptoms slightly, but resolution will not occur without antibiotic therapy.

Do only very specific movements bring on the pain? If it is only movement to one side that causes pain, an ear infection, abscess,

When to Get the Vet

Contact your dog's vet if:

- Your dog seems wobbly or unstable.

- Your dog cries out with every movement.

- Only specific movements, such as on one side of the body, bring on the pain.

mass, or injury could be the source of the pain. If the pain is brought on by any movement to either side or any movement up or down, there is a strong possibility that your dog is suffering from a protruding intervertebral disc. This is a situation that demands veterinary attention, and probably examination by a neurologist.

My Dog Cries Out When He Tries to Turn His Head

My Dog
Cries Out When She Tries to Stretch

Stretching is often the first thing a dog does when rising from its place of rest. Often accompanied by a yawn, the classic butt-in-the-air, front paws extended posture seems to mean the day is starting off right. If that stretch is interrupted by a vocal complaint, it is certainly a sign that something is bothering your dog, but rarely is it a grave matter.

What to Look For

Observe your dog for a few minutes, checking for any signs of discomfort and listening for more cries. If she'll let you, give her a massage. A gentle but firm massage is a great way to detect sore muscles, ligaments, or tendons. Also try gently opening your dog's mouth to get a good look inside.

What to Do

Logically speaking, any dog that suffers from a serious injury is unlikely to even attempt her morning stretch. To begin the stretch and be interrupted by a sharp pain or even a surprise twinge of discomfort is, on the other hand, most likely the result of some form of musculo-skeletal pain that may resolve on its own. Here's what to do:

What does your dog do after the vocal complaint? If you hear only one vocalization and then your dog goes back to normal, it was probably just a muscle cramp. However, if your dog's discomfort seems to continue, conduct a more thorough examination of all your dog's limbs. (See "My Dog Is Limping" on page 185.)

Does your dog object to any aspect of a thorough massage? Gently massaging your dog could elicit a cry if you touch a sore muscle, ligament, or tendon. These are all parts of the musculoskeletal system that, if bruised or injured in some way, could cause your dog to cry out upon stretching.

If you are able to isolate a point of discomfort, what you do will be determined by the severity of your dog's reactions. If your dog complains when specific joints or muscle groups are manipulated, try giving her a weight-appropriate dose of buffered or enteric-coated aspirin. (See "How to Treat Your Dog with Anti-Inflammatories" on page 24.) This will likely provide rapid relief.

Does your dog object to having her mouth examined? If opening your dog's mouth wide enough to get a good look inside is enough to elicit the same complaint you heard during the stretch, it may have been the yawn that caused the pain. Did you notice any injury to the inside of the mouth, infected teeth, bleeding gums, etc.? (See "My Dog Is Bleeding from His Mouth" on page 34 for more information.)

Does your dog have any swellings or areas of redness on her skin? An insect bite or bee sting during a stretch could easily prompt a spontaneous yelp from your dog. Look closely by brushing the coat in all directions in any area where your dog seems the least bit sensitive.

Cold compresses and sometimes a weight-appropriate dose of Benadryl will help dramatically.

All in all, since your dog felt well enough to begin a normal stretch, much of what caused her to vocalize was probably the surprise of feeling a sudden, unfamiliar sensation. If a reasonably thorough investigation on your part reveals nothing, relax, but continue to observe her behavior closely for the next few days.

Warning

Not every dog likes to have her mouth pried open or even her lips lifted to expose the teeth and gums. This is especially true if your dog's mouth is clenched shut in an attempt to protect something painful inside. Don't expect to solve this problem quickly and efficiently. Your dog doesn't necessarily understand what you're trying to do, so expect this to take some time. Go slowly and speak soothingly.

My Dog Cries Out When She Tries to Stretch

My Dog
Cries Out When He Breathes Deeply

For most oxygen-dependent creatures, a nice deep breath of fresh air is always a pleasure. If your dog begins to cry out any time he tries to take such a breath, there is most certainly something wrong. The reasons for such a reaction are varied, but are most likely related to your dog's respiratory, digestive, or musculoskeletal system.

What to Look For

Start your assessment by going over in your mind the events in your dog's routine for the past two days. Scrutinize his meals, water consumption, urinary and bowel habits, and his level of play and general activity. Next move on to a general physical exam, focusing on his respiratory rate and pattern, his rib and chest comfort, and his entire musculoskeletal system, particularly all four of his limbs.

What to Do

Now ask yourself a few questions:

Did your assessment reveal any changes in your dog's appetite or bowel habits? If so, be concerned with possibility of gas-trointestinal problems such as gas, bezoars (balls of hair and/or plant matter that stay stuck in your dog's stomach for long periods of time), or obstructions. All three of these can be quite serious. If your dog's behavior persists for more than a few hours, and the offer of warm, moist food doesn't appeal to him, see your vet right away.

Do your dog's cries seem irregular (not coming in any sort of pattern)? If the vocalizations are irregular and all else seems fine, you can probably afford to wait a bit longer before having to seek your veterinarian's help.

Did your physical examination reveal any specific difficulty related to the quality of your dog's respirations or their rate? If your dog's respirations are rapid and ragged, difficult and moist-sounding, or shallow and high-pitched, it is worrisome enough to ask your vet for advice and probably request a set of chest films as soon as possible.

Did your physical examination uncover any limb injury or discomfort? If so, it is probably worth having your vet take a look and suggest treatment, considering that the related discomfort is enough to induce him to vocalize merely due to the pain induced by breathing. Don't panic, but try to schedule with your vet within a few days.

My Dog Cries Out When She Tries to Move Her Leg

The quality of dogs' lives depends heavily on their ability to move about. Since they are "pack" animals, they are accustomed to living in close proximity to others of their own kind, and as domesticated animals they have adopted humans as an extension of their "pack."

Within that "pack," there are rules of behavior that need to be observed and some of the most important ones relate to the rules of elimination. In short, without the ability to urinate and defecate in an appropriate location, away from the sleeping and eating areas, dogs appear to feel a sense of shame. They need to be able to choose their location for each activity they perform. Without this mobility, they can become depressed and moribund. Most dogs are fairly stoic, so if the effort to move a leg results in a vocal sign of pain, as well as an obvious problem in walking or even getting up, you may have a serious problem.

What to Look For

Observe your dog for a few minutes to determine what types of movement are causing her pain. Look at your dog's leg without touching it, if that causes her pain. Check for bleeding, swelling, or changes in angle or position of the limb.

Dogs are quite good at hiding their injuries. It's a safe bet that the leg that's bothering your dog is tucked beneath her. This makes it hard to look at!

If your dog will let you, try manipulating her other legs first. This will give her a feeling of reassurance and introduce her to the idea of having her limbs moved in a pain-free manner. It will also give you a basis for comparison once you get to the limbs she is hiding beneath her.

If your dog is in so much pain that she won't let you near her, wait for 30 to 60 minutes before attempting any further examination. During that time, try observing your dog for signs that might help pinpoint the affected limb. She might lick or chew at the site or repeatedly attempt to test that limb in an effort to rise from a resting position. Rear leg injuries tend to be more common, especially in larger dogs.

What to Do

The questions below are designed to help you assess the nature and location of the problem. Rarely is there an instance of an injured leg that an owner can solve at home, unless it is a minor bruise or superficial cut that requires no veterinary care. In these cases, localized treatment and time are in order. (See "How to Control Bleeding" on page 18, and "How to Treat Your Dog with Anti-Inflammatories" on page 24.)

Is there an obvious injury to one of your dog's limbs? If you noticed any bleeding, swelling, or changes in angle or position of the limb, follow the directions for "How to Transport an Injured Dog" on page 20 and get right to the vet.

Did you notice a puncture wound? Sometimes insect or animal bites will cause swelling and pain. Larger punctures suggest larger animals' teeth, such as those of another dog. Smaller holes might be the result of cat or insect. If your dog was bitten by another animal that you don't know, she needs to be seen by her veterinarian for a rabies booster vaccination.

If you suspect an insect bite, watch your dog carefully for signs of an allergic reaction, such as swelling, itchiness, or even difficulty breathing. Follow the directions in "Treating Your Dog's Allergic Symptoms" on page 25. A weight-appropriate dose of Benadryl has the added benefit of acting as a mild sedative. Be sure to let your dog's vet know that you gave her Benadryl, however, as this sedation may otherwise be confused with lethargy.

When to Get the Vet

Leg pain is usually pretty clear cut. If it improves significantly within an hour, it does not require veterinary involvement. However, if it does not improve within an hour or seems to be getting worse, get your dog to the vet!

My Dog
Cries Out When He
Tries to Urinate

All normal healthy dogs should urinate in comfort. The production of urine and its subsequent elimination is an essential means of ridding the body of waste products that would otherwise remain in the bloodstream, acting as toxins. If your dog shows even the least amount of distress while attempting to urinate, you need to figure out why. A dog that goes for an extended period of time without urinating will get very sick and could die.

Males are more likely to become obstructed than females due to the increased length and narrower diameter of the male urethra. An obstruction may be the case if a male dog repeatedly attempts to urinate without success. Remember that some dogs will do this after they have successfully urinated, just trying to mark their perceived territory. Pay attention to what has immediately preceded these attempts! If your dog is struggling to urinate and cannot due so, get him to a veterinary clinic right away because this is a medical emergency. The reasons a dog would feel discomfort while urinating range from simple, treatable issues like urinary tract infections (UTI) to more complex problems, such as urinary bladder crystals and kidney or bladder stones. On rare occasions, pain while attempting to urinate may be due to a fractured penis. Yes, male dogs have a bone in theirs, and it can get fractured!

What to Look For

Observe your dog's penis as he tries to go to the bathroom. Note whether any urine is actually coming out.

If he will allow it, get a good look at his genitals to see whether there is any unusual swelling or redness associated with his penis or his scrotal area (and his testicles if he is intact).

My Patient's Story

Just a few months after being adopted by a local family, Diego was strolling along the sidewalk and lifted his leg to urinate on, of all things, a fire hydrant. Carol, his owner, told me that he suddenly started crying out and struggling as though he had been shot. With the help of a friend, she eventually succeeded in calming him down and rushed home to call me to have a look at him. She said there was blood in his groin and he was acting very protective of the area.

Diego had already distinguished himself as a "special needs" dog in terms of his behavior, so I sedated him before even attempting a thorough examination of his genitals. What I discovered was a large puncture wound right beside his penis, which I was able to clean and stitch quite neatly.

Carol later discovered that the fire hydrant Diego had chosen to christen happened to have a hook attached to it for hanging the cap during a fire. He had apparently impaled himself on it while lowering his leg after urinating. Subsequent to Diego's episode, the city removed all such hooks.

If your female will allow it, check her for swelling, redness, or any increase in pigmentation that would indicate excessive licking of the area.

Collect a urine sample to examine and possibly take to your veterinarian. This can be tricky, but the most successful technique for females is to use a clean pie plate slid beneath her as she squats. For males, a clean glass jar can be used to catch urine midstream or a few drops as they leak out. Always wear rubber gloves to avoid getting any urine on yourself in the process. Once you have the sample, drop it off with your vet as soon as possible, since time and temperature can alter the sample significantly.

What to Do

So how do you figure out why your dog is having trouble? Ask yourself the following questions:

Is your dog a male or a female? Male dogs are much more likely than females to experience pain on attempts to urinate due to the aforementioned anatomical differences. In addition, intact males will have greater potential for partial obstructions based on prostate enlargement or the presence of high sperm counts.

Did you see unusual swelling or redness? These are all signs that the problem may be localized to the genitalia or that your dog is doing his best to solve the problem by licking the area. However, dogs are rarely capable of doing so and if they were you wouldn't be witnessing the ongoing discomfort that you're trying to solve right now. Most often, your vet should be consulted. This step will generally result in a much more rapid resolution of the problem.

Does your dog have a history of urinary tract infections? Since this is probably the most common reason for discomfort on urination, it is worth investigating before the others. If your dog has a fever (see "How to Check Your Dog's Temperature on page 17), seems to drink more than usual, or acts a bit lethargic in addition to the urinary problem, it may be another UTI. If so, you will need your vet to help treat it appropriately.

Is your dog urinating successfully in spite of the discomfort? If your dog is still able to produce a significant amount of urine, the situation is not as grave as it would be if a urinary tract obstruction were suspected. Collect a urine sample and have it analyzed by your vet.

Is there blood in the urine? A little blood in the urine is often present during a UTI, but it is also present in cases of urinary

When to Get the Vet

If your dog is complaining and incapable of producing anything more than a few drops of bloody urine, it is an emergency!

tract crystals, stones, trauma, and neoplasia (tumors). If there is blood, always play it safe and see your veterinarian.

Does your dog appear to be in pain other than when he attempts to urinate? If there is evidence of pain not associated with urinating, your vet should see your dog.

My Dog
Cries Out When She Tries to Defecate

Like urination, defecation is important to a dog's health and sense of well-being. Although it is not as immediately critical as the ability to urinate, if for some reason your dog cannot defecate, the effects can be quite dramatic.

My Dog Cries Out When She Tries to Defecate

What to Look For

What you need to do is try to determine whether your dog is in pain because she is trying to pass some foreign body through her intestinal tract or because she is experiencing an inherent source of pain, such as cramping, constipation, anal sac inflammation, or gastroenteritis. Failure to defecate is an issue that you can afford to wait on as long as your dog continues to behave normally in all other ways. If she begins to vomit, refuse food, or act noticeably lethargic, your veterinarian should be consulted.

What to Do

After observing your dog, ask yourself the following questions:

Is your dog defecating successfully in spite of the pain? If so, what does the feces look like? If it is black and tarry, there is probably some bleeding occurring early in the gastrointestinal (GI) tract, near the esophagus and stomach. If there is red blood in it, the bleeding is coming from somewhere further along in the GI tract, closer to or from the colon. Since rectal bleeding is serious, consult your vet.

If the feces is covered in mucus, this indicates irritation of the intestinal lining. Putting your dog on a bland diet may help you solve the problem at home. (See "My Dog Is Pooping Everywhere" on page 254 for more information on this.)

Is your dog still energetic and interested in food and water? If so, chances are that whatever is causing the discomfort in her attempts to defecate is not emergent. If the problem doesn't improve or resolve on its own within three days or with the use of a bland diet for two to three days, then X-rays may be called for.

Is your dog vomiting? Difficulty with defecation combined with vomiting is very serious. Seek immediate veterinary help.

Is your dog dragging her bottom on the floor or ground? This is usually a sign that your dog is having problems with her anal sacs or with parasites. (See "How to Empty Your Dog's Anal Sacs" and/or "How to Treat Your Dog's Intestinal Parasites" on page 23.)

Does your dog often attempt to eat inappropriate items? Dogs that are prone to consuming inedible items, such as dirty clothing and used tampons, are more likely to have obstructions of foreign bodies. If you suspect that this has happened, your dog may eventually pass the item by forcing it out rectally, but waiting too long for this to happen can be risky. As soon as your dog begins to act sick or lethargic, get her in for an examination by her veterinarian.

When to Get the Vet

Any substantial amount of bleeding from your dog's rectum, especially if combined with lethargy, is an emergency!

My Dog
Keeps Yelping

My Dog
Keeps Yelping

"Will you please get that dog to shut up?" Instead of getting angry with your neighbor for screaming this request or, worse yet, taking it out on your dog, how about trying to find out what's bothering him to begin with? It shouldn't be that difficult and if successful, you, your neighbor, and the dog will rest easier as a result.

What to Look For

Start by taking your dog for a walk to distract him while you assess whether he has an orthopedic reason for all the yelping, such as an injury or arthritis. If his gait and weight-bearing ability seem normal and you see no evidence of other injury, move on to performing thorough eye, ear, and neurological exams like the ones in "My Dog Is Drooling Excessively" on page 90, "My Dog's Eyes Are Bulging" on page 171, and "My Dog Is Stiff" on page 200.

What to Do

Exam completed, ask yourself the following questions:

Did your investigation reveal any orthopedic issues? If so, you can start by treating your dog with an appropriate anti-inflammatory (see "How to Treat Your Dog with Anti-Inflammatories" on page 24), or you can have him evaluated immediately by an orthopedic specialist. The choice should be based on the level of discomfort your dog is experiencing and not on how obnoxious your neighbor's complaints are.

Did your oral exam reveal any dental issues? If so, you should be able to treat the dental problem at home if it is not too dramatic. (See "My Dog Is Drooling Excessively" on page 90 for what to do.) In addition, you should use an anti-inflammatory to reduce whatever pain he is experiencing. (See "How to Treat Your Dog with Anti-Inflammatories" on page 24.) If the discomfort is marked, your attempts may be improved by the use of a topical anesthetic such as Anbesol, following the directions just as you would for yourself.

Does nothing except distracting your dog get him to stop yelping? Maybe your dog is just tired of being left by himself. Try setting him up with a play group, doggie day care, or a daily dog walker for some exercise and fun. This may make your neighbor and your dog happy.

PART 14: MY DOG IS HAVING BEHAVIOR PROBLEMS

PART 14

MY DOG IS HAVING BEHAVIOR PROBLEMS

My Dog Is
Acting Funny

Canine behavior is a well-documented area of study. Most of us are familiar with the concept of "pack mentality," and many of us can predict how our dogs will behave in a given situation. But what happens when your dog is acting differently than you are accustomed to? What should you look for and how do you identify what aspect of her behavior is different?

Most dog owners, especially first-time puppy owners, find themselves questioning many of their pet's patterns of behavior. Eating style and urinary and defecation behaviors are sometimes confusing to a puppy owner. These questions are often easily answered in the literature provided by a breeder or pet store. However, once dogs have reached adulthood and their owners have learned more about their normal routines, breaks from those routines are more easily identified. At this point, an owner's questions about unusual behaviors can be addressed more seriously.

My Dog Is Acting Funny

What to Look For

You've already likely spent some time observing your dog to have noticed that she is acting funny. If needed, take a few more minutes to observe her with the following questions in mind.

What to Do

Ask yourself the following questions:

Is your dog walking like a "drunk"? A drunken walk is a serious sign. Dogs that exhibit this behavior should have a thorough physical and neurological exam and blood testing should be done to check for dehydration, hypoglycemia, electrolyte imbalance, chemical toxicity, and organ disease or signs of stroke, seizure activity, or vestibular syndrome.

Does your dog seem confused or disoriented? Confusion and disorientation are alarming, especially in a young dog. A thorough physical should include an eye exam to check for visual problems and an ear exam to check the health of the dog's ears and her ability to hear. All the concerns listed above for a drunken walk should also be included.

Does your dog recognize you and respond when you call? Failure to recognize or respond to owners is a grave sign. Once again eyesight and hearing should be checked as well as the dog's sense of smell. Blood testing and a thorough neurological exam will help to determine whether this abnormal behavior is the result of a recent stroke or seizure, or because of a chemical imbalance or toxin exposure.

Is your dog licking or eating unusual things? Licking or eating unusual material such as dirt, plants, fabric, or floors can be a short-lived phase or be due to some dietary insufficiency. If it persists, a veterinary check, including an oral exam, blood testing, and a thorough evaluation of the dog's diet should be performed.

When to Get the Vet

Unusual behaviors may be difficult to duplicate on command or in front of your vet, but can often be explained if witnessed by a professional. If worrisome behaviors persist, yet are only exhibited at home, try either seeking the help of a veterinarian who makes house calls or filming the behavior and then showing it to your vet. If the behavior can't be explained by the usual means, your vet may perform a CAT scan to check for brain lesions.

Is your dog acting needy? Neediness is a subjective evaluation when applied to dogs, but it is most often a sign that something is bothering her, either physically or emotionally. Because dogs are pack animals, they will seek the help of their most trusted or reliable family members when they need help or reassurance. In the process of consoling your dog under such a circumstance, you should try to check for injuries or other reasons why she would seek your attention. If simple explanations such as loud noises, strangers, or unfamiliar animals or surroundings are not part of the picture, your veterinarian may notice something you don't.

My Dog Is
Pressing His Head into Corners

Aside from the rare occasion when a dog has an itchy spot on his head, there is never a good reason for a dog to be pressing his head into corners.

What to Look For

Conduct a neurologically focused exam, such as the one outlined in "My Dog's Head Is Tilted" on page 203.

What to Do

Quickly ask yourself the following questions:

Has your dog suffered any recent head trauma? If the trauma was serious enough to cause head pressing, it is safe to assume that you should not delay, but should have your dog evaluated by a veterinarian as soon as possible. Most of the side effects of head trauma that can cause head pressing are grave.

Is your dog blind? Blind dogs can often be found stuck in corners, apparently pressing their heads against the walls.

They can be helped out of the corners, though, and some of them are capable of functioning quite well in the home they are familiar with.

Does your dog suffer from allergies? Dogs with dramatic environmental and/or food allergies might possibly head press in an effort to reduce their discomfort. These dogs, when escorted away from the corners, may continue to seek a variety of surfaces against which to continue their rubbing and/or pressing. They will, however, be perfectly capable of walking in a controlled, balanced manner with no head tilt or gait discrepancies.

Do you notice any asymmetry or other abnormality when you examine your dog's eyes? These findings usually suggest some intracranial problem and simply confirm how important it is to get your dog to a veterinarian for evaluation.

My Dog Is Pressing His Head into Corners

When to Get the Vet

- Whenever a dog presses his head against walls or into corners, it is a sign consistent with serious neurological disorders, intracranial diseases, or head trauma. If your dog is doing it, be alarmed. Conduct a brief physical exam and get your dog to a veterinarian as soon as possible.

- Has your dog recently gotten into any unusual chemicals or medications? Since many toxins have a direct effect on the nervous system, it is common for exposure to result in abnormal behaviors or neurological symptoms. Some products may even cause temporary blindness. If you know what chemicals or medications your dog has possibly ingested or inhaled, call the ASPCA National Animal Poison Control Center at 888-426-4435 for immediate advice. Plan to make a trip to the nearest animal emergency facility as well.

My Dog Keeps

Tucking Her Tail between Her Legs

Dogs usually tuck their tails between their legs as a defense mechanism. This can demonstrate fear, submission, or both. From a medical viewpoint, though, it can be a sign that a dog is experiencing pain or discomfort of some sort. A quick physical exam can usually help determine the reason and possibly help you decide on a course of action.

What to Look For

Start this exam by doing something you know will relax your dog or make her feel comfortable and happy. Remove her from any threats, loud noises, or distractions.

If the tail tucking continues, get her to stand squarely and balanced and perform a slow, firm-but-gentle evaluation of her spine by using your middle and index finger to "walk" down her spine. Start at the base of your dog's skull and work your way down to her tail, stopping at the spaces between the vertebrae to press, probe, and then release, checking for signs of pain or resistance.

Next, cautiously lift your dog's tail to examine her anal region for evidence of injury. Finally, place your dog on her side and gently massage/squeeze all the regions of her abdomen to see if there is any sign of discomfort.

What to Do

Ask yourself a few questions to determine what to do next:

Did the tail-tucking stop once you got your dog into her comfort zone? If so, the tucking action is probably just a behavioral response to perceived threats or frightening people or noises. Your dog is probably submissive or fearful in general and may benefit from more frequent exposure to a variety of people, animals, noises, and situations. This tactic will be most successful with you nearby for confidence and to provide positive reinforcement in the form of tasty treats.

Did your dog demonstrate any signs of discomfort during your spinal exam? Crying out, growling, snapping, flinching, or dropping to the floor during the probing of your dog's intervertebral spaces usually indicates some form of spinal injury or disease. Usually, if the problem is significant there will be more than just some tail-tucking to suggest it. When a tucked tail is the only sign, the disc spaces most commonly involved are the ones closer to the dog's tail. Try using an anti-inflammatory such as a dose-appropriate buffered or enteric-coated aspirin to see whether there is improvement. Always give it with food and only if your dog has never had problems with gastric or intestinal bleeding in the past. See "Treating Your Dog with Anti-Inflammatories" on page 24 for directions on dosing.

Did you notice any unusual swelling, bleeding, or discharge near your dog's anus? Perianal injuries, growths, and infections can cause enough discomfort to prompt your dog to tuck her tail. Refer to "My Dog Has a Discharge from Her Anus" on page 119 for advice on evaluating what you might discover in the area. Also see "How to Empty Your Dog's Anal Sacs" on page 23 for directions on how to empty your dog's anal sacs if they are full and you are brave.

Does your dog appear to have a pained abdomen? Generalized illness and abdominal pain in particular are often reasons for tail-tucking. If you are able to rule out behavioral, spinal, and perianal reasons for the tucking, get your dog's veterinarian's help as soon as possible in determining the underlying reason.

My Dog Is Barking at Night

My Dog Is
Barking at Night

Admittedly, a dog's bark in the middle of the night is never anyone's idea of a lullaby. If that dog happens to be *your* dog, not only do you have to check to see why he is barking, but you have to apologize to your neighbors the next day. After you have ensured that your family is safe and there is no evidence of intruders or wild animals invading your home, it would be wise to try to identify the cause of your dog's agitation.

What to Look For

Your physical exam in these instances should focus primarily on overall health and nighttime environmental factors. Conduct a thorough eye exam like the one in "My Dog's Eyes Are Red" on page 167 get an idea of whether his night vision may be a factor. A neurological exam by a neurologist may be necessary if you think your dog is exhibiting signs of nighttime senility, otherwise known as canine cognitive dysfunction.

What to Do

Now it's time to answer a few questions.

Is your dog a puppy? Young puppies find just about everything fascinating. Each day is full of intrigue and fun. Once everyone has gone to bed for the evening, though, a puppy's life takes a turn for the worse. Lack of playmates makes his nights boring. My suggestion is to supply some comfort and/or entertainment for the puppy. A nice cozy bed or crate should provide a comfortable place to rest. Usually a television or radio with the volume turned down low is enough to keep the puppy company.

Has your dog recently had a complete physical exam with blood work? Aging and ill dogs will often bark at night because the distractions of the day are no longer present to divert their attention from their own problems. Once they are all by themselves, they tend to focus on their own needs and issues. This makes them feel lonely and helpless. Barking is their cry for a friend.

Has your dog recently had his vision evaluated? Dogs with deteriorating vision have a tougher time seeing things in low light and darkness. Once night falls and the lights are turned down or off, many of these dogs will seek the comfort of their owners by barking.

My Dog Is
Barking Hoarsely

Dogs and barking seem to go together. Dogs tend to bark to attract attention to things they seem to think of as important, but sometimes they appear to be barking at absolutely nothing at all. I think it is safe to assume that many of us would like very much to be able to exert complete control over our dogs' barking, but aside from an appropriately timed growl, a dog's bark is often her most effective means of communication.

Thus, despite the fact that it may seem like a blessing when our dogs bark with hoarse "voices," it is always a surprise, as well as a cause for concern.

What to Look For

To investigate further, try taking a look down your dog's throat. Get a flashlight or take your dog to a spot with very good light. If you can, get someone else to help out.

Begin by petting your dog the way you normally would. In a few minutes, begin rubbing her ears and working your way to her muzzle. Place your left thumb on the right side of your dog's upper lip, just behind the large canine teeth. Place your left index and middle fingers on the left side of your dog's upper lip, just behind the large canine teeth. Do the same with

your right hand on her lower lip, and then open her mouth like a clam shell. (See the illustration on page 35.)

Take a good look inside her mouth and down her throat. Look for irritation and coatings on the tongue and back of throat. Check for masses and foreign bodies. Listen for coughing and to your dog's breathing.

What to Do

Next, ask yourself these questions:

Has your dog recently been barking for long periods of time? This could be a reasonable explanation for the change in sound. Like with people who have been yelling at athletic events, overuse can result in a sore throat and a hoarse voice.

Does your dog have a fever? Dogs with a hoarse bark and a fever may have an upper respiratory infection. In the case of many bacterial infections, a look down your dog's throat may reveal a thick coating on the tongue or back of the throat, ranging in color from white to yellowish or green.

Is your dog having difficulty swallowing? Dogs with viral or bacterial infections, masses, or obstructive foreign bodies in their throats may have difficulty swallowing. In such instances, your dog's veterinarian is the best one to have a look down your dog's throat to see what is causing the difficulty.

When to Get the Vet

Is your dog coughing or breathing with a raspy sound? While both these symptoms could be indications of bacterial or viral infections, they could also be associated with a form of paralysis that affects the nerves of the larynx. This is a diagnosis that can only be made by your veterinarian and should be made soon since this problem will often result in aspiration of your dog's food into the lungs, which, in turn, can cause pneumonia.

My Dog Is
Constantly Chasing Things

Whether or not we like to admit it, dogs are predators. Instinctually they chase animals down and kill them to survive. Centuries of controlled breeding practices have diluted that instinct in most breeds and altered it in others. So today, we're left with three categories of chasing—aggression, play, and herding. Your challenge is to determine which one your dog is displaying and then figure out how to handle it.

What to Look For

Take some time to observe your dog and think about his behavior. You might even want to make some notes. Ask yourself the following questions: What breed is your dog? Has this behavior always been a problem or is it a recent development? Is your dog on a new diet? Is your dog on a new exercise schedule? Are there other recent changes in your dog's behavior?

What to Do

Here's what to do, depending on the issue you found:

BREED ISSUE: Each dog breed has a fairly specific personality profile. Because of this, many of their behavioral patterns can be labeled as breed-specific. For instance, a Jack Russell terrier that continually chases down squirrels is quite normal and, some would say, just doing his job!

Similarly, if you find that your Shetland sheepdog is making a nuisance of himself at your child's birthday party by chasing the children around and nipping at their clothing, he's probably being driven by his deeply engrained instinct to herd. As annoying as it may be, he is trying to do what he perceives to be his job.

Those examples are the easy ones. More difficult to figure out is why your bichon frise is suddenly stalking your child and nipping her as she runs away, or why your mixed breed seems to have it in for that one kid who rides his bicycle by your house every day at 3:15 p.m. These are probably behavioral traits. Consider consulting an expert trained in animal behavior. Success comes in a variety of packages. For instance, a dog trainer might be all that is needed. In other instances, a certified pet dog trainer could help. Your dog's behavior, however, may require the help of a veterinarian who is board-certified in animal behavior. Seek your vet's advice and maybe a referral.

BEHAVIOR CHANGES: If any behavior—particularly chasing, stalking, or herding—is a new development in an adult dog, look for changes in your dog's environment that might have brought it on, such as new plants or chemicals that your dog could have been exposed to. For example, dogs, like people, can suffer from lead poisoning after repeated ingestion of lead-based paint in old houses. Lead poisoning can be easily confirmed with a blood test. If new plants or chemicals are present, remove them immediately and see whether the behavior dissipates over time.

DIET ISSUE: A sudden change in the food your dog is eating can have a dramatic effect on his behavior. Compare the ingredients in the new food with those in the old food, paying particular attention to the protein content. Occasionally, drastic increases in dietary protein can affect a dog's behavior. Try switching back to your dog's old food, changing to another food with percentages of ingredients similar to the previous food, or mixing the new food with the old food a little at a time to allow his system to adapt to the new food more gradually.

EXERCISE ISSUE: Dogs that are accustomed to a great deal of exercise come to depend on that activity. If that level of activity is suddenly reduced significantly, they will often resort to other forms of exercise or even destructive behavior to compensate. Try to return to the former exercise routine, or at least one that approximates it.

OTHER CHANGES: If there are other new behaviors, they may be explained by one of the above changes. If they are not explainable, if they have come on abruptly, or if they are alarming or aggressive in nature, a thorough neurological exam is probably appropriate. A major concern in such cases would be the development of an intracranial problem, such as a brain tumor or aneurysm. These might also be accompanied by other neurological symptoms, such as loss of balance, asymmetric pupils, changes in visual ability, altered gait, changes in appetite or thirst, or persistent barking.

When to Get the Vet

Contact your dog's vet if:

- Your dog is aggressive to people or animals.

- You notice any of the "other changes" listed on the left.

My Dog Is
Attacking
People or
Animals

My Dog Is

Attacking People or Animals

Canine aggression is a serious and worrisome behavior. While it can be corrected, the process most often requires the help of an expert animal behaviorist or dog trainer. It can be slow, difficult, and frustrating, and success is rarely achieved without absolute commitment from the owner and family.

Thankfully, not every case of aggression is a behavioral pattern. Some can be episodic and attributed to medical issues.

What to Look For

Cautiously perform an overall exam of your dog, including all aspects of her head, neck, spine, muscles, and limbs, searching for any signs of pain, discomfort, or mental instability. Refer to "My Dog Is Drooling Excessively" on page 90 for a thorough oral exam, "My Dog Is Stiff" on page 200 for a spinal exam, and "My Dog Is Limping" on page 185 for a musculoskeletal exam.

What to Do

Ask yourself the following questions to figure out what to do next:

Is your dog an adult or a puppy? Puppies that show aggressive behavior toward children and other animals usually do so as a means of establishing dominance. Human parents often make the mistake of excusing such behavior in their puppies, explaining it away with phrases like "She didn't mean it. After all, she's only a puppy!" Trust me, puppies may not mean to hurt anyone, but they do mean to bite. This behavior needs to be corrected from the moment it appears. "Puppy kindergarten" classes are a great way to learn more about such behavior and the methods necessary to deal with it. Adult dogs are more difficult to train away from true aggression.

Is this a new and sudden change from your dog's normal behavior? Sudden changes in behavior, particularly those involving aggression, may suggest illness, pain, exposure to toxins, or intracranial changes. If your normal, affable adult dog suddenly turns aggressive, have her examined as soon as possible to check her blood for signs of illness and toxin exposure.

Your veterinarian will also want to examine her body for evidence of pain. A neurological exam, possibly including a CAT scan, would also be advisable to check for evidence of spinal pain, recent seizure activity, or brain tumors.

Has your dog been neutered or spayed? If your dog is an intact adult, aggressive behavior may be territorial in nature. Unless you are planning to breed or show your dog, the first signs of aggression should be a strong argument for having the appropriate procedure done.

Has your dog recently suffered an injury?
Pain of any type can cause dogs to become irritable, defensive, and in many instances, aggressive. If pain is the reason for your dog's aggressive tendencies, treat the source of the pain and you may have your normal happy dog back.

My Dog Is
Afraid of Strangers

Most dogs, like humans, go through developmental stages during which they evolve from a stage of fearlessness to one of fear of all strangers, and eventually, with any luck, finally arrive at a state where they are capable of evaluating people as individuals. Some dogs, however, appear to get stuck in that middle step and remain fearful of all strangers. In some cases, depending on the breed of dog, this fear will take on behavioral manifestations, ranging from the most abject submission to the most violent aggression. Either of these can be objectionable, and the latter is completely unacceptable as well as dangerous. Before you give up on your dog as a lost cause, it may help to try to understand what prompts your dog's specific behavior pattern, with the hope that it may be correctable.

What to Look For

Your examination of your fearful dog should be an attempt to rule out any injury or disease that could be causing pain or discomfort. This pain might be inducing your dog to guard himself for fear that anyone he doesn't implicitly trust could cause further harm.

First, focus on all four of your dog's limbs, manipulating them in every direction. Check your dog's mouth and ears, then thoroughly examine his eyes. Moving on, check your dog's vision by testing his menace reflex, as outlined in "My Dog's Eyes Are Bulging" on page 171. Finally, test your dog's response to bright lights, loud noises, and high-pitched sounds.

What to Do

Armed with the information you learned from your exam, ask yourself the following questions:

Does your dog flinch or yelp during any part of your examination? Even though this could simply confirm what a fearful dog he is, chances are that it points toward some underlying pain or fear of a specific body part being moved in a certain way. If you can identify the source of the pain, you may be successful in altering or reprogramming the instinctive response. A dog that instinctively protects a painful body part is likely to relax and become more accepting once the source of pain has been corrected.

Does your dog ever exhibit the objectionable behavior toward you? Although this is highly unusual, if it does occur it means that your dog's fear is worse than simply one of strangers, but is enough of a problem that it usurps the bonds of trust he has established with you. This is worse, and may make behavioral modification more difficult.

Warning

Don't ever assume that you can trust your dog under any circumstances. If at any time you feel threatened by your dog, the chemistry of your relationship is in serious jeopardy and you must get help to re-establish that chemistry or make a decision to remove the dog from your household.

Does your dog ever *not* exhibit the objectionable behavior toward a stranger? Selective fear is more common and it is much more promising in terms of potential for remedial intervention. Love, patience, and time may allow for a complete recovery. At this time you should sign up for training classes and try to remain optimistic.

My Dog Is
Afraid of Other Animals

Dogs are social creatures. Most of them enjoy playing and, in some cases, get into trouble because of their enthusiastic approach to social interactions with other animals. But what if your dog is suddenly afraid of other dogs, or other animals in general?

What to Look For

It is important in such cases to conduct the same series of examinations recommended in "My Dog Is Attacking People or Animals" on page 239 to assess whether there is any physical or medical reason for the change in behavior.

What to Do

When you find that your dog is fearful of other animals, you have a choice to make. Many dog owners opt to simply avoid other animals entirely. Other dog owners enroll their dogs in dog training classes to try to socialize their dogs. If you're leaning in that direction, ask yourself the following questions:

How old is your dog? Dog training classes are most effective when they are begun when a puppy is about four months old. Obviously, socializing your dog with other

dogs doesn't cover other species of animals, but most puppies that excel in these classes seem to carry their positive animal experience over to other species.

If your dog is an adult when he begins to show signs of animal fear, it is first important to make sure that there is no medical reason for the behavior.

Do you have any reliable, nonthreatening animal friends? If your thorough physical exam doesn't reveal any muscular, skeletal, or medical concerns, then the solution may simply be repeated positive interaction with a few reliable, nonthreatening animal friends. Call your friends with animals and try setting up a play group!

My Dog Is
Afraid of Children

Like a Norman Rockwell painting, a popular vision of American family life includes children and pets living in harmony. Unfortunately, not every dog fits into this idyllic portrait. Some behaviorists maintain that dogs with fear issues have had some negative experience at a critical time in their social development. As dogs tend to follow a similar pattern of social development to humans, this is possible but rarely confirmed. Genetics certainly could play a role as well. Regardless of the source, fear behaviors can prevent a dog from functioning as an accepted part of a family.

What to Look For

Conduct the physical outlined in "My Dog Is Afraid of Strangers" on page 241. In addition, try to establish whether it is the size, sound, pattern of movement, or the unpredictable nature of children that seems to most affect your dog.

What to Do

Ask yourself the following questions to get a sense of what to do:

When did you first notice your dog's fear of children? If your adult dog has recently begun showing these signs of fear, there may be some specific, treatable reason for them. If your dog showed signs of pain or discomfort during your physical exam, it is

possible that he is guarding the painful areas from potential contact. Since children pose more of a threat to stumble or bump into your dog, he may simply be trying to avoid such an incident. Treat the source of the pain, and you may succeed in resolving the fear issue as well.

If your dog is still a puppy and has begun to fear children but not adults, it is critical that he be repeatedly loved and cared for by children to help him to build a trust of them. The critical part of this "hyper exposure" includes protection of both the children and the puppy from any and all potential harm. Start by having children feed, walk, and play with your dog in completely calm, nonthreatening situations, and always with an adult supervising. As trust builds, focus on the positive aspects of the interactions between the dog and the children and try to duplicate them repeatedly.

How does your dog exhibit his fear?

Most dogs exhibit their fears in one of two ways: They either behave in a submissive, cowering fashion, or they compensate for their fears by adopting an aggressive, threatening disposition. If your dog tends to behave in the latter fashion, it is imperative that you seek professional assistance from an animal behaviorist before any children are injured. Keep in mind that some dogs will not respond to attempts at behavioral modification and will eventually have to be euthanized. Unfortunately, this is the cold hard truth when it comes down to dogs that pose a threat to humans. Yes, the thought of finding a house out in the country without children or other pets seems like the perfect solution for such a

Warning

Dogs that exhibit either aggressive or fearful behavior toward children should always be monitored in their interactions with children. And even then, the ground rules should be very clear and offer control and safety for the children.

dog, but the number of such available situations is so far outnumbered by the number of dogs like this it is staggering.

On the other hand, dogs that cower, roll over, and even urinate around children can often be worked with to build their confidence. This work should also be done with caution since dogs that are typically submissive can sometimes switch to behaving aggressively without warning.

My Dog
Is Afraid of
Shiny Floors

My Dog Is
Afraid of Shiny Floors

Shiny, slippery floors are a real bugaboo to many dogs, especially large breeds, and especially as they get older and arthritic and their vision and coordination begin to deteriorate. The important thing for you to do is to determine whether your dog's fear of these floors is more closely related to her visual acuity or her physical abilities. How do you figure this out?

What to Look For

Conduct your physical exam following the directions detailed in "My Dog Is Afraid of Strangers" on page 241. In addition, take your dog for a walk on a variety of other surfaces, including at least one nonreflective but slippery surface, such as linoleum. This may result in initial enthusiasm immediately followed by the same fear you've noticed with shiny floors.

What to Do

Next, ask yourself the following questions:

What does your dog do to display her fear of these floors? Most dogs simply balk at the prospect of crossing a shiny wood or marble floor. They will whine and struggle if you try to force them to cross. Occasionally, they will flop down on the floor and refuse to move. If your dog does any of these things, yet is happy to cross carpeted floors or even smooth but dull linoleum floors, chances are that this is a visual problem, not a physical one. Try using a flat or satin finish the next time you buff your floors!

Did your dog display any signs of deteriorating vision during your physical exam? Regardless of your dog's age, if her vision is faulty, she may be unnerved by the fact that she can't focus accurately on the surface under her paws. You have two choices if the visual compromise is perma-

nent. You can either use a cleaner that results in a duller, less reflective surface, or you can put down rugs or carpeting.

Does your dog show any other signs of illness? If your dog has some other illness or chronic disease, weakness may be contributing to her lack of confidence. Enlist your vet's help in correcting the source of weakness and you may resolve the problem.

Does your dog appear to be arthritic or experiencing joint pain? Pain is often the reason behind a dog's reluctance to cross a slick surface for fear of falling and incurring more pain. Try giving your dog a weight-appropriate dose of a buffered or enteric-coated aspirin and see whether the joint discomfort improves. If it does, maybe the fear of the slick surface will dissipate as well.

Keep in mind that aspirin is just a temporary fix—you will need to get your veterinarian to help you form a therapy plan that should include dietary adjustment, anti-inflammatory medication, and exercise.

My Dog Is
Afraid of Certain Objects

Fear of specific objects is a common occurrence in dogs. Newspapers, brooms, vacuum cleaners, and cars are typical ones. What the fear stems from varies from dog to dog and is probably dependent on each dog's individual experience. Since we can't very well conduct interviews with our dogs, we often choose to speculate on why they fear certain objects and then formulate plans designed to calm or control these fears. Most often, a dog's fear of certain objects stems from some degree of confusion, surprise, or a lack of understanding. For example, I find that my folding examination table, which I bring into client's homes with me, is accepted by most dogs upon my arrival. When I rest it on its side and begin to unfold it, however, many dogs show signs of fear and anxiety. They will often back up and bark at me and the table until they have time to assess the table for what it has become.

Another reason for dogs' fear of objects is the negative memory they associate with those items. For instance, a dog that has been repeatedly hit with its owner's belt may develop a fear of belts or even certain kinds of belts similar to the one he remembers. In other instances, there may be something unique about the specific object a dog is afraid of that makes it so threatening.

What to Look For

Conduct the same physical exam outlined in "My Dog Is Afraid of Strangers" on page 241, paying close attention to your dog's response to all the tests involving his vision. It is important to rule out any physical problems before you start evaluating what might end up being a behavioral issue.

What to Do

Ask yourself the following questions to try to ascertain what your dog is feeling:

Is it one specific object, a few individual objects, or an entire class of objects that your dog fears? The exercise of identifying what specific things your dog fears may help you arrive at an explanation for the fear, or at least hint at why the fear arose. Then you can take steps toward correcting or easing that fear.

Has your dog always had this fear or is it a new development? The time frame may very well help to identify a specific incident that brought on the fear response. Try to retrace or recreate any traumatic events involving the objects, but make sure the sequence occurs with a more

positive result. For example, if you are convinced that your dog was battered with a newspaper, try linking any sight of a newspaper with a food reward. Make seeing a newspaper create an expectation of a food treat and soon your dog will expect the sight of every newspaper to be the preview to something terrific.

Are there distinct smells or sounds associated with the feared object(s)? Smell and sound are often inextricably linked with objects in a dog's mind. If you can replace the smells and sounds with others, yet keep the object constant, you may resolve the fear response.

My Patient's Story

My English bulldog patient, Millie, suddenly refused to eat or drink, demonstrating a pronounced fear of her food and water bowls, both of which were stainless steel. She would run enthusiastically into the kitchen and look as though she was about to attack her food with gusto. Once she got within a foot of the bowls, however, she would hit the brakes hard and fearfully scramble backward about five feet. Finally, she would bark a few times in frustration and fear and leave the room.

We soon figured out that Millie was more than willing to eat and drink, just not out of those bowls. It turns out that she was frightened to death by her distorted reflection in the stainless steel! Can you imagine what a distorted English bulldog face looks like? I don't blame her!

My Dog Is
Peeing Everywhere

When adult dogs begin to urinate inappropriately, either in frequency or location, it is usually a sign of illness. The problem is that the mere thought of chronic illness and the potential costs associated with the care and treatment of it is often enough cause for owners to give up on their dogs and offer them for adoption, or worse.

What to Look For

Although a dog that is peeing everywhere is usually unwell, the first things to rule out are reasons other than illness. As mentioned in "My Dog Is Always Thirsty," a dog that's drinking more water will usually be peeing more often. So start by looking for reasons why your dog would drink more water than usual, such as pregnancy or changes in diet, weather, or exercise routine.

Next, check your dog's temperature (see "How to Check Your Dog's Temperature" on page 17 for instructions on how to do this). Then collect a sample of your dog's urine in a clean container (see "My Dog

Cries Out When He Tries to Urinate" on page 224 for advice on how to obtain a urine sample).

When to Get the Vet

Excessive and inappropriate urination is serious, not to mention inconvenient. If you can't come up with an easy explanation for it, the first step is to bring a urine sample in to your vet (in a clean container) to be analyzed. Follow up with your vet's suggestions without delay!

What to Do

Ask yourself the following questions to try to figure out what might cause more urine to be produced or prompt the urge to urinate more frequently:

Is your dog an intact male? If he is, it is possible that he has perceived a need to mark his territory. This could be a response to a nearby female coming into "heat." Or your dog may have an enlarged prostate gland causing difficulty maintaining a substantial stream of urine. This could cause the need for more frequent urinations and even some leaking of urine. Your vet should be able to confirm or rule out these possibilities and give you some advice on how to either treat or manage them.

Is your dog an intact female? If so, she might be pregnant or coming into "heat." The hormonal changes related to the estrous cycle are often associated with frequent urinations, and not all dogs are capable of holding it in until they can get outside. Alternatively, your dog might be pregnant, and the space occupied by the fetuses is leaving less room in her abdomen for urinary bladder filling. This would result in more frequent, low volume urinations. Pregnancy can be diagnosed by X-ray, ultrasound, or palpation, depending on how long ago your dog conceived. These reasons for urinary problems are usually treated by waiting them out, but your vet may be able to suggest some better ways to manage them for your individual dog.

Does your dog have a fever? If so, she might be suffering from an infection, particularly a urinary tract infection, which would cause both a feeling of urgency and an increased thirst. See your vet for immediate treatment.

Is the urine an unusual color? Very pale urine could mean that either your dog's kidneys are not functioning properly, or that she is drinking so much that the kidneys are being overloaded. Dark or bloody urine could mean a urinary tract infection, crystals or stones in the urinary bladder, blunt trauma to the abdomen, or even a mass in the bladder. See your vet right away if you notice this.

My Dog Is
Urinating Where
He Shouldn't

House training is an essential part of your dog's upbringing and one that is critical if your dog is to become and remain a welcome member of the household. If this breaks down at some point, there must be a reason and you best find the reason quickly, before your dog becomes "the enemy."

What to Look For

The purpose of this exam is very straightforward—to determine without question whether the inappropriate urinary behavior is either medical or behavioral in origin. Think back to your dog's food intake and output for the past three days, looking for even the slightest evidence of an increase in water consumption and/or urine production.

Next, take a close look at your dog's home environment, with an eye toward any changes that may have occurred in terms of people, objects, or scheduling.

Finally, perform a thorough physical exam on your dog to see whether there are any other issues that might be pushing him to urinate inappropriately. Follow the examination directions in "My Dog Is Straining to Urinate" on page 258.

What to Do

Now, answer the questions in "My Dog Is Always Thirsty" on page 83 as well as the following:

Is your dog an intact male or female? If so, there is a strong likelihood that the inappropriate urinary behavior is due to the compulsion to mark territory. Be sure to both clean the areas repeatedly in your house where your dog has urinated and deny your dog access to those areas in the future. Make sure that the appropriate places to urinate are always available to your dog while he is restricted from the other places. If all else fails, ask your vet for the name of a reliable animal behaviorist.

Is your dog drinking an excessive quantity of water? This could be caused by conditions such as diabetes, infection, and

Cushing's syndrome. Your dog's veterinarian can perform the blood tests needed to confirm or refute these possibilities.

Is there blood in your dog's urine? This could indicate a urinary tract infection, crystals in your dog's urine, kidney or bladder stones, or urinary tract tumors. In any case, your veterinarian should be consulted as soon as possible.

Have you had any recent visitors to the house? If so, and especially if they had their dogs with them, your dog may be responding to their smell by covering it with his own.

My Dog Is Urinating Where He Shouldn't

My Patient's Story

David called me one day to report that Madonna, his Sheltie, was having accidents all over the house. "Doc, I don't know how much more of this we can take. You know my wife and I both work and if we have to come home to many more of these surprises we're either going to have to get rid of the dog or end up divorced!"

Later, after we had gone the route of doing blood testing and dietary experimentation, with no real improvement, David was describing to me how Madonna hated to walk in the snow. It dawned on me that maybe the brutal winter we were having might be responsible for Madonna's issues.

"David," I said, "I know it may sound crazy, but get your extension cord and a hair dryer and go out and dry off an area of grass where Madonna likes to do her business and see if that helps." The remainder of the winter was free of Madonna surprises—and David is still happily married.

My Dog
Urinates When Strangers Approach

Whenever a dog urinates in response to a stranger, it should be considered a sign of submission. This behavior can occur as a simple "squat and pee" maneuver, or it can take on the appearance of an elaborate ritual that includes cowering, tucking the tail, lowering the head, and looking very sheepish. In its most dramatic form, a dog will actually roll over on her back and urinate in place, often getting it on herself in the process.

What to Look For

There's really no need for an exam here. You understand the problem and I'm sure just want to fix it as soon as possible.

What to Do

The solution to this problem involves not only building your dog's confidence in herself, but also in building her confidence in you and your methods of dealing with dangerous situations.

The most successful means of breaking a dog's submissive urination habits is to have all strangers approach her with a minimum of excitement. They should speak in as unemotional a manner as possible and they should not engage her directly in any way. This way she should feel no threat or pressure.

Give your dog a reward for every interaction she engages in with no urinary behavior. Over time, this positive reinforcement with minimal threat and minimal excitement should promote confidence and minimize the need for submission.

My Dog Is
Pooping Everywhere

The canine digestive tract is quite similar to that of a human being. Dogs' elimination behavior, however, is not. While they will almost never defecate in an area where they eat or sleep, they will choose a location in which to defecate based on a complex assortment of instincts and sensations. In short, when a dog "goes" in a spot that seems inappropriate to us, it is either due to a medical issue, such as diarrhea, or a behavioral one.

What to Look For

Take a look at your dog's stool to see whether it's normal, formed stool, or diarrhea.

What to Do

Now, ask yourself the following questions to figure out how to proceed:

How old is your dog and how recently did you get him? Inappropriate defecation behavior in puppies and recently acquired, young dogs is most often accidental, and these episodes are easily corrected by more strictly regulating your dog's feeding and walking schedule.

It is important to realize that these "accidents" are not the dog's fault. In fact, correcting the problem is in *your* control, not your pet's. Sometimes a conversation with your veterinarian or a dog trainer can help you plan a schedule that will work.

Are we talking about normal, formed stool or is it diarrhea? As already suggested, most dogs hate to defecate in locations that they are not accustomed to. Medical reasons, such as diarrhea, though, can force them to eliminate before they can issue a warning bark or even make an effort to get outside or wherever it is that they typically go. If the stools are loose or watery, don't expect the problem to resolve until you have corrected the diarrhea. Most of the time, a dog's diarrhea is caused by some form of dietary indiscretion—such as his foray into your leftover Chinese food. So diarrhea can often be corrected by instituting a strictly controlled bland diet.

A good initial plan to try is to withhold all food for twelve to eighteen hours, then start by introducing the blandest diet possible, in small quantities. Try a 50/50 mix of boiled beef or lamb and boiled or steamed rice. This can be prepared by cooking the meat in boiling water, skimming the fat off, and then draining the meat in a colander. If you wish to make a large batch, it will keep in the fridge for a few days, or you can separate and freeze it and reheat as needed. You can also use human baby foods instead of boiling the meat, but stick to brands that have only pure meat without vegetables or grains mixed in.

Offer small amounts of the mixture every two to three hours. Continue this until the stools begin to firm up or, after two days of trying, the ongoing diarrhea forces you to see your vet.

Is your dog completely healthy? A healthy adult dog rarely begins to defecate inappropriately all of a sudden. If your dog's stool is soft or watery, and the bland diet suggested doesn't seem to work, check more closely for other signs of illness, such as blood or mucus in the stool, which could suggest an inflammatory process, exposure to toxins, or even parasites. Persistent diarrhea with mucus and/or blood should prompt a visit to your dog's vet.

Are the stools formed? If this is the first time this has happened and the stools are formed, look closely back on the last two weeks of your dog's life. Try first to figure out whether there have been any signs of illness in your dog over that period. If there have been none, switch your attention to yourself to identify any unusual patterns of behavior that your dog might

be reacting to. I rarely accuse dogs of vindictive behavior, but some will react dramatically to changes in their owners' lifestyles, and particularly to the company they keep!

Have you recently made any changes in your dog's diet? Dietary changes either in content, amount, frequency, or scheduling can result in a dog needing to eliminate at a time he is not used to. This may catch him by surprise and result in a not-so wonderful surprise for you. Even a new brand of dog treat or a little leftover restaurant food could have this effect.

Have there been any recent changes in your dog's environment? From the most dramatic home renovations to something as simple as changing the away message on your telephone answering machine, changes in what your dog hears, sees, and smells throughout the day can affect his bowel habits. If the inappropriate eliminations have come on suddenly without any medical reason, look hard at your dog's surroundings for an explanation.

My Dog Is Pooping Everywhere

My Dog Is
Dragging Her Bottom

Dogs can do some pretty amazing things. One talent they have yet to develop, however, is the ability to scratch their own bottoms. Yes, they are certainly adept at licking the area, but this is not always enough to accomplish the task at hand. When licking isn't enough to satisfy them, they will often resort to dragging their bottoms on the floor, sometimes referred to as "trucking" or "scooting." While this is certainly an obvious indication that your dog's rear is bothering her, it doesn't tell you why.

What to Look For

The best way to examine your dog's hindquarters is to put on a pair of rubber exam gloves and, while she remains standing, lift her tail up and have a good look. Here's what to do:

Once your dog's tail is elevated and her anus is easy to see, look all around the area for injuries, irritation, growths, or bulges. Try to use one gloved finger to feel the edges of her anus for bulges and to check for irritation or discharge.

The best way to refer to anything unusual that you might see in relation to your dog's anus is to identify its location as though you were talking about a clock. So, if your dog has a dark spot at the top of her anus, closest to her tail, you would say that it was located at twelve o'clock.

What to Do

Here's what to do, depending on what you found:

DIARRHEA: Has your dog recently been having bouts of diarrhea? Some dogs that are otherwise perfectly healthy will drag their hind ends on the ground in an attempt to remove any residue from the loose bowel movements. Try cleaning your dog's anal area with a warm, moist cloth or towel.

Has your dog been having loose or irregular bowel movements for quite some time? Sometimes after having had loose or irregular stools, a dog will develop abnormally full anal sacs, which cause discomfort. (Anal sacs are actually scent glands similar to the ones we find so objectionable in skunks, but less developed in

Contact your dog's vet if:

- You see a wound around your dog's anus.

- You see any discharge coming from your dog's anus.

- You see growths around or in your dog's anus.

GROWTHS, SWELLING, OR IRRITATION: These are fairly common in the region around a dog's anus. Growths should always be seen by a veterinarian when they are first noticed. Treat swelling by applying cold compresses. You can treat irritations at home with a topical antibiotic ointment, such as Bacitracin, or a steroid, such as hydrocortisone. If they don't work after a few days, call your dog's vet.

What if you see none of these? It's probably safe to treat your dog with cleansing, warm compresses, and gentle pressure.

size and offensiveness.) Another clue that your dog might have full anal sacs is if her rectum appears to be bulging in the five and/or seven o'clock regions. A dog scoots to try to alleviate the feelings of discomfort and fullness. Try cleaning your dog's anal area with a warm, moist cloth or towel and see "How to Empty Your Dog's Anal Sacs" on page 23 for help with anal sac issues.

WOUNDS OR DISCHARGE: Do you notice any wounds or discharge in the area around your dog's anus? Discharge of a viscous, sticky nature could indicate an infection, and almost any type of wound or infection to this region will prompt your dog to rub her bottom to try to solve the problem or at least make it feel better. If you do see wounds and/or a sticky discharge, especially if it is yellow to green in color and malodorous, get your veterinarian's help right away.

My Patient's Story

At first, I admit, I thought it was funny—the way my dog was scooting around the floor on her bottom. I remember my uncle had an old dog that used to do that. He called it "flop butt," and his friends told him his dog had hemorrhoids. When it went on, I realized there was something wrong. I took a closer look, and I didn't see any of those hemorrhoids, but she did seem a bit puffy, so I took a big wad of paper towels, pressed them up against her butt and squeezed. She let out a yelp and tried to bite me, but then seemed to change her mind. I noticed a nasty smell and realized that there was a blob of stinky goo in the paper towel. I chucked it out, got some more moist towels, cleaned her up, and dried her with a cotton facecloth. She seemed much better after that.

Thomas
Burlington, MA

My Dog Is Dragging Her Bottom

My Dog Is
Straining to Urinate

When your dog urinates, it should always be a comfortable process. In addition, whether your dog is male or female, the flow of urine should be steady and strong. If your dog's attempts to urinate seem to require more effort than usual, there is probably a reason—one that should at least be examined more closely.

My Dog Is
Straining to
Urinate

What to Look For

The first and most important part of an attempt to assess a dog's abnormal urinary behavior should be to look closely at his or her genitals. This process should begin like any other belly-rubbing session and continue as such while you look carefully for signs of recent licking, chewing, or scratching. These signs would be in the form of saliva staining (a coppery discoloration of the fur), redness of the skin, wounds, or excoriations. While looking your dog over, check carefully for any other changes in the appearance of your dog's skin, such as blisters, rashes, or pigmentation. Also take note of any signs of discharge from the area or directly from your dog's genitals.

What to Do

Is your dog a male or female? Each of the sexes has its own reasons for straining to urinate. An intact male might appear to be straining when he is simply trying to mark that one last bush even though his bladder is virtually empty (of course he'll probably repeat this effort many times before the walk is over!). A female in heat might appear to be straining to urinate when, in truth, she is just responding to hormone-related changes and sensations that urge her to urinate despite the fact that her bladder is empty. Both of these instances should be considered normal and require no intervention or even concern. Subtle variations of these cases, though, should alert you to the possibility that your dog needs some help.

Is there blood in your dog's urine? With the exception of females in heat, every instance of bloody urine should be addressed immediately. In many cases of urinary tract infection, a course of antibiotics may solve the problem in short order. Other related issues, such as crystals or stones in the urinary tract, may be significantly more challenging to correct. All of them will require the help of your veterinarian.

Does your dog's urine stream appear thin and/or weak? This is worrisome, particularly if your dog is male, since an enlarged prostate gland will tend to put pressure on the male urethra, restricting the flow of urine. Urinary crystals can also act as partial or complete obstructions to the male urethra, blocking the flow of urine and creating a very uncomfortable dog. In females, a diminished urine flow may simply mean that she has less urine than usual, but if there is also blood in the urine you should be concerned that there may be crystals, stones, or even a soft tissue mass presenting an obstruction to the flow of urine. Once again, if there is blood, you should have your vet check her out.

Did your examination reveal any signs of infection, abnormal growth, or injury? Infections that cause urinary frequency, discomfort, or straining are often easy to treat, but because there are so many more serious problems that could cause your dog to strain to urinate, it is always best to get your veterinarian's opinion.

My Dog Is
Straining to Defecate

The act of defecating may vary somewhat in terms of how long it takes your dog to complete the act and how much effort is required to do so. Any time your dog must actually strain to produce a bowel movement, you should take the time to try and figure out why. Reasons could include the presence of an intestinal obstruction or foreign body, gastroenteritis, intestinal masses, cramping, impacted or infected anal sacs, intussusceptions, hernias, or something simple like diarrhea or constipation.

What to Look For

If your dog is in the unenviable position of crouching unsuccessfully in repeated attempts to defecate, the first thing to do is to get a good look at her anus and the surrounding area. There is no reason to feel embarrassed or shy about this! Check for anything that looks abnormal, such as asymmetry of the opening itself or the surrounding tissues. Look for bulging or redness of the regions adjacent to the anus or protrusion of tissue from its edges.

What to Do

Now, ask yourself the following questions:

Has your dog recently been suffering from diarrhea? If your dog is straining to defecate after a recent bout of diarrhea, it should not surprise you. A bland, reduced quantity diet may solve the problem, but if your dog continues to strain for more than two days, seek your veterinarian's counsel. (See "My Dog Is Pooping Everywhere" on page 254 for information on a bland diet.)

Does your dog often chew or swallow things she shouldn't? Dogs that habitually steal inedible objects and chew or swallow them are prone to suffering from intestinal obstructions. Your dog's straining could be an attempt to pass such an object. Unfortunately, there is little you can do other than offer food, liquids, or even a lubricant type of laxative, such as cod liver oil.

Did you notice anything protruding from your dog's anus? If so, try to identify exactly what it is. If it is something you feel confident won't cause any trauma on the way out, don your rubber gloves, use some K-Y jelly to lubricate the area around the object, and grasp it firmly. Have someone else distract your dog while you slowly and gently withdraw the item. Have plenty of paper toweling or other absorbent material nearby, since there may be a quantity of semi-formed to liquid feces trapped behind the obstruction, waiting to squirt out! If you cannot identify the

My Dog Is
Straining to
Defecate

- If the straining continues for more than two episodes, consult your veterinarian.

- If your dog begins to vomit in conjunction with making repeated unsuccessful attempts to defecate, it is urgent that you see your vet for help.

protruding object or material, it is best left to your veterinarian to figure out, but be sure to do so immediately.

Did you see blood in your dog's rectal region? Bleeding from the rectum when you have already noticed your dog straining is a serious sign. (See "My Dog Is Bleeding from His Anus" on page 43.) Always seek veterinary advice in such cases.

Does there appear to be bulging in the five o'clock and/or seven o'clock regions of your dog's anus? This suggests that your dog may have full, impacted, or infected anal sacs. While some owners are willing to attempt to solve this problem at home, your dog's vet is really the one to handle this responsibility. If you wish to try, see "How to Empty Your Dog's Anal Sacs" on page 23. If you are successful, look at the material that you have expressed from the anal sacs. If it is viscous and tan like motor oil, that is normal. If it is yellowish and creamy to cheesy, with or without blood, the sacs are infected and need treatment by your veterinarian. If the material is dark brown to black and shiny, almost metallic in appearance, it means that the sacs have been impacted for quite some time and should be monitored closely by both you and your vet for future problems.

When was your dog's last normal bowel movement? If you realize, in the midst of being concerned about your dog's unsuccessful attempts to defecate, that it has been two days or more since your dog's last normal bowel movement, it is wise to at least have a conversation with your veterinarian. If your dog also looks or acts depressed or lethargic during this time period, get her in to the vet right away.

How to Get Your Dog to Defecate

Laxatives are often an effective way to help your dog in her efforts to eliminate. They vary in their ease of use and their methods of accomplishing their goal. The lubricant types—such as petroleum jelly and cod liver oil—work by simply coating the gastro-intestinal surfaces, allowing material to "slide through" a bit more easily. The bulk laxatives—such as Metamucil, raw bran, and Lactulose—provide a bulky, indigestible substance for the alimentary tract to work on, forcing other materials out in their path through the stomach and intestines. The final types of laxatives are the propulsive types such as Ex-Lax and Dulcolax. These stimulate the muscular contractions of the digestive tract to move things along more rapidly. When using any of these, only do so on the advice of your vet, or with caution. It is easy to convert a constipated dog to one with a bad case of diarrhea if you're not careful.

PART 16: MY DOG SMELLS FUNNY

My Dog Has a Funny Smell Coming from His Ears

There is nothing quite like the ripe smell of infected dog ears for clearing a room! And when it's your dog that's the culprit, there is little else you will be able to focus on until you have at least gotten a handle on what the problem is and how to deal with it. A few easy steps should have you well on your way to a solution.

What to Look For

When your goal is to thoroughly examine your dog's ears, start by observing your dog at rest. Concentrate on how he holds his ears and moves them before you even attempt to approach them yourself.

When your dog is awake, grab a flashlight and some treats or toys. Your next step is to gain your dog's trust and calm him while preparing to focus on the physical exam of his ears. Try talking to him soothingly while you pet him elsewhere. Gradually work your way closer to the ears in a casual, relaxed manner. Food bribes and chew treats are often wonderful distractions.

Since the smell is what first drew you to them, follow your nose to the areas that seem the most pungent. Explore the entire area of his head associated with his external ears before moving on to the inside of his ears. Once there, get a close look at the full extent of his internal ears and as far into his ear canals as your eyes, a flashlight, and your dog's tolerance will allow.

My Dog Has a Funny Smell Coming From His Ears

Warning

Always be cautious when you manipulate ears that you suspect are infected. They can be quite sensitive!

What to Do

Now ask yourself a few questions to figure out how to proceed:

Did your exam reveal any puncture wounds or lacerations? Infected wounds are a common source of foul ear odor. Start by cleaning the wounds and treating them, following the directions supplied in "How to Clean a Wound" on page 18 and "How to Dress a Wound" on page 19. If the wounds are too serious or disgusting, leave them to your veterinarian to treat appropriately.

Did you notice accumulated blood, pus, or other discharge inside your dog's ears? Fungal and bacterial infections of the ears, as well as mite infestation, can result in the accumulation of a significant amount of discharge and debris. Fungal (often yeast) infections usually cause a fermenting smell with a brown, waxy discharge that can border on being quite soupy. Bacterial (often staphylococcal) infections are also quite stinky. The discharge is usually pus, which is yellowish to green. These infections tend to need both topical and systemic therapy. Get your dog in to see his vet within a few days.

Mite infestations can also be the original problem in ear infections. The characteristic sign is that the material in your dog's ears is granular and dark brown, like coffee grounds. If this is the case, follow the directions in "How to Treat Your Dog's Mites" on page 22.

My Dog Has a Funny Smell Coming from Her Mouth

Most dogs don't have minty fresh breath unless their owners are supplying the breath mints. Because dogs tend to enjoy spending time in close proximity to their owners, the normal smell of their breath is usually quite familiar to those owners. If you suddenly notice that your dog's breath has changed to something different and objectionable, trust your nose and find out why.

What to Look For

Conduct a thorough oral exam like the one described in "My Dog Is Drooling Excessively" on page 90. Pay particular attention to any signs of injury or infection of all the tissues outside and inside your dog's mouth.

What to Do

Next ask yourself the following few questions:

Did your examination reveal any infection, injury, or bleeding? These tend to be the primary reasons for the onset of foul breath. By effectively treating infection, usually with antibiotics, the odor tends to fade away fairly quickly. So place a call to your vet.

Oral injuries and the associated bleeding will usually result in an unpleasant, yet distinctive odor. As long as there is no infection involved, controlling the bleeding is usually enough to correct the unpleasant smell. (See "How to Control Bleeding" on page 18.)

During your exam, did you notice any growths, swellings, or redness of your dog's gums? Abnormal growths and swellings of your dog's mouth should always be seen by your veterinarian. They could be the source of the unpleasant odor and could certainly be serious enough to demand immediate attention.

Redness alone could be evidence of gingivitis, an inflammatory process of the gums that can often cause bad breath. If this is the case, try gently brushing or rubbing your dog's teeth and gums with a pleasant-smelling toothpaste to see whether matters improve. If they don't improve in a few days, check with your vet.

My Dog Has a Funny Smell Coming from His Skin

What does your dog smell like? Of course you know his scent exactly, but like the smell of a spouse or friend, you would be hard pressed to identify it specifically. When and if it changes dramatically, however, you'll probably be quite capable of identifying precisely how it is different. If the change is unsavory, investigate immediately before it evolves into something more worrisome.

What to Look For

Put on a pair of rubber gloves to protect your skin. Proceed as slowly and thoroughly as possible and conduct a complete examination of your dog's entire body. Search for anything unusual, paying strict attention to changes in shape, color, texture, temperature, and sensitivity of your dog's skin and hair.

What to Do

Next, ask yourself a few questions:

Does your dog have dry, flaky skin? This type of skin, often coupled with dandruff and changes in skin color, may be the result of a skin condition known as seborrhea. It is often treatable by using the proper shampoos containing chlorhexidine and/or benzoyl peroxide, or other appropriate medications. It's usually okay to try one of the over-the-counter varieties of canine dandruff or seborrhea shampoos sold at pet supplies stores before resorting to your veterinarian for help. Unless the smell is so horrendous that not a soul can tolerate it, you should be able to stick to the shampoo treatment for a week to ten days and solve the problem.

Does your dog's skin feel oily, but still flakes and smells? This too could be the result of seborrhea. Try the same routine outlined above.

Did your exam reveal any sign of the four I's (injury, inflammation, irritation, or infection)? If the signs are minor, follow the directions in "How to Clean a Wound" on page 18 and "How to Dress a Wound" on page 19. If they seem more serious, see your vet.

My Dog Has a Funny Smell Coming from Her Anus

Face it. Your dog's anus is not supposed to smell like a bouquet of roses! If the typical smell of your dog has been replaced by a distinctly foul odor that appears to be emanating from her hind quarters, though, there is probably a problem. The problem could be something quite grave, but more likely it is something simple and quite treatable.

What to Look For

Start by reviewing your dog's recent bowel habits. Consider the frequency and regularity of bowel movements as well as their color and consistency.

Next, conduct a comprehensive examination of your dog's entire rectal region by lifting her tail and looking closely. It may help to have a friend distract your dog with treats, comfort, and affection.

What to Do

Asking yourself the following questions should help you figure out what to do:

Has your dog been suffering with recent bouts of diarrhea? The diarrhea alone could be responsible for the objectionable odor. Try a bland diet for a few days (see "My Dog Is Pooping Everywhere" on page 254 for more information on this diet).

Did your exam reveal bulges at five o'clock and/or seven o'clock on your dog's anus? If so, your dog probably has full or even impacted anal sacs. If you're up to it, try following the directions in "How to Empty Your Dog's Anal Sacs" on page 23.

When to Get the Vet

If your exam revealed any open wounds or signs of infection in your dog's rectal region, see your vet for the appropriate treatment. Infections and open wounds in this very delicate region require the skills of your veterinarian in order to set your dog straight.

My Dog
Fell from a Height

If your dog ever falls from a height greater than a few feet, it should merit a thorough examination at least by you and possibly by your vet. Falls are uncommon incidents in the lives of four-legged creatures and since they come as a surprise, they often end in awkward landings. The outcome of these landings varies tremendously, depending on the size and breed of the dog, the height from which the dog fell, the surface on which the dog lands, and the nature of the landing. I have seen one dog sustain a frightful fracture by simply stumbling along a flower bed border, and I've seen another dog that fell from a third floor window not sustain more than a bruise! Crazy things can happen when a dog is caught by surprise, so if your dog has a significant fall, assume the worst and hope for the best.

What to Look For

Gently stroke your dog's hindquarters, gradually working your way forward toward his head. By rubbing in circles, using light pressure, and speaking in a soothing voice, you will calm your dog while gaining knowledge regarding where he is tender.

Once you have covered most of his body with your guarded circular massage technique, move on to his head. If he's wearing his collar, this would be a good time to attach his leash. Some dogs that have suffered head injuries will suddenly try to run away, risking further injury in their disoriented, off-balanced condition. With a leash attached, you can prevent this.

Next, examine your dog's head carefully, but only superficially at first. Remember, your dog has just taken a serious fall and he could have fractured any number of bones, so each touch and manipulation must be performed with the utmost care.

- If your dog has fallen from a height, always approach him with caution! Because such falls often result in head injuries, your dog may be stunned, confused, or disoriented. This could cause some unexpected or unusual behavior. Be prepared by being overly cautious. Clear all people and objects away from your dog and get a large bath towel or blanket to use as protection and as a stretcher if needed. Also get your dog's leash.

- Not every dog likes to have his mouth pried open or even his lips lifted to expose the teeth and gums. This is especially true if your dog's mouth is clenched shut in an attempt to protect something painful inside. Go slowly and speak soothingly.

Look at his eyes, paying close attention to the size, symmetry, and movement of his pupils. Look for any evidence of cuts, swelling, blood, or bruising anywhere on his head and neck.

Carefully lift your dog's lips and check the color of his gums. Press his gums and then release and note how the color changes. Next check his ears for signs of bleeding.

Next observe your dog's breathing pattern. Finally, without manipulating his head or limbs, tempt him with a treat to rise on his own and support his own weight.

What to Do

As you slowly, gently, and carefully examine your dog, ask yourself these questions:

Is your dog exhibiting any signs of pain? Try to focus on what areas of his body really bother him. If the pain is substantial, an ER visit is appropriate, regardless of the pain's location. In general, if the pain is isolated to the limbs, you've got a little time, but if the pain is in the abdomen or thorax, have him seen in an emergency facility right away.

Has your dog vomited since the fall? If so, this could be a sign of head trauma and concussion. Check also for evidence of confusion or disorientation. In-hospital observation is recommended.

What do your dog's gums look like? They should be pink. If they are very pale, your dog is probably in shock, a condition in which most of your dog's blood pools in his abdomen in order to keep his vital organs and brain safe, warm, oxygenated, and supplied with nutrients.

When you press on the gums, the pink color of his gums should blanch, or become pale for a moment, then return to pink within two seconds. If the gums are pale to begin with or if they take longer than

When to Get the Vet

Falls are serious business and often require veterinary attention. If your dog is in great pain, shows signs of shock, is having breathing problems, or has a swollen or distended abdomen, get him to a veterinarian immediately.

two seconds to return to pink after you press them, rush your dog to an emergency hospital right away.

Does your dog's breathing pattern look or sound strange? Raspy, rough, wheezy, or high-pitched respirations are all of concern and worth having observed in a hospital setting. Very shallow breathing can signify painful respirations or a diaphragmatic hernia, two more reasons to hurry to an emergency facility.

Is your dog's abdomen swollen or distended? When abdominal organs such as the liver and spleen are injured in a fall, internal hemorrhaging may occur. Get him to the hospital immediately!

My Dog Was
Hit by a Car or
Heavy Object

My Dog Was
Hit by a Car or Heavy Object

Most every dog owner has at least one harrowing *hit-by-car* story to tell, and some of them are downright gruesome. If your dog gets hit by a car, unless she jumps right up and runs to you wagging her tail, she should be thoroughly examined by your veterinarian.

Try to remember three important things. First off, it's more important to seek timely care for your dog than it is to get the name of the driver who hit her. Second, even the most grotesquely fractured bones will mend when the proper veterinary care is administered. Finally, dogs are resilient creatures, especially when they have owners who really love them.

What to Look For

This is one of the most thorough yet delicate examinations to carry out because fractures and spinal cord injuries may exist. Remember, in most hit-by-car incidents the best thing you can do is figure out how best to get the dog to an emergency center without causing further injury to the dog or yourself.

If you witnessed the accident, you probably already have an idea of how serious the injuries may be. If your dog is not moving, try to get an idea of whether she has lost consciousness. While you're doing this, have someone get a blanket, board, or a stretcher if you happen to have one. Follow the directions in "How to Transport an Injured Dog" on page 20 and get her to the veterinary hospital.

If your dog is conscious, first check for any signs of bleeding, then follow the directions from "My Dog Fell from a Height" on page 266 for examining a dog with suspected fractures. Pay particular attention to the areas where there is evidence of blood.

What to Do

Next, ask yourself the following questions:

Is your dog in pain? This may seem like a silly question, but some dogs that are severely injured may be only partially conscious or in shock. This state of awareness could change at any moment, so be guarded in your approach to examining the dog. Obvious pain is all the more reason to be cautious in your efforts to help. Use a large towel or blanket and a muzzle to keep both your dog warm and protected and to protect yourself. Then, get her to an emergency center.

When to Get the Vet

If your dog is unconscious, in pain, or bleeding, get her to a veterinary emergency care center immediately!

Is your dog bleeding? If so, follow the directions in "How to Control Bleeding" on page 18. If there is pain and/or an obvious fracture associated with the bleeding, you'll have to make a judgment call on whether to apply pressure to control the bleeding at the risk of causing more pain. If the bleeding is substantial, try to control it while protecting yourself from harm. Then, get the dog to an emergency center!

My Dog Was Hit by a Car or Heavy Object

My Dog Was
Rescued from a Car Accident

An automobile accident can be just as dangerous for dogs as for their human companions. In many cases, dogs will suffer more devastating injuries simply because they are less likely to be seated in a safe position or be wearing a suitable restraint. Unlike a human's, a dog's first reaction following a crash is often to escape from the vehicle, so that he can assess his own wounds and gather his wits. Be aware of this instinct and exercise extreme caution when attempting to control and examine your dog following such an accident.

What to Look For

Because the results of a fall and a crash can be quite similar, conduct the examination outlined in "My Dog Fell from a Height" on page 266.

What to Do

As you slowly, gently, and carefully examine your dog, ask yourself these questions:

Is your dog exhibiting any signs of pain? Try to focus on what areas of his body really bother him. If the pain is substantial, an ER visit is appropriate, regardless of the pain's location. In general, if the pain is isolated to the limbs, you've got a little time, but if the pain is in the abdomen or thorax, have him seen in an emergency facility right away.

Warning

In examining any dog, even your own, that has suffered a powerful blunt trauma, never assume that the dog recognizes you or understands that you are trying to help! He may struggle violently or try to bite. Go slowly and carefully.

Has your dog vomited since the accident? If so, this could be a sign of head trauma and concussion. Check also for evidence of confusion or disorientation. In-hospital observation is recommended.

What did your dog's gums look like? They should be pink. If they are very pale, your dog is probably in shock, a condition in which most of your dog's blood pools in his abdomen to keep his vital organs and brain safe, warm, oxygenated, and supplied with nutrients.

When you press on the gums, the pink color of his gums should blanch, or become pale for a moment, then return to pink within two seconds. If the gums are pale to begin with or if they take longer than two seconds to return to pink after you press them, rush your dog to an emergency hospital right away.

When to Get the Vet

Car accidents are serious business and often require veterinary attention. If your dog is in great pain, shows signs of shock, is having breathing problems, or has a swollen or distended abdomen, get him to a veterinarian immediately.

Warning

Because automobile accidents often involve flying glass, metal, and assorted debris, your dog may have sharp foreign bodies penetrating his skin. These objects may hurt you if you are not careful. Also, they may be large enough to cause more damage when removed than if left alone. Don't be impulsive!

Does your dog's breathing pattern look or sound strange? Raspy, rough, wheezy, or high-pitched respirations are all of concern and worth having observed in a hospital setting. Very shallow breathing can signify painful respirations or a diaphragmatic hernia—two more reasons to hurry to an emergency facility.

Is your dog's abdomen swollen or distended? When abdominal organs such as the liver and spleen are injured in a fall, internal hemorrhaging may occur. Get him to the hospital immediately!

My Dog
Was Rescued
from a Burning
Buliding

My Dog Was
Rescued from a
Burning Building

If your dog has just been rescued from a burning building or even exposed to smoke and/or fire for a short while, expect there to be serious side effects within the next twelve to thirty-six hours. In most cases of smoke inhalation, the most serious effects do not occur immediately, but after a number of hours have passed and the body's inflammatory response sets in.

What to Look For

Your examination of a dog following emergence from a burning or smoking building should be brief and preferably conducted while transporting the dog to a twenty-four-hour veterinary hospital. Look for evidence of irritation of all mucus membranes, specifically the conjunctival tissues around the eyes and the tissues of the mouth and gums.

It will also be helpful to rub the dog down gently with a large light-colored or white towel slightly moistened with cool water. The light color will make any soot, cinders, blood, and other removed materials that come off your dog much easier to identify. The towel will also cool down the dog's external temperature while also

When to Get the Vet

- The best course of action following a dog's exposure to smoke and/or fire is to seek veterinary care and observation. Be sure this is done through a facility with twenty-four-hour care.

- If your dog is coughing or having trouble breathing, get her to the hospital immediately. Oxygen, antibiotics, fluids, and/or steroids may be required to stabilize her.

Years ago, I got an emergency call from someone's neighbor in Newton, MA. "Doctor, our neighbor's house is on fire and we think their dog is inside. Could you come right away because we're sure the dog is going to need some help once they get him out!"

When I arrived, the firemen were just pulling the dog's melting carrier out of the house with the dog inside. We managed to get Leo, a black Labrador retriever puppy, out of the carrier before it completely collapsed, but the neighbor got some of the melting plastic on her hand, which burned her badly before she was able to get it off. By using cold wet towels, we got the remainder of the melted plastic off Leo's fur and his subsequent respiratory condition took about as long to resolve as her hand took to heal.

giving you an idea whether there are any areas of her body that may have been in contact with burning embers or melting household materials like plastic or rubber.

What to Do

Ask yourself the following questions next:

Are your dog's mucus membranes red and irritated? Offer your dog cool water to drink to cool her mouth. Also, flush her eyes out with water or sterile saline. If your dog's eyes are swollen and red (like she has conjunctivitis), apply an ophthalmic antibiotic ointment, such as Erythromycin (Iloticin), to both eyes. If you have no such ointment, a sterile saline flush will help.

Does your dog have any smoldering or melted material stuck to her fur? Be sure to comb or brush it out. You may need to moisten it with cool water before attempting to remove it.

My Dog Was
Rescued from a
Frozen Lake

When a dog is rescued from icy cold waters, the first order of business is to bring his body temperature back to normal and thus maintain circulation to all his body parts. The second priority should be to maintain the dog's blood glucose within normal range. The third area to pay attention to is the respiratory system, ensuring that there is enough oxygen being delivered to all the tissues of the dog's body.

Whenever a dog is exposed to extreme cold, the body automatically does whatever is necessary to preserve core body temperature, protecting the organs most vital to the animal's survival. The longer the exposure, the poorer the circulation to the dog's extremities, so to avoid frostbite and eventual tissue death, act swiftly and efficiently.

What to Look For

Forget the exam, forget figuring out the details of how the dog fell through the ice or off the dock, and immediately perform the steps outlined below.

What to Do

Begin by rubbing the dog down with large, absorbent towels or blankets, preferably warm ones. Exchange wet ones for dry ones until the dog is dry.

Continue by offering the dog some warmed but bland food. If he shows no interest, try rubbing some Karo corn syrup or pancake syrup over his gums to allow the mucus membranes to absorb glucose into the bloodstream.

Finally, observe your dog's breathing. Is it labored and moist-sounding? It is quite possible that he has aspirated some water during the incident. He may cough some of this up, but if he doesn't he should eventually be able to resorb it over the next few weeks. This is probably the time to check with your veterinarian for further advice.

My Dog Was
Sprayed by a Skunk

Without a doubt, this is one of the most common animal emergency calls made in areas where skunks abound. While it doesn't constitute a true medical emergency, it does present an immediate, emergent need for resolution to the owners of the reeking dog! In addition, there are some side effects from the event that, if left untreated, could cause your dog some serious problems further down the road.

What to Look For

From a distance, get an idea of where your dog got sprayed. Since most dogs get sprayed directly in the face while they are running down the skunk, this is more a question of determining whether it was a direct hit. Direct hits are more likely to cause corneal ulceration and injury, while the indirect ones tend to resolve more quickly with minimal care.

What to Do

Here's what to do next:

Is your dog squinting and rubbing her nose and face? If so, you'll need to thoroughly flush and medicate her eyes as outlined in "How to Flush and Treat Your Dog's Itchy, Irritated Eyes" on page 21.

When to Get the Vet

Corneal abrasions or ulcers may result from the spray and/or your dog's subsequent self-trauma, especially if your dog is a brachycephalic breed, such as a bulldog or Boston terrier. (These dogs are distinguished by their protruding exposed eyes, extremely short, pushed-in noses, and small nostrils.) If your flushing and home medication don't appear to resolve your dog's symptoms, seek help from your vet. Long-standing corneal injuries can result in scarring and partial loss of vision.

Is your dog running around, trying to rub her fragrant self on everyone and everything within reach? This is a positive sign. If all else seems right with your dog, start in immediately on your bathing and rinsing routine. Save yourself a mess and a fiasco by ignoring what your parents, friends, and your parents' friends tell you about bathing your dog in tomato juice! This is an old wives' tale!

The best concoction for ridding the odor is a mixture of hydrogen peroxide, liquid dish soap, and baking soda. By mixing the three ingredients in the following proportions and pouring some in a spray bottle, you can use a two-pronged approach to de-skunking your dog without the unavoidable mess of bathing your dog with Del Monte's finest!

Here's the recipe: 32 ounces hydrogen peroxide, 2 ounces liquid dish soap (such as Palmolive, Joy, or Dawn), and 2 ounces baking soda.

Get a friend or family member to help you with the next part. Hold your dog outside or in the bathtub and use a sponge to bathe her with the mixture. Your helper can use the spray bottle—set to jet—to hit spots that need extra attention, and set to fine spray to cover larger areas. It helps to rotate using the concoction with water rinses and a mild shampoo. About three times through this rotation should achieve near perfect results.

My Dog Was
Quilled By A Porcupine

If your dog returns from an adventure outside looking like he was just feasting on a large cactus, he has probably been quilled by a porcupine. These quills present no threat to your dog's overall health, but they are very uncomfortable and can sometimes elicit a dramatic inflammatory response. This will look like swelling, irritation, and itchiness.

What to Look For

Most porcupine quills lodge themselves in the flesh of a dog's head and neck, especially the face and muzzle, since the reason for the quilling is typically the dog's attempt to bite the porcupine.

You'll need to do a careful exam of your dog. Look closely for evidence of quills near the eyes, nose, and mouth. Sometimes they are trickier to spot than you would imagine, since they are often quite thin and rather colorless in addition to being buried deeply. Be patient and careful. Try to identify all the quills and keep a count of how many you suspect there are before you attempt to remove the first one.

Removing Porcupine Quills

What to Do

What you'll need to do for your dog depends on what you found during your exam. Ask yourself the following questions:

Is your dog's face or muzzle swollen and itchy? If so, your dog is most likely very uncomfortable. Before attempting to do anything about the quills, try applying a cold compress to his face to both reduce the swelling and ease the discomfort.

Also consider administering a weight-appropriate dose of Benadryl. (See "Treating Your Dog's Allergic Symptoms" on page 25.) This will help reduce the swelling and itchiness while mildly sedating your dog, both of which are good to accomplish prior to attempting any quill removal.

Are the quills sunk deeply into your dog's flesh or are they only superficially buried? If the quills are only superficially attached, you may be able to simply pluck them out by wearing a pair of thick leather gloves, grasping them firmly, and pulling. This may be difficult if they are sunk deeper than the superficial layers of skin because the quills have barbs that make backing them out a challenge. If you find it impossible to do so, more dramatic sedation by your dog's veterinarian will probably be necessary, and the quills will have to be surgically removed (or, if they are lodged in your dog's lips, pushed through his lips and pulled out of his mouth using a pair of pliers).

Warning

Be careful during your exam, because you can be injured by quills that you may not see at first. Protect yourself by wearing gloves and going slowly, as your dog is probably frightened and in pain.

My Dog
Is Coughing

If your dog coughs a few times, it is rarely worth a second thought. If the coughing is repetitious, unusually harsh-sounding, or results in retching and even vomiting, it is definitely worthy of your concern. What does the coughing mean, exactly, and how serious is it?

What to Look For

Observe your dog for a few moments without touching her. Evaluate her breathing pattern; look for signs of a struggle to catch her breath and sounds that would indicate the presence of fluid or secretions in her lungs or airway. Listen closely when she coughs for the various sounds produced in the process. Look for evidence of a discharge from her eyes, nose, or mouth. Finally, think about her behavior over the past few days, looking back for any indications that there may have been signs of illness leading up to this moment.

What to Do

A few questions asked and answered should help you figure it out.

Has your dog recently been groomed at a salon or housed at a boarding facility? Whenever a dog is exposed to a number of other dogs in a closed environment, there is a high risk of exposure to respiratory pathogens. *Kennel cough* is a common result, especially in dogs that have not been properly vaccinated. To avoid this, only patronize facilities that require the appropriate vaccinations. To treat the problem once it occurs, seek the help of your veterinarian. Do not simply use an over-the-counter cough medication because it may mask your dog's symptoms while allowing the infection to worsen.

Does your dog have a history of heart disease? Dogs with cardiac insufficiency of any kind are prone to accumulating fluid in their lungs, which often results in

If your dog has a bloody discharge coming from her mouth, nose, or eyes, waste no time getting help from your vet.

exercise intolerance and a moist, productive cough. If this is the case, your dog should be evaluated by a veterinarian and, in all likelihood, will need to be placed on medication.

Does your dog have a discharge from her mouth, nose, or eyes? If you notice a clear to gray discharge, it is possible that allergies are the problem. Try using a weight-appropriate dose of an antihistamine, such as Benadryl or Claritin, to see if the coughing improves. Check with your vet first. If the color of the discharge is yellowish to green, it usually signifies infection and will probably need veterinary attention.

Has your dog recently been fighting an infection of some sort? Viral and bacterial infections and combinations of the two

(which often happen in cases of kennel cough) are common causes of worrisome coughs in dogs. Your dog's immune system certainly has the capacity to fight a bacterial infection, and many viral illnesses run their course within a few days. However, if your dog is becoming fatigued by the coughing, seems lethargic, or feels like she has a fever, your vet should be consulted right away.

Does your dog often suffer from respiratory allergies? Dogs with respiratory allergies may cough after exposure to any of the allergens they are sensitive to. If this has happened in the past, you probably already know what to do. If your dog has asthma, your vet has probably already given you an appropriate course of action.

If you fear that your dog has an as-yet undiagnosed respiratory allergy, the first step should be to confirm what new exposures have taken place and work toward avoiding them. HEPA filters in your heating/air conditioning may help. If the symptoms are serious enough, your vet may recommend allergy testing and even desensitization injections.

My Dog Is
Coughing

My Dog Is Sneezing

A sneeze here and there is a normal event in a dog's life. You and I probably feel like it's a good thing to sneeze once in a while. Repeated sneezing, however, is not normal and may indicate a serious problem. If it goes on for too long, it may even lead to bleeding, and the sneezing will then turn into a bloody spray. If your dog is sneezing more than you think is normal, there are a few things you can do in order to get a better idea how serious it is.

My Dog Is Sneezing

What to Look For

Start your assessment by offering your dog a drink of water. Occasionally a drink alone will clear the oronasal passage of some irritant and resolve the sneezing. Next, look your dog straight in the eye and get an idea if there are any asymmetries of his eyes, face, or muzzle. If you have some sort of protective face- and eyewear, use it to prevent getting oral or ocular exposure to your dog's nasal discharge. Listen carefully to your dog's breathing in between the sneezing episodes. Try blocking first one nostril, then the other, to determine whether there is any form of partial or complete obstruction in either of the nasal passages. Use your flashlight and try to get a look into each of your dog's nasal openings.

What to Do

Ask yourself a few questions to figure out what to do next:

Does your dog suffer from allergies?
Respiratory allergies are often the cause for seasonal bouts of episodic sneezing. If your dog has allergies to various seasonal plants or pollens, this may explain the sneezing and your dog may respond well to an antihistamine such as Tavist, Claritin, or even Benadryl. In general, check with your vet for dosage and to confirm that your dog has no specific additional health risks that would prevent you from using them safely.

Has your dog been outside and/or unsupervised for any period of time recently?
Inquisitive dogs are prone to sniffing new and interesting plants, objects, and substances, some of them dangerous. Any of these things can be inhaled, resulting in partial or complete obstruction of a nasal passage, pain, inflammation, and the resultant sneezing. Sometimes, even after one of these is evacuated, the irritation it has caused will promote continued

sneezing episodes. A bee sting is a perfect example and one that can continue to get worse with time if left untreated. If at any time during your evaluation of your dog's sneezing, the symptoms worsen, get him to your vet immediately.

Did you see any swelling or asymmetry to your dog's face? Blunt trauma and insect bites or stings are common causes of facial swelling associated with sneezing. If blunt trauma is suspected, get him to your vet. If an insect bite or sting is your suspicion, as long as his breathing is not labored or wheezy, a dose of Benadryl may reduce the swelling and could even solve the problem.

Does there appear to be any sign of infection? Any yellow to green discharge from the nostrils, eyes, or mouth could explain the sneezing and point you toward your veterinarian for medical treatment.

Did you see any bleeding from your dog's nostrils? Though it is possible that repeated sneezing will traumatize your dog's nasal passages enough to cause bleeding, any blood from his nostrils is enough to merit a visit with his veterinarian.

Does the airflow through your dog's nostrils seem difficult or uneven? Nasal inflammation or obstruction will result in difficulty passing air through those openings. If this is the case, and the use of over-the-counter antihistamines like Benadryl, Tavist, or Claritin results in no improvement, seek your veterinarian's help.

My Dog Is
Always Seeking Heat

Many dogs, being pack animals, enjoy the comfort provided by body heat. They like to snuggle with humans and other dogs, but they will make due with a spot by a radiator or a roaring fire. This is perfectly normal. If a dog is *never* seen anywhere but beside or in direct contact with a source of heat, it should be considered unusual, if not pathologic. At any rate, this sort of behavior merits further investigation.

What to Look For

In examining a dog that is constantly seeking heat, start by evaluating the dog's environment. Is it warm enough to allow you to feel comfortable without wearing more than a thin layer of clothing?

Conduct a partial neurological examination as well, like the one outlined in "My Dog's Eyes Are Bulging" on page 171. Continue by donning your gloves and conducting a total head-to-tail skin check. Finally, review your dog's recent eating, drinking, bowel, and urinary habits.

What to Do

Now ask yourself the following questions:

Does your dog shiver when she isn't near a heat source? If so, and if you too feel chilled in this environment, try turning up the heat! If the room is perfectly comfortable, yet the dog is still shivering, look to another cause for your dog to have lost her temperature-regulating ability.

Has your dog recently suffered a head trauma or serious fever or infection? Any of these could result in the loss of a dog's ability to regulate her body temperature. This loss will often resolve once the cause has been corrected.

Does your dog have any significant skin problems, such as rashes, irritations, infections, or hair loss? Many of these problems, when coupled with heat-seeking behavior, suggest an endocrine disorder. Most common among dogs is hypothyroidism, a treatable disease caused by either an underactive thyroid gland or a problem with the dog's pituitary gland. Blood testing can confirm or disprove this as the cause of your dog's compulsion.

Has your dog recently shown increases in appetite, thirst, urination, or defecation? These symptoms often occur in conjunction with endocrine disorders or infections. Your veterinarian can do the necessary blood testing to make the diagnosis.

My Dog Is
Always Seeking Cold

With the exception of those breeds with exceptionally thick coats, especially the Nordic breeds, dogs are not inclined to seek cold without some very specific reason. If your dog is not one of those breeds, and unless it is summer time or the temperature is above 80°F, there must be something awry.

What to Look For

Because the reasons for cold-seeking behavior are limited, your examination should be focused on your dog's neurological and endocrine status. This can be accomplished by following the same routines outlined in "My Dog's Eyes Are Bulging" on page 171 and "My Dog Is Always Seeking Heat" on page 281.

What to Do

You will need to answer the following questions to uncover the reasons for your dog's unusual behavior:

Does your dog pant or appear to be overheated unless he is in a below 60°F environment? If the ambient temperature of your house or apartment is above 80°F, it could be normal for your dog to be showing signs of overheating. Turn up the air conditioning and see whether that solves the problem. If it doesn't, or if the temperature in the home is already reasonably cool, look for other reasons to explain why your dog may have lost his temperature-regulating abilities.

Has your dog recently suffered a head trauma or serious fever or infection? Any of these could result in the loss of a dog's ability to regulate his body temperature. This loss will often resolve once the cause has been corrected.

Does your dog have any significant skin problems, such as rashes, irritations, infections, or hair loss? Many of these problems, when coupled with temperature-regulating issues, suggest an endocrine disorder. When the behavior is of the cold-seeking variety, both hyperadrenocorticism

(Cushing's disease) and hypoadrenocorticism (Addison's disease) should be explored.

Individually, the symptoms listed above could be responsible for a dog's desire to seek cold to soothe his otherwise hot, irritated skin. Before assuming the worst, and if your dog is otherwise bright, alert, and responsive, try bathing him with a soothing, moisturizing shampoo and gently drying him with a soft, warm towel. If this does not result in improvement, move on to further diagnostics.

Has your dog recently shown increases in appetite, thirst, urination, or defecation? These symptoms often occur in conjunction with endocrine disorders or infections. Your veterinarian can do the necessary blood testing to make the diagnosis.

When to Get the Vet

If your dog is a greyhound or other breed with particularly low body fat, be conscious of the potential for a dangerous condition called malignant hyperthermia, which can be fatal if not treated immediately.

My Dog
Just Had a Seizure

Seizures are not ever, under any circumstances, normal or even okay. The sight of your dog convulsing on the floor, legs pumping furiously, teeth chattering, foaming at the mouth while losing bowel and bladder control is a frightening one indeed. If your dog has one for the first time, your *physical* response should be to follow the directions outlined below. Your *intellectual* response should be to regard this as evidence that your dog has a very serious problem, but one that may be either curable or at least manageable.

My Dog
Just Had
a Seizure

Following the seizure, write down a detailed description of the event. Be specific about what happened leading up to the seizure, including what and when your dog last ate, the duration and degree of the episode, how it ended, and what behaviors your dog exhibited for the minutes and hours following the seizure and until full recovery was achieved. Try not to leave anything out! All these details are important because they may lead to a treatable diagnosis instead of the usual one of idiopathic epilepsy, which means epilepsy of unknown origin. Seizure disorders aren't often curable, but they are usually treatable.

What to Look For

Because seizures are the result of the disorganized firing of multiple neurological connections within the brain, focus your examination on your dog's nervous system. Start by performing an examination like the one outlined in "My Dog's Eyes Are Bulging" on page 171. Continue by thoroughly examining your dog's ears as outlined in "My Dog Has a Discharge Coming From His Ear" on page 113. Complete your exam by following the directions from "My Dog Keeps Falling Down" on page 188. This should give you an idea of whether you should be more worried that your dog might have sustained a head injury, developed a brain tumor or some systemic illness, or simply gone far too long without eating anything.

What to Do

Now, ask yourself the following questions:

When did your dog last eat and what did the meal consist of? If your dog has become hypoglycemic from exertion without enough nutrition over an extended period of time, she could easily have had a seizure from a lack of glucose needed by the brain to function normally.

If you suspect this to be true, rub some Karo corn syrup or pancake syrup on your dog's gums to help boost her blood sugar, then make a concerted effort to keep her on a reasonable and predictable diet in the future.

Has your dog recently been suffering from a systemic illness, high fever, or infection? Any of these could be the cause of seizures. If you have an idea what the underlying problem is, you may be able to avert any further seizures by gaining control of that problem.

Has your dog been showing new signs of illness? Increased urination, appetite and/or thirst, lethargy, jaundice, and loss of balance are all signs of problems that could lead to seizures. If your dog has experienced any of these prior to having a seizure, have the dog seen by a veterinarian to evaluate the new symptoms.

When to Get the Vet

- Has your dog recently ingested, inhaled, or been exposed to any unusual medications, foods, animals, substances, or chemicals? A single, isolated seizure or the first of a series of seizures can easily be induced by exposure to a variety of substances, including chemical toxins and the toxins produced by animals and insects. If you know what your dog has been exposed to, call your vet or the ASPCA National Animal Poison Control Center at 888-426-4435 to seek immediate advice.

- Whenever a dog has a seizure, a veterinary appointment is appropriate. At the least, simple treatable causes should be investigated. If medication is needed, it is always best to start sooner rather than later to avoid the suffering involved with further seizure activity. Most vets, though, will delay start of treatment until a dog has had at least two and possibly even three seizures. This is a way to avoid a lifetime of unnecessary seizure control medication.

My Dog Just Had a Seizure

My Dog Is
Is Shaking
His Head

My Dog Is
Shaking His Head

When it comes to dogs, any minor itch, tickle, irritation, or sting is enough to prompt them to shake a little in order to bring relief. When you see your dog shaking, therefore, it is no big deal. If the shaking persists, however, and it consistently involves one part of your dog's body, it is cause for concern. When it is his head that he keeps shaking, there are a number of distinct possibilities that could be the reason, and some of them may require swift action.

What to Look For

Begin your examination by following the directions outlined in "My Dog's Head Is Tilted" on page 203, paying particular attention to your dog's ears. In addition, check your dog's skin carefully for any signs of dryness, irritation, infection, wounds, or parasites. If you notice any one of these, the sooner you treat your dog with the appropriate medication, the better chance he has for a rapid recovery.

What to Do

Here's what to do next:

Does your dog have any evidence of an ear infection? Even a mild yeast infection is enough to induce a dog to shake his head frequently. Follow the directions for cleaning your dog's ears in "How to Clean and Treat Your Dog's Dirty and/or Infected Ears" on page 24.

Does your dog have any swelling of his ears? Sometimes a dog with an infection or other irritation of his ears shakes his head so much that he bangs it against something, which can cause a blood blister on the ear. This is called an aural hematoma, and it will certainly cause your dog to shake his head even more. This problem usually needs simple surgical intervention.

Does your dog have evidence of an injury or infection? The discomfort from a wound or a local infection of any part of your dog's head could cause him to shake his head. Clean and treat the wound or infection, and the shaking may stop.

Aural Hematoma

Has your dog recently suffered a head trauma? Trauma to the head can result in a number of problems that might cause a dog to shake his head. If the results of the trauma are not serious, the head shaking should diminish and eventually cease with time.

Does your dog's balance seem unstable? Dogs that have balance issues from any source—such as head trauma, stroke, inner ear infection, or vestibular syndrome—will frequently shake their heads to attempt to relieve the symptoms themselves. For more advice on how to proceed, follow the directions in "My Dog Keeps Losing His Balance" on page 190.

When to Get the Vet

Has your dog recently gotten into any unusual chemicals or medications? Since many toxins have a direct effect on the nervous system, it is common for exposure to result in abnormal behaviors or neurological symptoms. Some products may even cause temporary blindness. If you know what chemicals or medications your dog has possibly ingested or inhaled, call the ASPCA National Animal Poison Control Center at 888-426-4435 for immediate advice. Plan to make a trip to the nearest animal emergency facility as well.

My Dog Is
Is Shaking
All Over

My Dog Is
Shaking All Over

In the course of a day, most dogs will scratch, rub, chew, or shake some part of their bodies a great number of times. Such behaviors are normal and to be expected. If, however, such behavior is restricted to shaking and it involves your dog's entire body, be concerned. The reasons for shaking that takes over a dog's entire body are limited.

What to Look For

With this in mind, you need to first evaluate your dog's neurological status, then assess his nutritional, endocrine, and immune status.

Start by conducting an ocular/neurological evaluation like the one outlined in "My Dog's Eyes Are Bulging" on page 171. Continue by donning your gloves and thoroughly examining your dog's skin from head to tail, checking for any and all abnormalities. In the process, get an impression of whether your dog appears to be overheated and/or if her skin seems hypersensitive to your touch.

What to Do

Next, ask yourself these questions:

What did your dog last have to eat and how long ago was it? Hypoglycemia, a shortage of glucose (blood sugar) in the bloodstream, is a common cause of "the shakes." If hypoglycemia becomes dramatic enough, the trembling or shaking can progress to outright seizure activity. If you are even mildly suspicious that your dog's blood glucose is below normal, rub Karo corn syrup or even pancake syrup on your dog's gums to get some much-needed glucose into her system.

Similarly, poor nutrition can result in electrolyte imbalances that can result in muscle cramping and/or seizure-like symptoms. This is helpful to know but difficult to assess. It is a good reason to avoid poor quality foods, but also a reason to call your vet if you suspect it is the reason behind your dog's shaking.

Did your dog's neurological exam reveal any abnormalities? Overall body shakes can be a form of a seizure. And seizures can be caused by intracranial problems, signs of which can be ocular asymmetries, imbalance, and abnormalities of body carriage. The best advice? If the shaking occurs more than once in a twenty-four hour period or if one episode lasts for more than a few minutes, see your vet and request a neurological consult.

WHEN TO GET TO THE
VET

- If your dog ever exhibits seizure-like symptoms following any form of head trauma, take her to an emergency facility immediately!

- Has your dog recently gotten into any unusual chemicals or medications? Since many toxins have a direct effect on the nervous system, it is common for exposure to result in abnormal behaviors or neurological symptoms. Some products may even cause temporary blindness. If you know what chemicals or medications your dog has possibly ingested or inhaled, call the ASPCA National Animal Poison Control Center at 888-426-4435 for immediate advice. Plan to make a trip to the nearest animal emergency facility as well.

Has your dog been showing new signs of illness? Increased urination, appetite and/or thirst, lethargy, jaundice, and loss of balance are all signs of problems that could lead to seizures. If your dog has experienced any of these prior to having a seizure, it is important to have the dog seen by a veterinarian to evaluate the new symptoms.

Has your dog recently suffered any form of head trauma? The concussive forces of head trauma are enough to cause a variety of neurological symptoms. If your dog's shaking behavior was preceded by trauma to the head within the past thirty-six hours, the two are probably linked.

Has your dog recently been suffering from a systemic illness, high fever, or infection? Any of these could be the cause of shaking, trembling, or other seizure-like activity. If you have an idea what the underlying problem is, you may be able to avert any further shaking by gaining control of that problem.

My Dog
Is Shaking
All Over

My Dog Is
Shivering or Trembling

Like humans, dogs shiver or tremble for a wide variety of reasons. They will most commonly do it when they are cold, hungry, anxious, or frightened. Some dogs will do it if their blood sugar is dangerously low or immediately prior to having a seizure. Some of these are fairly alarming reasons, so it is best to try to figure out the reason why.

What to Look For

Evaluate your dog's overall health first by mentally reviewing your dog's past few days, including his appetite, thirst, and bowel and bladder habits. Assess your dog's current environment for temperature, comfort, stress, and potential or perceived threats. Finally, perform an overall body evaluation like the one described in "My Dog Is Stiff" on page 200.

What to Do

Ask yourself the following questions to ascertain how to proceed:

Did your mental review reveal any inconsistencies in your dog's routine over the past few days? Inconsistencies in behavior could easily be caused by electrolyte imbalances, hypoglycemia, nausea, or the undesirable side effects of being thrown off a normally predictable medication schedule. The sooner your dog's routine returns to normal, the better.

Does your dog show any signs of pain or discomfort? Pain is often a cause of trembling. If you suspect that pain is the reason behind your dog's problem, try treating the pain with an anti-inflammatory (see "How to Treat Your Dog with Anti-Inflammatories" on page 24).

Did your examination and mental review uncover any potential stresses and/or fears that might be adversely affecting your dog? Sometimes something as simple as a distracting treat or walk is enough to break the cycle of fear/stress and the shivering/trembling complex of behavior. In other cases, serious medications are needed to get a dog under control. These circumstances require the help and judgment of your veterinarian.

My Dog Is
Weak and Lethargic

Weakness and lethargy are both symptoms that prompt immediate action by most veterinarians. If your dog is looking weak and/or lethargic, you need to go through an immediate exam to determine whether an urgent trip to your vet is needed or if just a few readily available household items might solve the problem.

What to Look For

This isn't a physical exam. Instead, quickly run through this mental checklist to verify that:

- Your dog has eaten recently, but not to excess.

- Your dog has had enough to drink, but not too much.

- Your dog has not recently been running herself ragged for more than an hour straight.

- Your dog has not recently suffered any blunt trauma to any part of her body, especially her head.

- Your dog has not recently had access to any toxins or chemicals.

- Your dog has not been suffering from any recent illness.

- Your dog has no history of anemia or blood loss.

- Your dog is not currently taking any medications. (If she is, be sure to have the medication and the dosage handy.)

What to Do

Now, quickly ask yourself the following questions:

Did your mental checklist turn up any inconsistencies? If so, track them down and try to determine whether they could be the source of your dog's weakness. Follow the appropriate course of action, if it seems reasonable, at home. If not, see your veterinarian.

If your mental checklist does not fill you in on your dog's condition, try performing the examination outlined in "My Dog Is Stiff" on page 200 for clues as to which direction to follow to arrive at a diagnosis.

My Dog's
Nose Is
Wet/Dry
When It's
Usually
Dry/Wet

My Dog's
Nose Is Wet/Dry When It's Usually Dry/Wet

Are you an optimist or a pessimist, glass half full or half empty? This may seem irrelevant, but the issue of dry versus wet is like that when it comes to dogs' noses. If a dog owner asks the question, "Should my dog's nose be dry or wet?" or "Is it a dry nose or a wet nose that means my dog is sick?," there is no correct answer. The truth is that some dogs' noses are cold and moist most of the time, while others spend most of their lives with warm, dry noses.

What to Look For

There's probably no need to exam your dog any further. You've already identified what you think is going on.

What to Do

Ask yourself one simple question:

Does your dog seem healthy otherwise?
If you are concerned about your dog's health and you suddenly notice that his nose seems hot and dry, don't get overly worried unless you know for sure that his nose is ordinarily cool and moist.

Likewise, if his nose is suddenly cold and wet, it should only raise your awareness if warm and dry is his usual state and he also seems a bit off recently. As in most cases, it is the overall picture that makes for reasonable worry, not one isolated sign. Focus on your dog's other symptoms first, then come back to his nose.

My Dog
Is Wheezing

Unusual breath sounds are always alarming. When you are suspicious that your dog's respirations are abnormal, the first step is to identify the type of sounds you are hearing. A true wheeze is a vibrational sound that occurs when air is forced through a narrowed passageway where the walls are in close proximity to one another. By definition, wheezes occur as part of an obstructive disease or event.

Another possible explanation for wheezing is when tissues that are normally tightly stretched over or attached to other nearby tissues are suddenly loosened or freed from their normal tethering and are rendered loose enough to flap. If you can pinpoint the origin of your dog's wheeze, you may be able to diagnose her problem.

What to Look For

Before you get started with your examination, think about your dog's past few days' activities and behavior, including what she has eaten, what and who she has played with, and what sorts of unusual products and/or chemicals she might have been exposed to.

Next, take a moment to simply observe your dog, counting respirations per minute and noting how much effort she is putting into each breath. Dogs that are struggling to breathe will appear to be using their sides much more than those that are breathing comfortably. They will also tend to keep their mouths open in a typical panting posture.

Next move in closer to your dog and just listen, following your ears to the area where the wheezes seem to be loudest. Most often this will lead you to your dog's mouth or nostrils. Perform a thorough oral exam like the one described in "My Dog Is Drooling Excessively" on page 90 to get an idea if the obstruction is something that is physically apparent. While you're looking inside your dog's mouth, pay attention to the color of her mouth and tongue. If your dog's distress progresses further, her mucus membranes, including her tongue, may begin to turn gray to purple in color. If so, you should head to a veterinary hospital right away!

What to Do

Now ask yourself the following questions:

Does your dog suffer from allergies of any kind? If so, a wheezing episode could easily be brought on by exposure to either a food, plant, or other inhalant allergen. Try a dose of Benadryl before it gets worse. (See "How to Treat Your Dog's Allergic Symptoms" on page 25.)

Did your physical exam reveal any foreign bodies or other mechanical airway obstructions in your dog's throat? If so, use your good judgment to decide whether an attempt to remove the object is wise or if you are better off taking an immediate trip to see your veterinarian. Don't ever try such an action unless you are either sure that there is no chance of doing your dog any further harm, or that she is in such immediate danger that to wait would create a life-threatening situation.

Has your dog just completed an intense period of physical exertion? If so, let her rest and cool down for a minute or two before jumping to the conclusion that there is a problem. Some dogs, and particularly certain breeds such as pugs and bulldogs, are prone to wheezing after exercise due to the nature of their respiratory systems. Think about how hard it is for a pug or a bulldog to breathe even while at rest!

When to Get the Vet

- If your mental review alerted you to any potential exposure risks and if you are pretty sure what the specific products/chemicals might be, call the ASPCA National Animal Poison Control Center at 888-426-4435 for immediate advice. Plan to make a trip to the nearest animal emergency facility as well.

- Along the same lines, if you suspect that your dog has been bitten or stung by an insect, take immediate action to avoid total airway obstruction. If you have it, administer an appropriate dose of Benadryl and get to your vet immediately. (See "How to Treat Your Dog's Allergic Symptoms" on page 25.)

My Dog Is Wheezing

My Dog's

Tongue Hangs Out in a Strange Way

The normal canine jaw and the teeth it supports are designed to efficiently and effectively crush, tear, and chew prey until it is in a form capable of being swallowed. The canine tongue is a highly coordinated muscle designed to maneuver and manipulate that food to promote the efficiency of the chewing process. It is shaped and situated in such a way as to protect it and preserve it in a warm moist environment at all times, ready to fulfill its role.

As you might imagine, it's not a good thing if a dog's tongue is hanging out. If that highly specialized muscle is allowed to hang out of the mouth for extended periods of time, it could dry out, lose some of its sensitivity, and prevent your dog from properly eating, swallowing, and digesting. In short, other than when your dog is panting, it is abnormal for his tongue to be hanging out in an unusual manner.

What to Look For

Conduct a thorough oral exam like the one described in "My Dog Is Drooling Excessively" on page 90.

What to Do

If your oral exam reveals anything significant, address it in whatever way is appropriate (see "My Dog Is Drooling Excessively" on page 90 or other relevant chapters). If it reveals no abnormalities, check with your veterinarian about arranging a neurological consult.

My Dog Is
Panting
Heavily

My Dog Is
Panting Heavily

Dogs tend to pant a great deal. Because they don't sweat the way humans do, panting is their way of cooling down when they are overheated, in a particularly warm climate, after exerting themselves. This is not, however, the only reason why dogs pant.

Panting is also an important way for dogs to oxygenate their blood. Their bodies, like ours, have many complex feedback mechanisms, and a significant number of them result in an increase in respiratory rate (what we call panting). In other words, your dog's panting may be a normal response to an unusual and possibly abnormal condition. Assuming that the panting you're noticing is excessive, the first thing to do is try to explain it.

What to Look For

This is a simple one. Think for a moment about your dog's environment and what she's been doing lately.

What to Do

Next, ask yourself the following questions:

Is the ambient temperature high and/or has your dog been exerting herself more than usual? If so, the panting should subside in a few minutes provided the dog is kept cool and calm.

Has your dog eaten or drank an unusual food or liquid or an unusually large amount recently? If either is the case, your dog may be overfull to the point of discomfort, or on the verge of vomiting. Be ready to clean up a mess!

Has your dog been out of your sight for any period of time recently? If so, your dog may have sustained an injury. Check your dog's entire body for signs of pain or injury. Any kind of pain or significant discomfort is reason enough for a dog to pant excessively. Relieve the pain, and the panting should stop.

Is your dog being treated for any ongoing illness? Many chronic illnesses—such as Cushing's disease, chronic renal failure, and congestive heart failure—can cause panting either directly or by inducing electrolyte imbalances, which then, in turn, cause increased respiratory rate. This is an issue best addressed by your veterinarian.

Is your dog taking any medication? A variety of medications can cause panting (especially prednisone). Ask your vet whether the medication your dog is taking might be responsible.

When to Get the Vet

- While normal panting serves a useful function, abnormally excessive panting is often a sign of serious problems. Brachycephalic breeds—such as bulldogs, pugs, and Boston terriers—have particular difficulty recovering from heat-related exhaustion because of their physical structure. (These dogs are distinguished by their protruding exposed eyes, extremely short pushed-in noses, and small nostrils.) Don't ignore these dogs' panting if it lasts for more than ten minutes at rest in a cool environment. Think about it. Have you ever needed more than ten minutes to catch your breath, even after strenuous exercise?

- If your dog's panting doesn't subside in a few minutes, move on to a more thorough evaluation of the dog. Start by checking her mucous membranes. If the normally pink, moist tissues of the mouth and tongue are turning bluish purple (hypoxia) or are ghostly pale (shock), get your dog to an emergency facility immediately!

- Does your dog have a fever? Sometimes a body temperature of higher than 102.5°F will cause a dog to pant in an attempt to reduce its fever. (See "How to Check Your Dog's Temperature" on page 17 for instructions on taking your dog's temperature.) If your panting dog has such a temperature elevation and isn't simply overheated, it may be due to infection. See your veterinarian right away.

Index

[Note: Page numbers in italics indicate illustrations.]

A

abdomen
  after car accident, 271
  after fall, 268
  how to examine, 97, 98,
    142–143
  pain in, 234
  swelling of, 139–140
abscesses, how to treat,
  25–26. *See also* anal sacs
accidents
  fell from height, 266–268
  hit by car, 268–269
  hit by heavy object,
    268–269
  quilled by porcupine,
    276–277
  rescued from burning
    building, 272–273
  rescued from car acci-
    dent, 270–271
  rescued from frozen lake,
    274
  sprayed by skunk,
    275–276
aggression. *See* attacks;
  fears
allergies, how to treat, 25,
  153
anal sacs, 188, 257, 260–261,
  265. *See also* anus
  how to empty, 23, 24
  impacted, *44*
animals, fear of other, 243
anti-inflammatories, how to
  use, 24
anus. *See also* anal sacs
  bleeding from, 43–45
  discharges from, 119–121,
    234, 257
  foreign objects in, 165–166
  irritated rump skin and,
    55
  rubbing or licking of,
    159–160
  smells from, 265
  swelling and, 234, 257

armpits
  growths in, 131–132
  scratching, rubbing, or
    licking of, 158–159
ASPCA National Animal
  Poison Control Center
  phone number, 67
aspirin, how to administer,
  24
attacks, on people or animals, 239–241
aural hematoma, *287*

B

back
  irritated skin on, 53–54
  scratching, rubbing, or
    licking of, 157–158
  swelling of, 144–145
bald spots, 70–71
barking. *See also* crying out
  problems
  hoarse, 236–237
  nighttime, 234–235
bathrooming issues. *See*
  elimination issues
behavior problems
  acting strangely, 229–231
  attacking people or ani-
    mals, 239–241
  barking at night, 234–235
  barking hoarsely, 236–237
  chasing constantly,
    237–239
  fear of certain objects,
    247–248
  fear of children, 244–245
  fear of other animals, 243
  fear of shiny floors,
    245–246
  fear of strangers, 241–245
  pressing head into corner,
    231–232
  tucking tail between legs,
    233–234
Bernese mountain dog, 95
blanket stretcher, *20*

bleeding problems
  anus, 43–45, 234, 260
  calluses, 61–62
  ears, 30–32
  eyes, 28–30
  how to assess severity of,
    17–18
  how to control, 18, *18*
  mouth, 34–36, 91–92, 214
  neck, 37–38
  nipples, 208
  nose, 32–34
  paws, 38–40, 64, 80
  rectum, 166
  skin, 41–42
  sneezing and, 281
  stools, 227
  urine and, 226, 250, 252,
    258–259
  vagina, 212
blepharospasm, 173
blindness, 175, 231–232
blisters
  on genitals, 68–69, *69*
  in mouth, 66–67
  on skin, 64–66
bloodshot eyes, 168–169
bones, examining of, 186–187
bottom, dragging of, 227,
  256–257
bowel movements. *See* elimination issues
box carrier, *20*
brachycephalic breeds
  heat exhaustion and, 297
  skunks and, 275
breathing problems
  after fall, 268
  crying out and, 221–222
  sneezing and, 280–281
  wheezing and, 293–294
bulging eyes, 171–173, *172*

C

calluses, on elbows, 61–62
car accident, 268–271
castration, 206

chasing, constant, 237–239
cherry eye, 125, 168, *181*, 183
chest, irritated skin on,
  52–53
chewing, crying out and,
  213–215
children, fear of, 244–245
chocolate, ingestion of, 103
chronic uveitis, 180
circles, walking in, 198–199
cloudy eye, 170
coat. *See* fur problems
cold, seeking of, 282–283
cold compresses, 156, *182*
collars, irritated skin and, 50
conjunctivitis, 168, 169,
  183–184
coughing, 278–279
crying out problems
  breathing, 221–222
  chewing, 213–215
  defecating, 226–227
  head and, 217–218
  legs and, 222–223
  mouth and, 215–217
  stretching, 219–220
  urinating, 224–226
  yelping, 228–229

D

dark areas
  in eyes, 179–180
  in mouth, 57–59
  on skin, 59–61, 130–131
defecation. *See* elimination
  issues
dehydration
  how to check for, 27, 85
  how to handle, 27
  lip smacking and, 102
  thirst and, 84, 86
  vomiting and, 100
dental problems
  crying out and, 214
  drooling and, 91–92

facial swelling and, 137
    yelping and, 228-229

depression, hunger and, 88

diabetes, 109

diarrhea, 254-257, 260, 265
    how to manage, 23

diet. *See* food

discharges
    anus, 119-121, 234, 257
    coughing and, 279
    ears, 113-115, 262
    eyes, 111-112, 182
    nose, 116-117, 140
    skin, 117-119
    vagina, 212

disorientation, 230

dog trainer, 238

drooling, 90-93

drunken walking, 230

E

ears
    anatomy of, 31
    aural hematoma, 287
    bleeding from, 30-32
    circling and, 198
    discharge from, 113-115, 262
    foreign objects in, 161-162
    growths on, 30, 125-126
    head shaking and, 286
    how to clean and treat, 24-25
    irritated skin on, 47-48
    mites and, 22, 32, 114-115, 262
    neck and, 50, 155
    scratching or rubbing of, 149-151
    smells from, 261-262
    swelling of, 138-139
    ticks and, 31
    tilted head and, 204

eating and drinking problems
    chocolate ingestion, 103
    drooling, 90-93
    feces ingestion, 106
    gagging, 93-94
    gulping, 95-96
    hunger issues, 87-90
    lip smacking, 101-102

plant ingestion, 104-105
regurgitating, 97-98
swallowing strangely, 95-96
tampon ingestion, 106-107
thirst issues, 83-87, 251-252, 282, 283
vomiting, 99-100
weight gain or loss, 108-110

eczema, 79

elbows, irritated skin on, 61-62

electrical cords, 67

elimination issues
    blood in stools, 45, 227
    checking of stools, 254-255
    cold-seeking and, 283
    crying out when defecating, 226-227
    crying out when urinating, 224-226
    defecation difficulty, 259-261
    defecation everywhere, 254-255
    dragging of bottom, 227, 256-257
    feces ingestion, 106
    heat-seeking and, 282
    urination around strangers, 253
    urination difficulty, 258-259
    urination everywhere, 249-250
    urination in inappropriate places, 251-252

Elizabethan collar, *42*

emergency poison control phone number, 67

epidermal collarettes, 68-69, *69*

erection, constant, 209-210

exercise, importance of, 238

exophthalmic dogs, 112

eyes. *See also* third eyelid
    anatomy of, 29
    bleeding from, 28-30
    bloodshot, 168-169
    bulging, 171-173
    dark pigment in, 179-180
    discharge from, 111-112, 182
    growth on eyelid, 123-124
    growths on, 29, 30, 112, 149
    how to flush, 21, *21*
    pupils different sizes, 177-178
    pupils large, 174-175
    pupils small, 176

rapid movement of, 189, 204
red, 167-168
scratching or rubbing of, 148-149, 178
squinting, 173-174
styes and, 183-184
yelping and, 229

F

face
    growth on, 121-122
    irritated skin on, 45-46
    removing porcupine quills from, 276-277, *277*
    swelling of, 136-137

fainting, 192-193

falls, 188-190, 266-268

fears
    of certain objects, 247-248
    of children, 244-245
    of other animals, 243
    of shiny floors, 245-246
    of strangers, 241-242

feces. *See* elimination issues

fire, rescue from, 272-273

first aid kit, suggested items for, 15-16

fleas, *22*
    dull coat and, 75
    ears and, 31-32
    how to treat, 22
    skin irritations and, 50, 54-55, 157

flies, in ears, 32

floors, fear of shiny, 245-246

footpads. *See* paws

foreign objects. *See* objects

fur problems
    bald spots, 70-71
    dull, dry coat, 74-76, 110
    hair loss, 57, 60
    hot spots, 72-73
    how to remove matted, 21
    matted fur, 77-78
    shedding, 78-79

G

gagging, 93–94

gastric dilation and volvulus (GDV), 143

genital problems
  blisters, 68–69, *69*
  constant erection, 206–210
  enlarged nipples, 207–208
  enlarged testicles, 205–206
  enlarged vulva, 211–212
  growths and, 133–134
  scratching, rubbing, or licking of area, 158–159
  strained urination and, 258
  swelling, 225

gingivitis, 35

glaucoma, 169, 172–173

glucose, getting into system quickly, 190, 274, 285, 288

greyhounds, 283

groin area. *See* genital problems

growths
  anus, 44–45, 160, 257
  armpit, 131–132
  ear, 30, 125–126
  eyelid, 123–124
  eyes, 29–30, 112, 149
  face, 121–122
  genital area, 133–134, 212
  leg, 134–135
  mouth, 35–36, 92–93, 128–129
  nose, 127–128
  skin, 130–131
  third eyelid, 124–125

gulping, 95–96

gums. *See* mouth

H

hackles, 144

head
  crying out when turning, 217–218
  pressing in to corner, 231–232
  shaking of, 286–287
  tilting of, 203–204

heat
  in house, 76

seeking of, 281–282

hemorrhagic blisters, 68

hot spots, 72–73
  how to treat, 26–27

hunger issues, 87–90

hygroma, 62

hyperhydrosis, 87

hypoglycemia. *See* glucose

hypothyroidism, 61, 79, 109

I

illness. *See* sickness, evaluating signs of

imbalance
  ears and, 150
  evaluating of, 190–191
  head and, 204, 217–218, 287
  stairs and, 197

injuries
  transporting dog after, 20–21, *20*
  treating superficial, 156

iris nevi, 180

itchiness
  anus, 159–160
  armpits, 158–159
  back, 157–158
  ears, 149–151
  eyes, 148–149, 178
  genital area, 158–159
  mouth, 154–155
  neck, 155–156
  nose, 152–153

J

joints, examining of, 186

K

kennel cough, 278

"knuckling" maneuver, 189, 190, 195, 202

L

lake, examining dog after rescue from cold, 274

laxatives, 261

leathery skin, 56–57

legs. *See also* walking problems
  crying out and, 222–223
  growths on, 134–135
  how to examine, 146
  inability to use, 193–196
  swelling of, 146–147
  tail tucked between, 233–234

lethargy
  as sign of sickness, 291
  weight gain and, 109

light sensitivity, 214, 216

limping, 185–187

lips. *See* mouth

Lyme disease, 218

M

malignant hyperthermia, 283

mange, 76

marking territory, 250, 251

massage, 145, 200–201, 220

masses. *See* growths

melanoma, 60

menace reflex, testing of, 167–168, 171–172

mites
  dull coat and, 76
  ears and, *22*, 32, 114–115, 262
  how to treat, 22

mouth
  bleeding from, 34–36, 214
  blisters in, 66–67
  crying out and, 213–217
  dark areas on and in, 57–59
  drooling and, 90–93
  examining after car accident, 271
  examining after fall, 267–268
  growths on, 35–36, 92–93, 128–129
  how to examine, 35, 58
  scratching or rubbing of, 154–155
  smacking of lips, 101–102
  smells from, 263
  tongue hanging strangely, 295

muzzle, homemade, *20*

myasthenia gravis, 96

N

nails. *See* toenails

neck
  bleeding from, 37–38
  how to manage injuries of, 27
  irritated skin on, 49–51
  scratching or rubbing of, 155–156
  swelling of, 139–140

neediness, 231

neutering, aggression and, 240

nighttime barking, 234–235

nipples, enlarged, 207–208

nose
  bleeding from, 32–34
  dark areas on, 57–59
  discharge from, 116–117
  growth on, 127–128
  irritated skin on, 48–49
  scratching, rubbing, or licking of,
    152–153
  swelling of, 139–140
  wet or dry, unusual, 292

nystagmus, 189, 204

O

objects
  being hit by heavy, 268–269
  bumping into, 199–200
  drooling and, 91
  in ears, 161–162
  gagging and, 94
  in mouth, 214–215
  in nose, 153
  in paws, 164–165, 186
  in rectum, 165–166
  regurgitation of, 97
  strained defecation and, 260
  in throat, 162–163, 294
  vomiting and, 100

oral warts, *129*

orchiectomy, 206

P

pain, how to evaluate, 22

panting, 143, 296–297

paraphimosis, 209–210

parasites. *See also* specific parasites
  anal scratching and, 160
  dull coat and, 75–76
  in ears, 30, 31–32, 151
  genital area and, 158–159
  how to treat intestinal, 23
  matted fur and, 78
  nasal swelling and, 140
  neck irritations and, 156
  skin discharge and, 119
  skin irritations and, 57

paws. *See also* toenails
  anatomy of, *39*
  bleeding from, 38–40
  cracked footpads on, 63–64
  dragging tops of, 202–203
  examining of, 186
  foreign objects in, 164–165

pigments. *See* dark areas

pitting edema, 147

plants, eating of, 104–105

poison control phone number, 67

poisonous plants, list of, 104–105

porcupine quills, removing, 276–277,
    277

puncture wounds, 223

pupils. *See* eyes

pustules, on genitals, 68

Q

quick, on toenail, *81*

quills, removing of, 276–277, *277*

R

rectum. *See* anal sacs; anus

red eyes, 167–168

regurgitation, 97–98

retrobular abscess, 214, 216

Rhodesian ridgeback, 158

ringworm
  bald spots and, 70, 71
  hair loss and, 60
  skin irritations and, 46, 47

rump, irritated skin on, 55

S

seborrhea, 79, 119

seizure, 284–285

shaking
  all over, 288–289
  of head, 286–287

shampoos, emollient-type, 56–57, 76

shedding, 78–79

shiny floors, fear of, 245–246

shivering, 290

sickness, evaluating signs of
  coughing, 278–279
  hanging tongue, 295
  panting heavily, 296–297
  seeking cold, 282–283
  seeking heat, 281–282
  seizure, 284–285
  shaking all over, 288–289
  shaking of head, 286–287
  shivering or trembling, 290
  sneezing, 280–281
  weakness or lethargy, 291
  wet or dry nose, 292
  wheezing, 293–294

skin problems. *See also* fur problems
  back irritations, 53–54
  bleeding, 41–42
  blisters, 64–66
  chest irritations, 52–53
  cold-seeking and, 283
  dark areas, 57–61, 130–131
  discharges, 117–119
  ear irritations, 47–48
  elbow calluses, 61–62
  facial irritations, 45–46
  footpad cracks, 63–64
  growth on, 130–131
  heat-seeking and, 282
  leathery skin, 56–57
  neck irritations, 49–51
  nose irritations, 48–49
  rump irritations, 55
  scratching and, 159
  smells and, 264

skunk, 275–276

smells, unusual
  anus, 265
  ears, 261–262

mouth, 263
skin, 264

smoke inhalation, 272-273

sneezing, 280-281

sock bandage, *62*

spine, examining of, 194

spraying, by skunk, 275-276

squinting, 173-174, 182

stairs, inability to use, 196-197

stiffness, 145, 200-202

stings
sneezing and, 281
vomiting and, 100

stools. *See* elimination issues

strangers
fear of, 241-242
urination around, 253

stretching, crying out when, 219-220

submissive behavior
tail between legs and, 233-234
urination and, 253

swallowing difficulties, 95-96, 237

swelling
abdomen, 139-140
anus, 234, 257
back, 144-145
calluses, 62
ear, 138-139
face, 136-137
genitals, 225
leg, 146-147
neck, 139-140
nose, 139-140

T

tail
tucked between legs, 233-234
tucked underneath, 189-190

tampon, ingestion of, 106-107

teeth. *See* dental problems

temperature, how to take, 17

testicles, enlarged, 205-206

third eyelid
growth on, 124-125
problems with, 168, 181-183

thirst issues

always thirsty, 83-85
cold-seeking and, 283
heat-seeking and, 282
never thirsty, 85-87
urination and, 251-252

throat, foreign objects in, 162-163, 294

ticks
in ears, 31
engorged, *45*
in genital area, 159
how to remove, 22-23
mistaken for growths, 122, 123, 126, 130
on skin, 45

tilted head, 203-204

toenails
bleeding from, 40
broken, 79-81
how to examine, 186
how to trim, *82*
quick in, *81*
strange growth of, 81-83

tongue, hanging strangely, 295

transport methods, for injured dog, 20-21, *20*

trembling, 295

U

urinary tract infections, 210, 224-226

urination. *See* elimination issues

V

vaccinations
coughing and, 278
nasal discharges and, 116-117
swelling and, 141, 145

vagina. *See* genital problems

vision, testing of, 167-168, 171-172

vomiting
after car accident, 271
after fall, 267
defecation problems and, 227
evaluating of, 99-100
how to force, 17
hunger and, 90
vulva, enlarged, 211-212

W

walking problems. *See also* legs
bumping into objects, 199-200
can't use stairs, 196-197
circling, 198-199
dragging paws, 202-203
fainting, 192-193
falling, 188-190
limping, 184-187
losing balance, 190-191
stiffness, 200-202
tilted head, 203-204

warts, oral, *129*

water, examining after rescue from cold, 274

weakness or lethargy, 291

webbing, examining of, 186

weight gain or loss, 108-110

wheezing, 293-294

Wobbler's syndrome, 217-218

wounds, how to clean and dress, 18-19, *19*

About the Author

Dr. Jake Tedaldi is a 1980 graduate of Harvard University, where he concentrated in English and American Literature and Languages. He remained at Harvard as a freshman advisor while working at Massachusetts General Hospital and McLean Hospital for two years.

Jake began his veterinary education in the fall of '86 and graduated from Tufts University School of Veterinary Medicine in 1990. He lives in Newton, MA with his wife, Ruth, their four sons, Max, Luke, Jude, and Dylan, and their Labrador retriever, Tilly. His mobile veterinary practice takes him on house calls throughout the greater Boston area.

Acknowledgments

I would be remiss if I were not to credit those people who have made it possible for this book to exist. These are the people who shaped my approach to life in general, and also my way of treating people, animals, and the relationships that exist between the two. These are also the people who fostered my interest in academics and the sciences in particular, helped me achieve my goals, and encouraged me when there were obstacles in my path. Finally, these are the people who facilitated the actual events that led to the creation of this book. Here goes:

Thank you, Mom and Dad (Eugene and Anne-Marie Tedaldi), for providing the kind of home where it was okay to raise a raccoon cub for three years; nurse injured crows, squirrels, and chipmunks back to health; and house an eleven-foot long boa constrictor for more than a year after I had left the house! Thank you to my three sisters—Jeana, Pat, and Claire—for teaching me that softer and kinder is always better.

Thank you, Sister Assumpta (Kathleen Fitzgerald), for making me understand how important it is to read, read, read, and to always be proud to be smart!

Thank you, Mr. Heckman, for not castigating me for getting that one drop of dilute HCL in Caroline Clarke's eye!

Thank you, Ms. Barbour, for teaching me that the letters after your name don't mean a thing unless you've got the goods to go with them.

Thank you, John Barnwell, for the clinical, cynical perspective on life, love, religion, the cosmos, dreams, and reality.

Thank you, Jules and Jeanette, for your emotional and financial support and especially "Nettie" for honing my vocabulary skills!

Thank you, Alicia Gordon and Ann Lower, for setting the wheels in motion.

Thank you, Max, Luke, Jude, and Dylan, for making me the proudest father on earth and for never allowing me to get away with even a borderline error in grammar, punctuation, pronunciation, diction, or syntax!

And finally, to Ruth, my wife, best friend, consultant, and confidante: Your love, trust, and confidence are what have given me the peace of mind to accomplish this. Thank you for believing in me enough to convince me to try, for trusting me when it would have been easy not to, and for never making me feel guilty about devoting time to a book about dogs. This is "our" first book. I love you.